CW00505428

THE EPISTLE OF THE APOSTLES

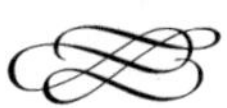

Early Christian Apocrypha

Julian V. Hills

Harold W. Attridge

Dennis R. MacDonald

VOLUME 1: *The Acts of Andrew*

VOLUME 2: *The Epistle of the Apostles*

THE EPISTLE OF THE APOSTLES

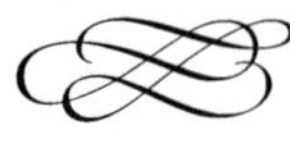

Julian V. Hills

Copyright © 2009 by Julian V. Hills

All rights reserved. Printed in the United States of America. No part of this book may be used or reproduced in any manner whatsoever without written permission except in the case of brief quotations embodied in critical articles and reviews. For information address Polebridge Press, P. O. Box 7268, Santa Rosa, California 95407.

Cover and interior design by Robaire Ream

Library of Congress Cataloging-in-Publication Data

Hills, Julian Victor.
The Epistle of the Apostles / Julian V. Hills.
p. cm. -- (Early Christian Apocrypha ; v. 2)
Includes bibliographical references and indexes.
ISBN 978-1-59815-017-9
1. Epistle of the Apostles--Criticism, interpretation, etc. I. Title.
BS2900.A7H54 2009
229'.9307--dc22

2009045381

CONTENTS

SERIES PREFACE

The series *Early Christian Apocrypha &* (*ECA&*), the first such publication by north American scholars, is designed as a study edition of early Christian apocryphal texts and related writings. These comprise the standard set of New Testament apocrypha (gospels, acts, epistles, apocalypses) along with other, some less well known, writings that emerged from the early Christian movement, such as homiletical, polemical, exegetical, and church order tracts. Writings reckoned "orthodox" and "heretical" by contemporaries and later authorities will be included.

The publisher and the editors have had several goals in mind. First, to provide quotable and lively renderings into modern U.S. English—satisfying both to the specialist and to the non-expert reader. Second, to offer full introductions and bibliographies that will situate the texts in question in their larger Christian and Greco-Roman contexts. Third, to supply brief commentary explaining technical aspects of the writing and the movement of the text.—storyline or theological argument. Fourth, to add "verse numbers" where previous editions gave only larger section or chapter numbers.

Where appropriate, the texts will be annotated with cross-references, not only within the biblical canon but also outside it—in due course supplying a network of interconnected references to assist comparative study. A full index of texts, biblical and non-biblical, will conclude each volume.

My thanks are due to
Alexander E. Schmid. of Marquette University,
for compiling the index to this volume.

SIGLA, ABBREVIATIONS, CONVENTIONS

Aaa	Lipsius-Bonnet, *Acta apostolorum apocrypha*
ANF	Roberts-Donaldson, *Ante-Nicene Fathers*
BAGD	Bauer-Arndt-Gingrich-Danker, *Greek-English Lexicon*
BDB	Brown-Driver-Briggs, *Hebrew and English Lexicon*
Crum	Crum, *A Coptic Dictionary*
DLLA	Dillmann, *Lexicon linguae aethiopicae*
fam. 1, fam. 2	Ethiopic mss identified as belonging to two distinct "families"; see Introduction, "Ethiopic"
GSLLA	Grébaut, *Supplément au Lexicon linguae aethiopicae*
LCDG	Leslau, *Concise Dictionary of Ge'ez*
LPGL	Lampe, *Patristic Greek Lexicon*
LSJ	Liddell-Scott-Jones, *Greek-English Lexicon*
MM	Moulton-Milligan, *Vocabulary of the Greek Testament*
NHLE	Robinson, *Nag Hammadi Library in English*
NTApoc ^{2}	Schneemelcher, *New Testament Apocrypha*
PSCSD	Payne Smith, *Compendious Syriac Dictionary*
PSTS	Payne Smith, *Thesaurus Syriacus*

<and>	words supplied *ad sensum*
[then]	words supplied to fill whole or partial *lacunae* (gaps)
columns	following Duensing (1925), *NTApoc* ^{2} (1991–92), and Elliott (1993): where both versions survive, the Ethiopic is presented on the left side, the Coptic on the right
»	indicates the place where the principal reference list of passages related by a common theme or expression is to be found
†	see the Additional Note, after the main translation

INTRODUCTION

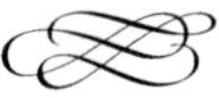

The *Epistula Apostolorum*, or "Epistle of the Apostles," is one of a handful of early Christian writings discovered, which is to say *rediscovered*, by western scholars in the late nineteenth century. This *Epistula* was greeted with considerable interest, even excitement. Kirsopp Lake (1872–1946), professor of early Christian literature and ecclesiastical history at Harvard University, told the world that it was "comparable with the Didache [first published in 1883] and the Odes of Solomon [1909] for its additions to our knowledge of the second century" (1920: 16). The great papyrologist Gustav Adolf Deissmann (1866–1937) claimed that of the many contemporary finds, including a large part of the *Acts of Paul*, the *Epistula* was "historically the most valuable" (1922: 44).

An outline of its contents will give some indication of what in this "new" writing caught the eye of these and other scholars:

Chaps. 1-6: In this "book" which begins as an apostolic "letter" (see note on 1:1), the apostles introduce themselves, and announce that they are writing to the whole church to warn believers about "Simon and Cerinthus"; they remind their readers of the basics of the gospel message, which includes a selection of brief miracle reports; this gospel summary concludes with a statement of faith that may be, in fact, an ancient "creed."

Chaps. 7-12: The apostles tell of their privilege of meeting the risen Lord Jesus; how in an epiphany reminiscent of the Gospel of John's "doubting Thomas" scene (John 20) he proved his physical post-resurrection reality to them; and what was the nature of their dominical commission: to listen to the "revelation" that will occupy the rest of the work.

Chaps. 13-18: The Lord reveals the mystery of his descent "through the heavens" and his incarnation; he urges the disciples to keep the Passover, which is specifically connected with expectation of his Second Coming; he even answers a question about *when* "the coming of the Father" will take place; the "new commandment" (cf. John 13:34) is given.

Chap. 19-26: The Lord exhorts the disciples to preach and teach the reality of resurrection; here the author quotes Psalm 3 in full—a frequent patristic proof-text for the resurrection, and the longest biblical quotation in the *Epistula apostolorum*; judgment will follow resurrection, but *hope* and *promise* are emphasized, rather than the inevitability of punishment; frequently in the exchange the Lord reassures the disciples that their questioning is welcome: it is a sign not of doubt but of a wish to clarify what they are to preach and teach.

Chaps. 27-30: The Lord also reports his descent into Hades (cf. 1 Pet 3:19) and preaching to the deceased patriarchs; the promise given to them is now available to all believers; the disciples express anxiety at the prospect of Jesus' departure from them; again, he reassures them that "those who do not see me" will be "more blessed" even than they (cf. John 20:29); as the disciples and their successors preach, they will be fortified by the power of God's spirit, so that they may teach even "the other nations" (so the Coptic text; "the Gentiles," Ethiopic).

Chaps. 31-39: Suddenly a new figure is introduced: "Look: You will meet a man whose name is Saul, which being interpreted means Paul" (31:1). The Pauline mission is thereby announced, not as in competition with but as complementary to the mission of Peter and the rest; but this new missionary moment also signals the coming of "signs and wonders"—a trumpet in heaven, a dragon reaching down to earth, stars falling from the sky, etc.—that will be the beginning of the End; these predictions are chiefly of concern because of the dissention the events are predicted to bring: relatives turning against children, disregard of neighbors, hatred, affliction, jealousy; even church leaders will be led astray; but just as the faithful will endure, so will the wicked be destroyed.

Chaps. 40–45: The disciples express dismay at the predicted fate of sinners, and learn that the Lord will "hear the prayer of the righteous" for them; a scheme of ministry is set out ("fathers, teachers, servants"; see chap. 41), possibly corresponding to actual clerical "orders" in the author's community; the disciples (and presumably their successors) are to administer "baptism of life and the forgiveness of sins" (42:3), though there is no mention of the Eucharist (but note the reference to the *agape*, or "love feast," in 15:6); the necessity of unity in the church is emphasized in a retelling of the parable of the Wise and Foolish Bridesmaids (cf. Matt 25:1–12) that speaks of *all ten* young women as "sisters."

Chaps. 46–50: In a final summons to preach and teach, the Lord insists that rich and poor are to be treated alike and to be equally generous with what they have; that the neighbor who has committed sin must be restored (cf. Matthew 18); and that each member of the community is to correct, rebuke, and exhort those on the outside who attack the believers; and, finally, that there will come "another teaching and conflict"—the heresy and fruit of heresy that the author has warned of at the outset.

Chap. 51: The *Epistula apostolorum* ends with the Lord's ascension in a scene similar to what is recounted in Acts 1. Angels accompany the Lord on his journey back to heaven, as he blesses the disciples with the words, "Go in peace."

Here, then, is a writing that breathes the spirit of the emerging "Catholic" (or "Great") church vs. "Gnostic" church debate. Indeed, a previous translator took the address ("to *all* people" in 1:1) to specify the recipients as "the Catholics" (see the note). At point after point it recalls the theology of Justin Martyr (d. ca. 165 CE) and of his pupil, the most famous opponent of Gnosticism, Irenaeus (d. ca. 200 CE). The date of Easter appears to be a matter of continuing controversy, and the author shows an acquaintance with a host of genres and sub-genres, including the church order, the apocalypse, and—as a unifying genre—the post-resurrection dialogue. More specifically, as Helmut Koester has observed, "throughout [the *Ep. apost.*], the specifically apologetic structuring of the various topics of the creed can be observed. Apocalyptic revelation has been replaced by doctrinal discourse" (Koester, 1971: 203). There is a general consensus that the *Epistula* is to be dated in the second half of the second century, and that it was written in Egypt or Asia Minor (for a concise review of the arguments, see Hill, 1999: 1–21; Hornschuh stands alone in dating the work as early as 120).

The theological language and idiom is most strongly reminiscent of the Gospel of John among New Testament writings. Hence, for example, though one of the miracles briefly reported is an exorcism (5:9 "he expelled demons from the possessed"), there is no suggestion of a supernatural battle with the devil, demons, Satan, etc., such as characterizes large parts of the Synoptic tradition but not John. And while the opponents are not John's "the Jews" (or "Judeans"), they are similarly personified, now as "Simon Magus" and "Cerinthus" and their followers—docetists (supposing that Jesus only "seemed" to be a physical being) and other proto-Gnostics, apparently. The most potent immediate danger, therefore, is not defeat in some metaphysical conflict but the prospect of eternal death through false teaching, apostasy, and the like.

In addition to much of the New Testament, the author was familiar with a wide range of Jewish and Christian traditions and texts. He or she also exercised considerable skill in composing this post-resurrection discourse, so that the body of the work exhibits a disciplined rhetorical structure, not merely a repeated "He said" and "We said" pattern imposed on dogmatic assertions. (For details, see the Additional Note on 12:3.) Redaction-critical study, focusing on structure and arrangement and the editing of previous traditional material, strongly suggests that the work was intended not as a private compendium of biblical and doctrinal truths but as an appeal to a specific community, or group of communities, to understand and live the Christian life according to a specific theological vision. Part of this vision, it seems, has been developed in conscious response to an early form of Christian Gnosticism. The modern student or even the casual investigator of earliest Christianity therefore stands to learn a great deal from this writing. Yet the *Epistula* remains a minor witness, a lesser voice, in modern reconstructions of the development of Christian life and thought. Why is this?

Several reasons may be suggested. First, though undoubtedly composed in Greek, the language of the New Testament and chief language of the earliest Christian mission, this document survives in other tongues: (a) in a single Coptic parchment codex of the 4th or 5th century CE; (b) in a single fragmentary page of Latin, of similar date; and (c) in more than a dozen Ethiopic manuscripts, dating from the 16th to the early 20th century, in which it is commonly part of a compendium of texts bearing the title *Maṣḥafa Kidān* ("Book of the Covenant"). Now, Coptic and Ethiopic, while essential to research in specific aspects of church history and textual criticism, are not part of the standard repertoire of language tools practiced by students of earliest Christianity—or at least, they were not at the time of this writing's rediscovery. To be sure, Coptic has achieved a new status since the discovery of the famed Nag Hammadi Gnostic Library, and especially the Coptic *Gospel of Thomas*. But Ethiopic, admittedly the language of survival of several extremely important intertestamental pseudepigrapha, including *1 Enoch* and *Jubilees*, is most often the domain of teachers of other *semitic* languages, more commonly associated with Old Testament studies. Hence, in part, the writing's relative neglect.

Second, no document that would fit this text's description is named or discussed in surviving early Christian writings, and, if there are any quotations of the work in extant patristic literature, none has yet been identified with confidence. Indeed, apart from the manuscripts themselves, there is no evidence that the early church even knew of the work! It speaks as if out of nowhere; and, not being part of a collection (such as the Dead Sea Scrolls or the Nag Hammadi Library), it appears to speak alone. The possible quotation in the Latin poet Commodian (probably mid-3rd cent.) detected by James (1922; also 1924: 488 n. 1) is more likely a proverbial or gnomic saying concerning the incorporeality of phantoms (see note on 11:8). In later literature there is only an abbreviated quotation of 13:1–14:2, valuable for other reasons, by the Ethiopian priest-king Ase Zär'a Ya'qob (1434–68 C.E.) (see Haile, 1982).

Third, the editions and translations published until now are either inaccessible to the average English-speaking reader or, from a technical perspective, out of date. For all its merits, the *editio princeps* of the Ethiopic text, published with French translation by Louis Guerrier (with Sylvain Grébaut) in 1913 (reprinted, 1982), can now be shown to have as its base an inferior manuscript. This is because Guerrier worked without knowledge of the Coptic—not to mention the fact that several good and relatively early Ethiopic manuscripts had not yet been discovered or catalogued. Conversely, the still standard edition of the Coptic text, published by the prolific German editor, translator, and historian Carl Schmidt (with Isaak Wajnberg) in 1919 (reprinted, 1969), was largely completed before Schmidt became aware of the Ethiopic witnesses. Many of the fragments that Schmidt printed, but only as scraps of unconnected words and phrases, can now be matched with meaningful parallels in the Ethiopic. Schmidt's book remains an indispensable resource for scholarly research; but it is extremely long and complex, hugely expensive, and not readily available even in college libraries. It is a real pity that Schmidt was not encouraged to issue a manual-sized edition. Recently Darrell D. Hannah has announced a new critical edition, forthcoming in the series Oxford Early Christian Gospel Texts (Hannah, 2008: 610 n. 32).

As for translations into English, the first, by Montague Rhodes James (1924, often reprinted), was based on Guerrier's and Schmidt's editions and translations, and presents a single, harmonized version in which only the major differences between the Coptic and the Ethiopic are noted. The second and currently dominant English translation, by R. E. Taylor, is in fact a rendering in English of Hugo Duensing's German translation (1925) as revised by C. Detlef G. Müller (in Schneemelcher, 1991). Consequently, there has yet to appear a translation directly from the original languages into English. In addition, the past few decades have seen an explosion of research on and publication of a substantial array of documents which share literary and theological features with the *Epistula*, especially the post-resurrection dialogues in the Nag Hammadi Library (see Robinson, 1987). In a number of places, phrases formerly judged obscure or indecipherable can be explained with reference to phraseology common to the genre of post-resurrection dialogue.

COPTIC

The Coptic manuscript of the *Epistula apostolorum* is housed in the Institut Français d'Archéologie Orientale, in Cairo. It is in the Achmimic dialect, though with some Subachmimic forms (on these dialects in general, see Metzger, 1977: 108–17; Wisse, 1995), and lacks all or most of chaps. 1–6, 21–22, 31–38, and 49–51. However—and this is an extremely fortunate situation—the Coptic codex ("book") has numbered pages. And since the average line-length in the surviving portions is very regular, and with it the number of lines per page, it is possible to state with confidence that the length of the original, unmutilated Coptic text must have been almost identical to that of the later Ethiopic version (this is set out in graphic form in Vanovermeire, 1962: 149–51). To be sure, even the surviving text has lacunae (gaps), which Schmidt and others have attempted to fill—Schmidt, of course, making most of his conjectures before even knowing of the parallel Ethiopic text. But at many points these lacunae can now be filled according not only to sense but also to actual wording, given the precise length of gap and size of letters.

For the most part, the Coptic and Ethiopic versions are in close agreement, and their differences can be accounted for by the particular features of the respective languages. (On the characteristics of Coptic and Ethiopic as "translation languages," see Plumley, in Metzger, 1977: 141–52; and Hofmann, in Metzger, 1977: 240–56.) In addition, there are numerous spelling mistakes and minor textual differences that are properly "inner-Ethiopic" and even "inner-Coptic" variants—copying errors, for example, or words capable of two meanings taken in different ways. Occasionally, however, it appears that the two recensions present a different underlying original text, perhaps going back to the Greek (examples given below). But where both versions are intact, in only one instance does the Coptic text actually lack an equivalent amount of text opposite more than a few words in the Ethiopic. This occurs in chap. 19: In both versions, in a saying reminiscent of John 10:38 and 14:10, Jesus says, "I am fully in the [*Eth.* my] Father and the [*Eth.* my] Father in me." In the Ethiopic, the disciples press him on this remark, after which he repeats the assertion. Given the characteristic question-and-answer exchange, it is more probable that the Coptic lacks the intervening sentences through haplography (the scribe having noticed and written something only once) than that an Ethiopian scribe has added them through dittography (duplication of material).

ETHIOPIC

The new translation of the Ethiopic text is based on a collation of fourteen manuscripts. The Ethiopian language used is *Geʿez*, or "classical Ethiopic," in contrast to modern Ethiopic, which is Amharic. Classical Ethiopic is the language in which the well-known pseudepigrapha *1 Enoch*, *Jubilees*, and the *Ascension of Isaiah* are preserved in their entirety, probably because the Ethiopian canon (that is, the authoritative collection of scriptures) was larger and looser than the standard western biblical canon of Old Testament and New Testament writings (see Cowley, 1974).

Five of the fourteen manuscripts of the *Epistula* were edited by Guerrier, who assigned to them the sigla (that is, identifying letters) *A, B, C* (all three in Paris), *K*, and *L* (both in London). To these five Wajnberg added one manuscript, to which he assigned the siglum *S* (Stuttgart). Since 1919, nine further manuscripts have become available, most of them through the *Ethiopic Monasteries Manuscript Library* (EMML) project and the microfilms of manuscripts made available through the Hill Monastic Manuscript Library (HMML) at St. John's University, Collegeville, Minnesota. The sigla assigned to them by the present writer (Hills, 1990) have been accepted by Noel (2000), and appear below. The full inventory of Ethiopic manuscripts consulted is therefore as follows (siglum; location; catalogue editor; library accession number with page numbers where available; probable date, by century):

A	Paris	Abbadie, no. 51 (pp. 60–63)	XVI cent.
B	Paris	Abbadie, no. 90 (pp. 100–101)	XVI cent.
C	Paris	Abbadie, no. 199 (pp. 199–201)	XVII/XVIII cent.
K	London	Br. Mus. Or. 795; Wright, no. 361 (pp. 270–75)	XVIII cent.
L	London	Br. Mus. Or. 793; Wright, no. 362 (pp. 275–77)	XVIII cent.
M	Ethiopia	EMML/HMML, no. 370	XIX/XX cent.

N	Ethiopia	EMML/HMML, no. 1945	XVIII cent.
O	Ethiopia	EMML/HMML, no. 2358	XVI cent.
P	Ethiopia	EMML/HMML, no. 6925	XVII/XVIII cent.
Q	Ethiopia	EMML/HMML, no. 7021	XIX cent.
R	Ethiopia	EMML/HMML, no. 7204	XVIII cent.
S	Stuttgart	Stuttgart Or. fol. 49	XV/XVII cent.
T	Lake Tana	Hammerschmidt, no. 35 (pp. 163–67)	XVIII cent.
V	Vatican	Cerulli Etiop., no. 151 (p. 108)	XX cent.

Those familiar with the basics of New Testament textual criticism—how the hundreds of extant manuscripts in Greek and other languages have been weighed and counted so as to establish a reliable text for study, public worship, and private devotion—may be surprised, or even dismayed, at the relative youth of even the oldest of these Ethiopic manuscripts. This is not only because good Greek manuscripts survive from very early in Christian history in papyrus fragments but also, from the third century on, in codex form, that is, as "books." It is also because even the Ethiopic translation of the New Testament is regularly referred to as a production of the fourth century or slightly later—as if we actually possessed fourth-, or at the latest sixth- or seventh-, century manuscripts or fragments (see, e.g., the listing in Metzger-Ehrman, 2005: 120–21). In fact, the oldest extant biblical mss in Ge'ez are in the 10th–12th century range (see Ullendorff, 1968). This makes them strikingly similar in age to the oldest Hebrew *Old Testament* manuscripts available before the fortuitous discovery of the Qumran library in 1947. The question naturally arises, then, whether there is the same general faithfulness to a received text in the Ge'ez *Epistula* as in the Hebrew Old Testament.

A fresh collation of these Ethiopic manuscripts reveals that they fall into two groups, to be designated "family 1" (fam. 1) and "family 2" (fam. 2), by analogy with "family 1" (f^1) and "family 13" (f^{13}) minuscule (small and cursive) Greek manuscripts of the New Testament (Metzger-Ehrman, 2005: 86–87). Fam. 1 comprises mss *BCKNO*; fam. 2, *LMPQRSV*. Manuscripts *A* and *T* usually follow fam. 1, but sometimes agree with fam. *2*. Within the Ethiopic recension, on text-critical grounds fam. 1 readings may usually be judged more primitive than those of fam. 2. They also regularly agree with the Coptic against fam. 2. However, fam. 1 is itself often either corrupt or contaminated with fam. 2 readings; and three fam. 2 mss occasionally preserve excellent readings, either individually or together. It turns out that the leading representative of fam. 2 is *L*—ironically, since this is the manuscript which served as the basic text for Guerrier's edition. (Again by analogy with New Testament Greek mss, fam. 2 appears to be the *Textus Receptus*, that is, the "Majority" text.) Additional evidence for this division of the manuscripts into two families is the testimony of manuscript *B*. Together with *K*, *B* is a strong representative of fam. 1. But *B* has suffered extensive scribal revision to bring it in line with fam. 2. Where it is necessary to report them, "corrections" in *B* (that is, the later, changed text) will be designated *B***, the "original" text (that is, the earlier, previous readings) *B**. Finally, within the two families of manuscripts, several smaller pairs or groups are apparent, especially *AT*, *BK*, *CN*, and *QR*. Naturally, the most probable reason for this is the dependence of one manuscript on another, or on a near relative.

FAMILY 1, FAMILY 2, AND THE COPTIC TEXT

In light of the foregoing, several principles have guided the selection of readings on which the translation in this book is based. First, where the Ethiopic text is clearly presenting the same subject-matter as the Coptic, the manuscript or manuscripts that are closest to the Coptic readings are generally preferred. Often this amounts to a simple choice between a shorter and a longer reading. This is especially the case when the distinctive readings of fam. 1 witnesses cannot be suspected of later theological motivation, while the fam. 2 reading may be. For example:

Ep. apost. 10:6
Copt. ⲧⲟⲧⲉ ⲁⲥⲃⲱⲕ ϣⲁ ⲡϫⲁⲓⲉⲥ
Then she went (back) to the Lord
Eth. fam. 1: *wa- 'emze gab'at xabēhu la-'egzi'*

For *la-'egzi'* ("the Lord"; *BKOS*) all other witnesses have *la-'egzi'ena* ("to our Lord"). Further, *BKRS* add "Jesus"; *Q* adds "Jesus Christ." The same phenomenon occurs in 10:9, where *BCKNO* have "the Lord," all others, "our Lord."

Ep. apost. 10:7
Copt. ⲡⲁϫⲉϥ ϫⲉ ⲙⲁⲣⲉ . . . ⲃⲱⲕ
And he said, "Go, . . ."
Eth. fam. 1: *wa-yebē teḥor*

For *yebē* ("he said"; *BKNOQR*) all other witnesses except *C* ("we said") have *yebēla*, "he said *to her*."

Ep. apost. 12:3
Copt. ϯⲛⲁϭⲱⲗⲡ ⲛⲏⲧⲛⲉ ⲁⲃⲁⲗ ⲛ̄ⲛⲉⲧⲙ̄ⲡⲥⲁϩⲣⲉ ⲛ̄ⲛ̄ⲡⲏⲩⲉ ⲙⲛ̄ⲛⲉⲧϩⲛ̄ ⲛ̄ⲡⲏⲩⲉ
I shall reveal to you what is above heaven and what is in heaven
Eth. fam. 1: *'ekaššet lakemu za-samāyāt wa-za-mal'elta samāyāt*
I shall reveal to you what is in heaven (*lit.* heavenly things) and what is above heaven

For *za-samāyāt* ("heavenly things," *ABCKNOT*; in Eph 1:3 for ἐν τοῖς ἐπουρανίοις), all other witnesses (i.e., fam. 2) have *za-ba-medr*, "what is on earth."

	Ep. apost. 13:3
Copt.	Michael . . . and Gabriel and Uriel and Raphael
Eth. fam. 1	Michael and Gabriel and Uriel and Raphael
Eth. fam. 2	Michael and Gabriel and Raphael and Uriel

Most of Ethiopic fam. 1 (*ACNOT*) gives the archangels' names in the order Michael, Gabriel, Uriel, and Raphael, as in the Coptic. All other Ethiopic manuscripts have Uriel and Raphael in reverse order—as, incidentally, in *Orac. Sib.* 2.215. A similar case, of possible linguistic or cultural interest but no likely theological significance, is in *Ep. apost.* 30:1, where the cardinal points are given in the order East, West, South, and North in the Coptic text but East, West, North, and South in the Ethiopic.

	Ep. apost. 13:4
Copt.	. . . ⲁⲟⲩ ⲥⲉⲃⲱⲕ ⲁⲃⲁⲗ ⲛ̄ⲧⲇⲓⲁⲕⲟⲛⲓⲁ
	. . . and fulfill the service
Eth. fam. 1	. . . *yetqanayu gebromu*
	. . . and do their (*sc.* the archangels') work of service

Before *gebromu* ("their work"), fam. 2 manuscripts *LMPQRSV* add *la-'ab ba-* ("[and serve] the Father in").

	Ep. apost. 14:5
Copt.	ⲁⲓⲟⲩⲱⲛϩ ⲁⲃⲁⲗ ⲛ̄ⲙⲁⲣⲓⲁ
	I appeared to Mary
Eth. fam. 1:	*'astar'aykewwā la-Māryām*

Fam. 2 representative *L* reads *la-dengel Māryām* ("to the virgin Mary"); *QRS* have *la-qeddest dengel* ("to the holy virgin"); and see note on 3:10.

	Ep. apost. 15:2
Copt.	ⲟⲩⲛ̄ ⲟⲩⲉ ϩⲛ̄ⲧⲏⲛⲉ ⲉⲩⲛⲁⲧⲉⲕϥ̄ ⲁⲡⲱ̄ϣ̄ⲧⲉⲕⲟ
	one of you will be thrown into prison
Eth. *M*	*1-'em-westētekemu yewaddeyewwo westa moqeḥ*

Here, the one Ethiopic witness that agrees with the Coptic is the generally unremarkable *M*. All other manuscripts have "one of you [*or* one of those] standing [*some add* with me]," likely under the influence of Mark 9:1 // Matt 16:28 // Luke 9:27; and the final phrase, "with me," is found in the Greek text of Mark 9:1 in D 565 it—but not in the "received" Ge'ez New Testament published by the British and Foreign Bible Society (p. 79; cf. Zuurmond, 1995).

Next, there are a few places where the difference between the Coptic and Ethiopic can be explained on the basis of two readings or senses of the same Greek word or, more commonly, in one or the other recension a slight misreading of a probable original Greek word. This is not to claim that the present Ethiopic manuscript tradition is wholly to be accounted for as the result of translation or translations directly out of the Greek, though this may in fact be so. Instead, the observation that matters is that the chain of transmission—perhaps Greek to Coptic, Coptic to Arabic, Arabic to Ethiopic—at some stage preserved different, even if erroneous, readings. The final, that is, the resultant text that has come down to us may have been preceded by several intermediary recensions, and it is not necessary—however desirable—to be able to track or conjecture the actual steps in the history of transmission. A few examples will illustrate the kind of differences that are found:

Ep. apost. 13:3

Copt. ⲉⲩⲙⲉⲩⲉ ⲅⲁⲣ ⲁⲃⲁⲗ ϩⲛ̄ ⲡⲟⲩϩⲏⲧ
they [*sc.* the archangels] *thought in their hearts*
that I was one of them.

Eth. *rassaykewwomu*
it seemed to them
that I was one of them.

Both readings naturally go back to the Greek expression δοκεῖν αὐτοῖς, which can be either personal ("I seemed to them") or impersonal ("it seemed to them that I . . .").

Ep. apost. 15:9

Copt. . . . until the day on which I come
with those slain on my account.
ⲙⲛ̄ ⲛⲉⲧⲁⲩϩⲁⲧⲃⲟⲩ ⲉⲧⲃⲏⲧ

Eth. . . . until I come from the Father
with my wounds.
mesla 'aṣle'teya.

The idea behind the Ethiopic reading is familiar not only from the "doubting Thomas" scene in the *Epistula apostolorum* itself, but also from various New Testament and later uses of Zech 14:5 ("they shall look upon him whom they have pierced"). The Greek reflected here is almost certainly μετὰ τῶν τραυμάτων μου. The Coptic is reminiscent of 1 Thess 3:13 ("the coming of the Lord Jesus with all his *saints* [*or* holy ones]"), the Lord's entourage now specifically envisioned as those who have died for him, that is, his martyrs: μετὰ τῶν τραυματίων μου (τραυματίας = "wounded man, one slain in battle").

Ep. apost. 41:6

Copt. It is *just as* (ⲕⲁⲧⲁ ⲧϩⲉ) you have said.

Eth. You have spoken *correctly* (*'artā'kemu*).

The Coptic likely reflects Greek καθὼς ἐλαλησατε (cf. Esth 6:10 LXX and v.l.), the Ethiopic καλῶς ἐλαλήσατε (cf. John 4:17; 13:13).

However, there are a few places where the Ethiopic readings, though diverging from one another in details, together seem to witness to a different underlying text. In such cases, it cannot be assumed that the Coptic tradition is the more primitive. For example:

Ep. apost. 9:3
Copt. ⲁⲩⲃⲱⲕ ⲁⲡⲙⲁ ⲉⲧⲙ̄ⲙⲟ ⲉⲩⲙⲁϩ ϩⲁⲙⲧⲉ ⲛ̄ⲥϩⲓⲙⲉ
ⲙⲁⲣⲓⲁ ⲧⲁⲙⲁⲣⲑⲁ ⲁⲟⲩ ⲙⲁⲣⲓⲁ ⲧⲙⲁⲅⲇⲁⲗⲏⲛⲏ
[Three] women went there (*sc.* to the tomb):
Mary, Martha, and Mary Magdalene.
Eth. *xaba ḥorā 'anest šalās*
Sārā wa-Mārtā wa-Māryām Magdalāwit
to which place went three women:
Sarah and Martha and Mary Magdalene.

For possible biblical allusions—whether primitive or by way of later "corrections" to the text—see the note. Neither reading can claim the immediate right to be judged the more primitive.

Ep. apost. 17:2
Copt. ⲁϣⲁ ⲡⲟⲩⲱⲛ ⲛ̄ϣⲉ ⲙⲛ̄ ⲡⲟⲩⲱⲛ ⲛϫⲟⲩⲧ ϫⲱⲕ ⲁⲃⲁⲗ
When the hundredth part and the twentieth part is fulfilled . . .
Eth. *'ama 100-wa-50-'ām tafaṣṣama*
When one hundred and fifty years are fulfilled . . .

Whether the expression regarding "parts" refers to years is an open question. Nor, similarly, is it at all certain that the Ethiopic number is simply an "updating" of the date for a somewhat later readership—similar to revisions in the date of Armageddon that have occasionally been issued by nineteenth- and twentieth-century millennial Christian groups. But if it were, we should expect to find even larger numbers in one or more manuscripts, as the Second Coming failed to materialize in the third and fourth centuries. But the entire Ethiopic text tradition transmits the one number.

Ep. apost. 27:1
Copt. ⲁï̈ⲉⲓ ⲁϩⲣⲏï ϣⲁ [ⲡⲙⲁ ⲛ̄]ⲗⲁⲍⲁⲣⲟⲥ ⲁⲟⲩ ⲁïⲧⲁϣⲉⲁⲉⲓϣ
ⲛ̄ⲛ̄ⲇⲓ]ⲕⲁ[ⲓⲟⲥ ⲙⲛ̄] ⲛ̄ⲡⲣⲟⲫⲏⲧⲏⲥ
I descended to [the place] of Lazarus and preached . . .
[. . right]eous ones and to the prophets
Eth. *waradku xaba 'Abrehām wa-Yesḥaq wa-Yā'qob*
xaba 'abawikemu wa-nabiyāt wa-zēnawkewwomu
I descended to the place of Abraham, Isaac, and Jacob,
to your fathers and the prophets, and preached . . .

Both Lazarus and the patriarchs are associated with Hades in Jewish and early Christian traditions (see the note). It is therefore not possible to choose between the Coptic and Ethiopic readings on grounds of theological antiquity alone.

Finally, in this connection it is worth pointing out that only in recent years has the prospect of complete and truly "critical" texts of the Coptic and Ethiopic New Testament begun to become a reality. George Horner's venerable Coptic editions are gradually being superseded by yet more sophisticated productions; and his Sahidic (1911–1924) and Bohairic (1898–1905) texts can only with limited confidence be extrapolated to represent readings in Achmimic or Subachmimic. As for the Ethiopic version, when in this volume a text is quoted as exhibiting the Ge'ez of a certain New Testament word or phrase, this is commonly on the authority of C. F. A. Dillmann's *Lexicon* or of the British and Foreign Bible Society text already referred to, except where a modern critical text is available. There is some value to such citation, in that some manuscript(s) somewhere—though maybe late and elsewhere unreliable—presumably preserve the cited or quoted Ethiopic reading. In other words, if, in the New Testament, Greek word "XXX" was at some point received as Ge'ez word "YYY," this at least allows the conjecture that the same Greek word lies behind our extant Ethiopic in the *Epistula apostolorum*—by whatever process, and via whichever intermediary versions, the transmission occurred. (On the possibility of achieving accuracy in retroverting extant Ethiopic to "original" Greek, see Miles, 1985; on the origin and character of the Ge'ez version of the Old Testament, see Knibb, 1999.) But the actual situation is more complex. To take an immediately relevant example, in the new critical edition of the Gospel of Matthew, Rochus Zuurmond (2001) is constrained to trace *four* Ethiopic manuscript traditions, not one; and he supplies samples of a fifth. The result is that to speak of "the Ethiopic version" is becoming an anachronism, just as for more than a century it has been recognized that the different parts of the New Testament were translated into Ge'ez in different eras.

THE LATIN FRAGMENT

The Latin fragment was first published by Josef Bick in 1908. A palimpsest (re-used parchment, over-written with a later text), it amounts to a single leaf of eighteen short lines (approximately twenty characters per line) in two columns on each side; the columns are numbered V, VI, VII, and VIII. In Schmidt's heavily restored text (1919: 21–22), it comprises *Ep. apost.* 12:1; 13:1–2; 13:3–5, and, without a break (though part of one word is illegible), 17:2–5. Words in italics are substantially restored:

col. V lines 1–3 = *Ep. apost.* 12:1:

1So we, wishing to prove that he had *truly* risen in the *flesh*, entreated. . . .

[15 lines faint or otherwise indecipherable]

col. VI = *Ep. apost.* 13:1–2:

[1] *What* he revealed to us are *these things that* he said: "When I came down *from the Father almighty and passed* by the heavens, I put on the *wisdom of the Father* and the power of the Holy Spirit by the power of *the Father*. [2]And I passed by the *archangels and* the angels in the appearance of their likeness, as if I were one of them among the powers and rulers and principalities—I *went through* them, since I possessed the wisdom of him who sent me.

col. VII = *Ep. apost.* 13:3–5:

[3] "The archangels Michael, and Gabriel and Uriel and Raphael—they openly (*palam*) followed me down to the fifth firmament, for they thought in their hearts that I was one of them; the Father gave me such power as this. [4]Then I equipped the archangels with a marvelous voice, to lead them up to the altar of my Father to serve and fulfill the service until I go to him; so I did by the wisdom of the likeness. [5] For I became all things

Col. VIII = *Ep. apost.* 13.5 (cont.); 17:2–5:

"in everything so that I might fulfill the will of my Father who sent me [. . .] [17:2]When the year is fulfilled, between Pentecost (*pentecosten*) and Unleavened Bread (*azyma*), the coming (*adventus*) the coming of my Father will take place." [3]But we said to him, "O Lord, now do you say you will come to us? How, as you say, can 'he who sent me' come?" [4]He said to us, "I am fully (*totus*) in the Father." [5][. . .] said, "How is it that you will leave us until your coming (*adventum*)? Where, then, can we. . . ?"

THE APOSTLES IN THE EPISTULA APOSTOLORUM

The apostles Peter, Thomas, and Andrew occupy a special place in the portion of the writing before the full "revelation discourse" of the resurrected Jesus begins. In *Ep. apost.* 9–12, they are invited by name to inspect the risen Lord's body. In contrast to the Gospel of John, in which "doubting Thomas" is encouraged to see and touch the body (though it is not clear that he does, in fact, touch it; see John 20:19–26) as a concession necessitated by his earlier absence from the upper room, here in the *Epistula* it appears that the participation of Peter, Thomas, and Andrew in the demonstration is a special privilege. That is, they are specially chosen witnesses.

Of even greater value to the student of early Christianity, however, may be the *list* of apostles that is given in chap. 2. Such lists can be indicative of various things: the author's dependence on one New Testament writing rather than another; the community's loyalty to one or more strand of apostolic tradition; the relative authority of one apostolic "name" over another. The list in *Ep. apost.* 2:1 (according to fam. 1 manuscripts) is as follows: John, Peter, Thomas, Andrew, James, Philip, Bartholomew, Matthew, Nathanael, Judas "the Zealot," Cephas.

It is at once striking that there are only eleven names here; the manuscripts are agreed on the number. Since the author almost certainly knows the book of Acts, the absence of Matthias can scarcely be an oversight. The most likely reason is that the author is following Acts rather strictly here: since the ascension has not yet been discussed (it will be reported in *Ep. apost.* 51), Matthias's name cannot yet appear (see Acts 1:13, also with only eleven named apostles). It is also possible, since there is no prediction of a replacement apostle, that in the author's mind *Paul*, the great apostle to the Gentiles, is the one to complete the number of the twelve (see chap. 31). Noteworthy is the early Greek *Liturgy of St. James*, in which the *diakonia* (deacon's prayers) include these names recited by the priest: "the holy apostles Peter and Paul, Andrew, James, John, Philip, Bartholomew, Thomas, Thaddaeus, Matthew, James, Simon, Jude, Matthias" (Brightman, 1896: 57, cf. 501).

Quite apart from such speculation, however, three things are to be noticed about the *Epistula*'s list. First, this is the earliest extant reference to "Peter" and "Cephas" as two separate persons (see Galatians 1–2; and Ehrman, 1990). Second, there are some minor differences in the manuscripts, as reported fully in the note; for example, ms *M* lacks "Matthew" and adds "James" after "Cephas." But exegetically the most important observation concerns a third point, that the order of the names *Peter, Thomas,* and *Andrew* corresponds to the order in which these three are addressed in the writing's version of the "doubting Thomas" story. Previous editions and translations did not show this, since the less reliable fam. 2 manuscripts reverse Thomas and Peter—doubtless under the influence of John 20. It may be possible to go further, and suggest that the apostle John, at the head of the list, is perceived as the spokesman or amanuensis of the college of apostles (see further Hills, 2008: 87–88). This would be entirely consistent with the often noticed "Johannine" character of the writing's theology and even dialogical style.

For comparison, the following New Testament lists may be quoted (> = surname, epithet, or "son of"):

Ep. apost. 2	**Matt 10:2–4**	**Mark 3:16–19**
John	Simon Peter	Simon Peter
Peter	Andrew	James > Zebedee
Thomas	James	John
Andrew	John	Andrew
James	Philip	Philip
Philip	Bartholomew	Bartholomew
Bartholomew	Thomas	Matthew
Matthew	Matthew	Thomas
Nathanael	James > Alphaeus	James > Alphaeus
Judas	Thaddaeus	Thaddaeus

Cephas	Simon > Cananaean	Simon > Cananaean
Judas Isacariot	Judas Isacariot	Judas Isacariot

Luke 6:14–16	**Acts 1:13**
Simon Peter	Peter
Andrew	John
James	James
John	Andrew
Philip	Philip
Bartholomew	Thomas
Matthew	Bartholomew
Thomas	Matthew
James > Alphaeus	James > Alphaeus
Simon > Zealot	Simon > Zealot
Judas > James	Judas > James
Judas Isacariot	[Matthias: Acts 1:26]

Full discussion of the variants is not possible here, but a few details are relevant to the list in the *Epistula apostolorum.* In Matt 10:3 and Mark 3:18, "Thaddaeus" has attracted several variant readings (see a critical Greek New Testament for the specific data). Most of these involve the name "Lebbaeus" as surname, forename, or substitute for Thaddaeus. Of more significance is the reading of the Old Latin in place of Thaddaeus: "Judas Zelotes." Bruce M. Metzger (1994: 26) suggests that "the name *Judas Zelotes* in several Old Latin manuscripts (compare also the same name in the fifth-century mosaic in the great Baptistry at Ravenna [Battistero degli Ortodossi]) may be a further assimilation to the previous name on Luke's list, 'Simon who was called the Zealot'" —Σίμωνα τὸν καλούμενον ζηλωτήν (Luke 6:15; cf. Σίμων ὁ ζηλώτης in Acts 1:13). Luke's term ζηλώτης (BADG, s.v. [p. 338a] "zealot, enthusiast, fanatic"; Eth. *qanāʾi*, as in *Ep. apost.* 2:1) replaces Mark's ὁ Καναναῖος (v.l. ὁ Κανανίτης; Mark 3:18 = Matt 10:4; and see John 14:22 v.l.), which may be a Greek transcription from the Aramaic root *qnʾ*, "to be jealous, zealous" (Jastrow, 1903: 1390b).

The various recensions of the *Apostolic Church Order* (*A.C.O.*) preserve similar lists. (Horner's edition, quoted throughout this book, gives this work the title, *Statutes of the Apostles*, following the 1691 partial edition by the great Ethiopicist Hiob Ludolf [1624–1704]). Schmidt (1919: 244–45), followed by, e.g., Schnackenburg (1968: 84 n. 32), even held that the *A.C.O.* is dependent on the *Epistula*. The lists are quoted here following Horner (1904: 127, 233, 295; see also 365; in one Eth. ms, Peter is placed before John; in both the Eth. and the Arab. recensions "James the brother of the Lord" is added at the end of the list). Also quoted is the list from the *Abyssinian Anaphora of our Lord* (Brightman, 1896: 228; cf. Cooper-MacLean, 1902: 246), that is, a representative Ethiopian eucharistic prayer plausibly influential in the later transmission of a list in Geʿez literature:

***A.C.O.* 1 (Eth., Arab.)**	***A.C.O. proem.* (Sah. Copt.)**	***Abyssinian Anaphora***
John	John	Simon Peter
Matthew	Matthew	Andrew
Peter	Peter	James
Philip	Andrew	John
Simon	Philip	Philip
James	Simon	Bartholomew
Nathanael	James	Thomas
Thomas	Nathanael	Matthew
Cephas	Thomas	Thaddaeus
Andrew	Cephas	Nathanael
Bartholomew	Bartholomew	James > Alphaeus
Judas	Judas > James	Matthias

Finally, the list in the *Constitutions of the Apostles* 6.14.1 (Funk, 1905: 335; ET in ANF 7. 456a) and its derivative in the Ethiopic *Didascalia* (Harden, 1920: 151; the Syriac and Latin versions of *Didascalia* 25 both lack the list; see Connolly, 1929: 210):

***Const. apost.* 6.14.1**	***Didascalia* (Eth.) 33**
Peter	Peter
Andrew	Andrew
James	James
John > Zebedee	John > Zebedee
Philip	Philip
Bartholomew	Bartholomew
Thomas	Matthew
Matthew	Thomas
James > Alphaeus	James > Alphaeus
Lebbaeus > Thaddaeus	Simon > Cananaean
Simon > Canaanite	Lebbaeus > Thaddaeus
Matthias	Matthias

James the brother of the Lord and Paul are added at the end of these two lists. The presence of Paul presumably attests to the same wish to profess the unity of the apostolic college as in the *Epistula* 31 and as already in *1 Clement* (especially chaps. 5 and 47), usually dated ca. 100 C.E.

THE EPISTULA APOSTOLORUM AND THE TESTAMENT IN GALILEE

Among the many source-critical questions still unanswered is the precise relationship between the *Epistula apostolorum* and a short apocalypse commonly referred to as the *Testament of Our Lord and Savior in Galilee*. An Ethiopic version of this document precedes the text of the *Epistula* in all the extant manuscripts; but there is either a fresh *incipit* ("title," usually of colored or ornamented opening words) or some scribal marker (whether ruled lines or a measurable space) between the two writings. Guerrier was the first to publish it, as the first eleven chapters of the *Epistula apostolorum*; but the page numbering in the Coptic text, already referred to, does not allow for this.

The potential significance of this separate tract of just a few pages is due to some considerable overlap between its eschatological teaching and *Ep. apost.* 35–37. Though actual word-for-word agreement is not extensive, there are some impressive parallels, including selective quotation of parts of Psalm 49 in its LXX wording. On the other hand, some detailed teaching about the Antichrist and the most precise geographical references (in Asia Minor) and chronological indicators (chiefly mid-third century) are not present in the *Epistula apostolorum.* Clearly, at some stage of composition or manuscript transmission the same writing lies behind both the *Epistula* and the *Testament*, or possibly one is the source of the other.

The matter is complicated by the fact that a very similar writing is found at the beginning of the huge church order known as the *Testamentum Domini*, usually dated to the early fifth century (see Rahmani, 1899; Cooper and MacLean, 1902; Beylot, 1984; Sperry-White, 1991). It is obvious that the subject-matter is not directly related to the bulk of the *Testamentum Domini*, which is a compendious set of ecclesiastical directions and liturgical prayers. Instead, the text serves to provide a post-resurrection setting for this church order material. Jesus' instructions for the new church therefore comprise the teaching that occupies the forty days of Acts 1:3, except that in place of instruction about the kingdom of God the disciples receive canon law and rubrics for worship—all very necessary as the church began to expand into new situations in new lands.

The full set of manuscript witnesses to the *Testament in Galilee* therefore comprises the following: (1) the Syriac and Ethiopic versions of the *Testamentum Domini* 1–11; (2) the Ethiopic versions of the *Testament* (there is an annotated French translation in Pérès, 1994: 113–24); and (3) the Ethiopic manuscripts' texts of the *Ep. apost.* 35–37, together with some Coptic fragments which seem to belong here. All of this material is being compared synoptically and will be used in the creation of a fresh edition and translation for another volume in this series of early Christian apocrypha.

A NEW TRANSLATION

The translation presented here reflects rather more of the idiom and sentence structure of the Coptic and Ethiopic texts than might be expected in a fresh, twenty-first century translation of an ancient work. There are several reasons for this. First, the texts being translated are not readily accessible except to those with research library privileges and with language training beyond the norm in the field of early Christian studies. Accuracy, even at the occasional expense of rhetorical appeal, has been the goal. Hence, for example, the retention of what will generally be reckoned an anachronistic "O" in the address "O Lord" in the Ethiopic version specifically when the Ge'ez text, or the best representatives of it, actually includes the prefix or suffix "O" over against the Coptic (see also 10:4, where the Coptic has ⲱ: ὦ, "O!"). Further, in general the standard or "first dictionary definition" of nouns and verbs has been used, especially in the translation of common New Testament and early church terms. From the Coptic and Ethiopic versions of the New Testament it is of course possible to learn what are the typical translation equivalents. Moreover, following the example of Hugo Duensing's German translation (1925), the English translation presented here includes, in parentheses, the actual Greek words present in the Coptic text as a further effort to allow the reader to hear at least echoes of the Greek original. To be sure, a review of other Coptic texts, including the Coptic New Testament, shows that Greek words present in the later version were not *necessarily* there in the original; sometimes more complex Greek words are replaced with simpler terminology. Here in the *Epistula*, the Coptic translator seems almost at will to have added δέ ("but, and") and γάρ ("for, because," though γάρ sometimes has no explanatory force even in Greek). Nevertheless, it is hoped that the momentary distraction of these parenthetical interruptions in the English will find adequate compensation in the value of seeing the Greek—in many if not most cases the actual words written in the mid-second century.

It will also be observed that the Coptic text preserves the names and titles of revered places and persons, commonly referred to as *nomina sacra*, in their abbreviated form: ⲓ̅ⲏ̅ⲗ̅ ='Ισραηλ, "Israel" (30:1); ⲓ̅ⲥ̅ ⲭ̅ⲥ̅ = 'Ιησοῦς Χριστός, "Jesus Christ" (7:2); ⲡ̅ⲛ̅ⲁ̅ = πνεῦμα, "spirit, Spirit" (22:1; 30:4; et al.); ⲥ̅ⲱ̅ⲣ̅: σωτήρ, "savior" (8:1; 10:5; 12:3) (see Van Groningen, 1940: 44–45 [§21.4 and fig. 12]; Layton, 2000: 34 [§41a]). As usual, Greek verbal forms are transcribed in an uninflected root form, identical in appearance to the second person singular present imperative. The usual variations in spelling due to itacism (the same sound) are found, e.g., ⲡⲣⲟⲫⲏⲧⲓⲁ: προφητεία, "prophecy" (19:18); ⲓⲣⲏⲛⲏ: εἰρήνη, "peace" (43:6). Both rough and smooth breathings are often reflected in an initial ϩ, e.g., ϩⲟⲙⲟⲗⲟⲅⲉⲓ: ὁμολογεῖν, "to confess" (39:10; 43:17); ϩⲩⲡⲟⲙⲟⲛⲏ: ὑπομονή, "endurance" (44:4); but ϩⲉⲑⲛⲟⲥ: ἔθνος, "nation, Gentile" (30:1; ⲉⲑⲛⲟⲥ in 30:5); ϩⲉⲛⲩⲃⲣⲓⲥ: ὕβρις, "arrogance" (38:4); ⲣ̅ⲩⲡⲟⲙⲉⲓⲛⲉ: ὑπομενεῖν "to endure" (38:4); ϩⲁⲙⲏⲛ : ἀμήν, "Amen" (16:3; 21:1; and passim); ⲧϩⲉⲗⲡⲓⲥ: ἐλπίς, "hope" (43:6) (for the orthographic principles involved, see Lambdin, 1983: xvii; Layton, 2000: 33–34 [§§39–40]). Greek ὡς ("as, just as, when") appears with the rough breathing (ʽ) at 10:1, but without it at 13:2.

Second, I have tried hard not to exaggerate either the *similarities* or the *differences* between the two major recensions. An analogy will be useful to explain the kind of restraint involved, again from textual criticism. In textual criticism, which is the art and science by which the best or "original" reading (or, as often, that of the "archetype") is sought among two or more "variant" readings found in the extant manuscripts, this maxim is often and rightly appealed to: "Choose the reading which best explains the origin of the others" (Metzger-Ehrman, 2005: 300). Just so, in translating two ancient versions side by side the translator is always conscious of the fact that for the most part—that is, except where a willful interpolator or "corrector" has been at work—the two witnesses ultimately derive from the same antecedent, sometimes referred to as the "Ur-text." So in any given passage, where a Coptic word or phrase and the corresponding Ethiopic are capable of a wide range of meaning, prudence requires that the translation first to be considered is that which reflects the respective terms' substantial overlap in semantic range or domain (for this concept, see, e.g., Louw and Nida, 1989: 1. vi–viii). One further case calls for special mention, since it concerns a term of some consequence. Ethiopic *te'zāz* ("commandment") appears first in 18:5, where, as already noted, Jesus issues his "new commandment." Thereafter, the same word (often with the possessive suffix *-eya*, "my") appears frequently opposite the certain Coptic *plural*, "commandments," even though Ge'ez does have a distinct plural form, *te'zāzāt*. Here, then, the singular must be used in the collective sense, as is found in other texts, though we would not know this for sure apart from the extant Coptic manuscript.

Finally, the relatively conservative method of translation adopted here is complemented by a rather fuller set of notes than might be expected to accompany a better-known apocryphal writing. As already stated, the *Epistula* shares terminology, themes, and motifs with a wide range of contemporary and near-contemporary writings. But this needs to be demonstrated, not merely asserted; and some sense of this range will, I hope, help to evoke some sort of historical and theological context for our further understanding of this promising but for now still little-known and enigmatic text.

HOW TO USE THIS BOOK

Epistle of the Apostles 65

teaching. [5]People will follow them and give allegiance to their riches, to their rituals, to their drunkenness, and to their bribes; and there will be partiality among them.

38 "But those who wish to see the face of God the Father, who show no partiality toward rich sinners, and who do not fear those who err, but correct them—[2]they, the wounded, will be with the Father; just as those who correct their neighbors will be saved, that is, a son of wisdom[a] through faith. [3]But if he has not become a son of wisdom he will hate and persecute and not turn to his brother, but will ignore and reject him. [4]But those who walk in truth and in the knowledge of faith in me, who have wisdom and knowledge and perseverance for the truth though they are despised as they strive for poverty, and endure it—[5]their reward is great,[b] since they are reproached, tormented, persecuted, destitute; and people are arrogant against them as they hunger and thirst. [6]But

[5]People . . . them . . . . . .

and their partiality . . . . . .]

38 "*But* (δε) [those who] wish to [. . . . . .] these will [not show partiality . . . . . . the] sinn[ers . . . . reprove their nei]ghbors, [he will be . . . a son] of *wisdom* (σοφια), since he [believes (πιστευε) . . .]. [3]*But* (δε) if [he is not] the son of *wisdom* (σοφια) . . . he will hate his neighbor, will turn against him and [*negl*]*ect* (απορει) him. [4]But those who *live their lives* (πολιτευεσθαι) in truth and in the knowledge of *faith* (πιστις), having *love* (αγαπη) for me—*for* (γαρ) they have *endured* (υπομεινε) *mistreatment* (υβρις)—people will despise them, since they walk in poverty and *endure* (υπομινε) those who hate them [and] reproach them. [5]They have been [tormented], destitute; people are arrogant against them as they walk in hunger and thirst. [6]*But because* (αλλα επει) they

38:2 [a]Cf. Lk 7:35
38:5 [b]Cf. Mt 5:12; Lk 6:23
38:6 [c]Cf. Rm 2:7
[d]Cf. 1Ths 4:17

38:2 • *wounded (qʷesulāna)*: Cf. 15:9, where Jesus foretells his coming "with my wounds." Here in 38:2 Guerrier (1919: [80] 220) emends the text to *qʷeṣṣulāna* ("crowned"), but with no manuscript support; cf. but *Barn.* 7.9 "the one that is accursed is crowned"; Herm. *Sim.* 8.3.6; 8.4.6.

37:5 *their rituals (ḥermatomu)*: Mss LPSV read *ḥertemennāhomu* "their depravity" (Duensing-Müller); in Phil 1:28 the same form translates αὐτοῖς . . . ἀπωλείας ("their destruction" [. . .]).
38:6 *in heaven (ba-samāyāt)*: Ethiopic mss CN *kama ʾenta samʿāt* "as martyrs" (cf. 50:4).

Cross references

Epistle of the Apostles translation

Notes on translation

Notes on original language manuscripts

THE BOOK OF THE REVELATION OF JESUS CHRIST TO HIS DISCIPLES

1 The book of what Jesus Christ revealed through the council of **1:1** [a]Cf. 3:9
the apostles, the disciples[a] of Jesus Christ, for all <people>, concern- **1:2** [a]Cf. 50:8
ing the false apostles Simon and Cerinthus; [2]about whom it is writ- **1:3** [a]Cf. Ac 15:7
ten so that no one associate with them—for in them is the deceit **1:4** [a]Cf. 1Jn 1:1
with which they kill people[a]—[3]so that you may be strong, and not [b]Cf. 31:12
falter, nor depart from the word of the gospel[a] that you have heard.
[4]What we have heard[a] and remembered[b] we have written for the

1:1 • *book*, or possibly "letter" (Duensing-Müller: "What Jesus Christ revealed to his disciples as a letter"). Ethiopic *maṣḥaf* can mean letter, as it does in, e.g., Isa 39:1; Esth 3:13; 2 Pet 3:16 (*DLLA*, *s.v.* *ṣaḥafa* [col. 1268]). But for "letter," *mal'ekt* is the preferred term, e.g., in the titles and colophons of all NT epistles; conversely, all ten NT instances of βίβλος ("book") are translated *maṣḥaf.* †

• *council:* Cf. Ignatius *Magn.* 6.1 "the presbyters in the place of the council of the apostles (εἰς τόπον συνεδρίου τῶν ἀποστόλων)."

• *for all <people>:* Similarly, Guerrier ("à tous") and Wajnberg ("für Alle"). Duensing-Müller translate "to the Catholics," presumably supposing an original τοῖς καθολικοῖς or πρὸς τοὺς καθολικούς. But though the term "catholic" is used of "the church," already in Ignatius *Smyrn.* 8.2; *Mart. Pol. inscrip.*, its earliest occurrence absolutely of "Christians" is apparently in the late third-century *Mart. Pion.* 19.4 (*LPGL*, *s.v.* καθολικός 1, 2 [pp. 690b–691a]). †

• *false apostles:* Probably for ψευδαπόστολοι, though the single NT use of the term is translated with the adjective alone (without the word "apostle[s]," the reading here of ms V), in the Ethiopic of 2 Cor 11:13: οἱ γὰρ τοιοῦτοι ψευδαπόστολοι = *'esma hallawu ḥassāweyān.* †

• *Simon and Cerinthus:* See further on 7:1, where the names of Simon and Cerinthus are reversed.

1:4 • *What we have heard:* Contrast AcJohn 88 "I cannot <either> *speak* or write to you the things which I have seen and heard." Duensing-Müller: "As we have heard (it)"; but *za-kama* here probably functions as a relative pronoun rather than as an adverb; see also 21:5; 30:2, 3.

• *remembered:* By the mid-second century "remembering" was becoming a technical term for the recollection and recording of earlier traditions about Jesus; see, e.g., Acts 20:35; *1 Clem.* 13.1–2; 46.7–8; Papias *frg.* 2 (*apud* Eusebius *Hist. eccl.* 3.39.3–4); further, Cameron, 2005: 91–95.

Title *The Book . . . :* Ethiopic mss PSV have "The Testament which [S: our Lord] Jesus Christ spoke and revealed . . . ," repeating "Testament" (*kidān*) from the title of the preceding *Testament in Galilee.*
1:2 *deceit: ḥebl*; mss OTV *ḥabl* "rope, cord" (cf. Job 18:10; Ps 140:5; Isa 5:18), but this is likely an orthographic variant, since confusion between *h* and *ḥ* (and other gutturals) is common in Ge'ez manuscripts. †

1:5 [a]Cf. Dan 4:1; 6:25; 1Pt 1:2; 2Pt 1:2
2:2 [a]Cf. 30:1
[b]Cf. 14:1
2:3 [a]Cf. 3:9; 5:7; 12:1; 1Jn 1:1; MPerp 1.6
3:2 [a]» 13:2
[b]» 1:6

whole world. [5]We greet you in joy, our sons and daughters, in the name of God almighty and in Jesus Christ. May grace abound upon you.[a]

2 We—John and Peter and Thomas and Andrew and James and Philip and Bartholomew and Matthew and Nathanael and Judas the Zealot and Cephas—[2]we write to the churches of the East and West, to those in the North and South,[a] announcing[b] and making known to you the things concerning Jesus Christ. [3]We have written about how we both heard him and touched him[a] after he rose from the dead.

3 And in that he revealed to us great, marvelous, and true things, we know this:

[2]Our Lord and Savior Jesus Christ, the Son of God,
is he who was sent[a] from God almighty,[b]
the maker and creator of what is named with every name;

1:5 • *sons and daughters (weludena wa-'awāledina):* The text specifies both genders, even though as in Greek the grammatically masculine plural "sons" can stand for both. Cf. *Barn.* 1.1 Χαίρετε, υἱοὶ καὶ θυγατέρες ("Hail, sons and daughters"), of which Kleist (1948: 167 n. 1) writes, "This salutation is unique in ancient Christian epistolography." †
2:2 • *we write,* literally "wrote" or "have written," but taken here as an epistolary aorist (ἐγράψαμεν; see Schmidt, 1919: 170 n. 1); in the NT, 1 John 2:14, 21, 26; 5:13.
3:1 • *we know this:* Duensing-Müller begin the chapter with these words. But the Ethiopic punctuation, admittedly not an infallible guide, suggests that the break occurs after "from the dead." †
3:2 • *named . . . name:* Cf. Eph 1:21; *Pr. Paul* (NHC I,*1*) A1.11–13; Irenaeus *Adv. haer.* 4.19.2. Guerrier orders the words slightly differently: "whose name is declared by all (things)"; cf. Exod 9:16 "so that my name may be declared throughout all the earth."

1:5 *We greet you ('ammāxnākemu)*: So Ethiopic fam. 1, probably reflecting Greek ἀσπαζόμεθα ὑμᾶς; cf. Rom 16:33; Ignatius *Trall.* 12.1. Duensing-Müller ("so we entrust it to you") follow fam. 2 mss BLS *'amāxannākemu.* †
1:6 *God:* Fam. 2 adds "the Father" (Duensing-Müller). "Father" is present in the creedal statement in 5:22. †
almighty ('axāzē kʷellu 'ālam), literally, "ruler of the whole world" (mss LP lack "whole"); also in 3:2; 5:22. †
and in: Ms O adds "his Son."
2:1 *We . . . :* The names differ slightly in the mss. Fam. 2 (as in Duensing-Müller) reverses Thomas and Peter, a significant difference in light of 11:7, where the disciples are invited to inspect the Lord's body in the order Peter, Thomas, Andrew. M lacks "Matthew" and adds "James" after "and Cephas"; S places "the Zealot" after Nathanael. There are similar lists in Matt 10:2–4; Mark 3:16–19; Luke 6:14–16; Acts 1:13; *A.C.O.* (Eth., Arab.) 1 (also Sah. Copt. *proem.*); *Const. apost.* 6.14.1; *Didasc.* (Eth.) 33. See the inventory of lists discussed in the Introduction. †
2:2 *churches:* Only mss LMO read the plural; all others have the singular (though likely in the collective sense), *la-bēta kerestiyān.*
3:2 *Lord and Savior Jesus Christ:* Mss ACNV lack "and Savior"; BO lack "Jesus Christ." Elsewhere in the writing the mss variously modify the titles of God and Jesus.

3 who is over all authorities,
Lord of lords and King of kings, Power of powers;
4 the heavenly one who sits upon the cherubim[a] and seraphim,
at the right hand[b] of the throne of the Father;[c]
5 by whose word he commanded the heavens
and built the earth and what is in it;
and defined the limits of the sea,
that it might not cross its boundaries,[a]
and opened the deep wells and springs,
that they might flow upon the earth both day and night;
6 who established the sun, the moon and the stars in heaven;
who separated light from darkness;[a]
7 who ordered Gehenna <into being>,
and in the twinkling of an eye commands
the winter rains and storms of snow and hail;
who causes the seasons to change and remain
at their appointed times;
8 who made humankind in his image and likeness;[a]
9 of whom the patriarchs and the prophets spoke[a] in parables;
and whom the apostles preached in truth
and the disciples[b] touched.[c]
10 <Him> we know: the Word who became flesh[a]
in the womb of the virgin Mary by the Holy Spirit,

3:4 [a]Cf. Dan 3:43 LXX (PrAz 32)
[b]» 19:11
[c]Cf. Mt 22:44; 26:64; Mk 16:19; Ac 2:33; Hb 1:3; 8:1; 12:2
3:5 [a]Cf. Jb 38:8–11; Ps 104:5–9; Prv 8:28–29
3:6 [a]Cf. 21:8; 39:3; Gn 1:4, 18; Is 45:7; Jer 31:35
3:8 [a]Cf. Gn 1:26
3:9 [a]Cf. Hb 1:1
[b]Cf. 1:1
[c]» 2:3
3:10 [a]Cf. 39:12; Jn 1:14

3:3 • *Lord . . . kings:* Cf. Deut 10:17; 1 Tim 6:15; Rev 17:14; 19:16; *1 Enoch* 9.4; *T. Mos.* 9.6; *Pr. Paul* (NHC I,*1*) A1.14; *Ps.-Clem. Hom* 3.72. The epithet "king of kings" had special significance in later Ethiopian tradition as the Geʿez for "emperor."
3:8 • *in his image and likeness:* Ethiopic *ba-'ar'ayāhu wa-ba-'amsālihu*, presumably for εἰκών and ὁμοίωσις in Gen 1:26. Further on *'amsāl*, see note on "parables" in 3:9.
3:9 • *patriarchs and prophets:* The first term is unambiguously "patriarchs" (*'abaw qadamt;* literally, "first" or "former fathers"); with "prophets" in, e.g., Irenaeus *Adv. haer.* 4.21.3. The phrase "fathers and prophets" occurs at 27:1; 28:3; 31:10.
• *parables:* Ethiopic *'amsāl* (in the singular or plural) = "likeness, form, image, proverb." The same word is translated "likeness" in 3:8; see further on the cognate *messālē* ("parable," or "picture" [Duensing-Müller]) in 5:21. †
• *. . . the disciples touched:* Or "who spoke in parables through the patriarchs and prophets and in truth through him whom the apostles declared and the disciples touched" (Duensing-Müller).
3:10 • *became flesh* (*kona šega*): The same words (though in reverse order) as in the Geʿez version of John 1:14 for σὰρξ ἐγένετο.

3:10 *the virgin:* Fam. 2 "the holy virgin"; and after "virgin," fam. 2 adds "carried (conceived)" (so Duensing); "hidden in her birth-pangs by the Holy Spirit" (Müller).

3:12 [a]Cf. Lk 2:7
3:13 [a]» 29:5

[11]and was born not by the lust of the flesh
but by the will of God,
[12]and was wrapped <in swaddling cloths>[a] in Bethlehem;
[13]—he who was to be killed was nursed and grew up,
as we saw.[a]

4 This is what the Lord Jesus Christ did:
[2]He was taken to school by Joseph and Mary his mother.
[3]And his teacher taught him saying, "Say alpha."
[4]He answered and said to him, "First you tell me what beta is;
then indeed you shall do what is true and real."

3:13 • *grew up (lehqa)*: Cf. 21:3 "I put on flesh and grew up"; Luke 1:80; 2:7; Justin *1 Apol.* 31.7.†

• *as we saw:* If the text is sound, the chief Lukan apostolic credential—presence with the Lord Jesus "beginning from the baptism of John until the day when he was taken up from us" (Acts 1:22; cf. Luke 24:48; Acts 2:32)—is here extended to include Jesus' childhood. The remark is perhaps intended to confirm the truth of the childhood story that immediately follows.

4:1 • *This . . . did:* The phrase probably serves as a superscription to the "miracle list" in chaps. 4–5; it has a counterpart in 13:1 "What he revealed to us is this: . . ." Further documentation and discussion of miracle lists, see Hills, 1993: 389–90; 2008: 38–44.

4:2 • *He was taken to school . . . :* Cf. *Inf. Thom.* 6.3; 14.2; Ps 119:99 "I have more understanding than all my teachers." Irenaeus (*Adv. haer.* 1.20.1) condemns the story, which he states is told by the Marcosians (mid-second century disciples of a gnostic teacher, Marcus); this group also used the *Acts of Thomas* and other presumed unorthodox writings. On the genesis of the school tradition, see McNeil, 1976.

4:4 • *then . . . real:* This concluding phrase is probably corrupt in all mss, and possibly belongs with 5:1. Other attempts to make sense of it include Duensing "And . . . true . . . a real thing which was done"; Müller "And truly (it was) a real thing which was done."

3:11 *and was born . . . :* The Ethiopic mss are united in reading the singular (*tawalda;* contrast John 1:13 οἳ οὐκ ἐγεννήθησαν = *'ella 'i- . . . waldu*), as do "several ancient witnesses, chiefly Latin (It b Irenaeus [lat] Tertullian Origen [lat] Ambrose Augustine Ps-Athanasius)" (Metzger, 1994: 168). On the significance of the Western reading, see Streeter, 1924: 70; Hornschuh, 1965: 106.

3:13 *. . . who was to be killed:* Both fam. 1 and fam. 2 are probably corrupt. After "Bethlehem" fam. 2 has "and was made known and" (so Duensing-Müller) but lacks "he was to be killed"; ms M has "that he might suffer" after "Bethlehem." †

4:1 *the Lord Jesus Christ:* So mss CK; "our Savior" O; AT "our Lord, that is, our Lord [*sic*] Christ"; fam. 2 "our Lord."

This . . . did: For *zanta gabra* ("he did this" *or* "these things") mss CN have *zanta tagazra* "this one [i.e., Jesus] was circumcised"; ms O *za-tagamra* "that which [*or* he who] was completed [*or* comprehended]."

4:3 *alpha:* Ms V adds "and beta."

5 Then there was a marriage in Cana of Galilee,[a]
and he was invited with his mother and his brothers;
and he made water into wine;
2and he raised the dead,[a]
and made the paralytic walk,[b]
and stretched out the hand[c] of him whose hand was withered;[d]
3and a woman who had suffered a hemorrhage for twelve years
touched the hem of his garment and was immediately cured.[a]
4And as we wondered and marveled at this glorious work that
he had done, he said to us, "Who touched me?"
5We said to him, "O Lord, a crowd of people touched you."
6He answered and said to us, "I perceived that power had gone
out of me."
7Right away that woman, having approached him, said to him,
"O Lord, I touched you."
8He answered and said to her, "Go, your faith has cured you."
9Then he made the deaf hear, and the blind see, and expelled
demons from the possessed, and cleansed lepers.[a]
10And the demon Legion, that possessed a man, found Jesus and
cried out, saying, "Before the day of our destruction has
arrived you have come to drive us out!"[a]

5:1 [a]Cf. 10:4; Jn 2:1–11
5:2 [a]Cf. Mt 11:5; Lk 7:22
[b]Cf. Mt 4:24; Mt 9:1–8; Mk 2:1–12; Lk 5:17–26; Jn 5:2–9
[c]Cf. 39:5
[d]Cf. Mt 12:9–14; Mk 3:1–6; Lk 6:6–11
5:3 [a]Cf. Mt 9:20–22; Mk 5:25–34; Lk 8:43–48
5:9 [a]Cf. Mt 11:5; Lk 7:21–22
5:10 [a]Cf. Mt 8:28–34; Mk 1:21–28; 5:1–20; Lk 4:31–37; 8:26–39

5:1 • *brothers:* The disciples are referred to as "brothers" in 10:2; 19:6; 32:4. †
• *and . . . wine: wa-maya rassaya wayna*, a phrase not in John 2 but found verbatim as a reminiscence in John 4:46 ἐποίησεν τὸ ὕδωρ οἶνον.
5:4 • *glorious work* or "miracle" (Duensing-Müller). *sebḥat* is the standard term for "glory" or "praise" (δόξα, αἴνεσις), but in the plural can translate ἔνδοξα, ἀρεταί ("glorious deeds, works"), as in Isa 12:4; 42:8, 12; 43:21 (see Brockington, 1967: 5); cf. *Ep. apost.* 13:5; 33:7; 36:11.
5:7 • *I touched you:* The woman's saving touch perhaps anticipates the *disciples'* touching of Jesus to verify his resurrection in 12:1.

5:1 *his mother and* is lacking in ms O.
5:2 *paralytic:* The noun is singular (*maḍāgʷeʿ*) in mss BKOQR, plural (*maḍāgʷeʿān*) in ACLMNPSTV. Whether the original Greek read the singular or the plural, the noun was almost certainly παραλυτικός ("paralytic") or equivalent, not χωλός ("lame," as in Duensing-Müller): the ten uses of παραλυτικός in the NT are with one exception translated *maḍāgʷeʿ* in the Ethiopic NT; the exception (Mark 2:10) has *dewuy* ("sick"), presumably to avoid repetition of "paralytic" in 2:9. †
withered: Ms M adds "and immediately it was restored, like the other <hand>"; cf. Matt 12:13 v.l.
5:3 *hem . . . garment (zafara lebsu):* Mss LMPSV *ṣenfa lebsu*, as in Matt 9:20 for τοῦ κρασπέδου τοῦ ἱματίου αὐτοῦ.

5:19 [a]Cf. Mt 14:13–21; 15:32–39; Mk 6:30–44; 8:1–10; Lk 9:10–17; Jn 6:1–13

11 Jesus rebuked him, and said to him, "Come out of this man
without harming him."
12 And he entered the swine and plunged them into the sea, and
they drowned.
13 Then he walked on the sea; and the winds blew, and he
rebuked them; and he calmed the waves of the sea.
14 And when we, his disciples, had no denarius, we said to him,
"Teacher, what are we to do about the tax collectors?"
15 He answered and said to us, "One of you, cast the fish-hook
into the deep, and catch a fish; he will find a denarius in it.
16 Give it to the tax collectors for me and for you."
17 Then when we had no bread except five loaves and two fish,
he commanded the people to sit down;
18 they numbered five thousand, besides women and children,
to whom we distributed fragments of the bread;
19 and they were satisfied, and there was <some> left over,
and we gathered up twelve baskets full of fragments,[a]

5:11 • *... without harming him:* Cf. Luke 4:35; AcPet. 11 "Peter said, 'You too, then, whatever demon you may be . . ., come out of the young man and do him no harm' " (*NTApoc*^{2} 2. 293); *Acts of Andrew* (Copt. *P. Utrecht* 1, lines 32–38) "The demon said to the apostle, 'I have never harmed any of his limbs . . ., so now I will leave this young man to whose limbs I have done no violence whatsoever' " (MacDonald, 1990: 250–51; *NTApoc*^{2} 2. 407).
5:13 • *he walked on the sea . . . :* Cf. Matt 8:23–27; 14:22–33; Mark 4:35–41; 6:45–52; Luke 8:22–25; John 6:15–21. These two sea miracles are frequently placed together in early Christian miracle lists.

• *and the winds blew:* The exact phrase is found, in a different context, in Matt 7:25, 27 (houses built on rock and sand); cf. John 6:18.
5:14 • *when we . . . :* This and the following miracle account (5:17–20) both begin with the phrase *'enza 'albena,* which would translate ἡμεῖς μὴ ἔχοντες or equivalent. With the story of the fish, cf. Matt 17:24–27. For Matthew's οἱ τὰ δίδραχμα λαμβάνοντες ("the collectors of the half-shekel tax" = *'ella ṣabbāḥta dināra yenašše'u*) *Ep. apost.* 5:14 has *masabbeḥān* = οἱ τελῶναι.
5:15 • *One of you . . . :* Bultmann suggests that since not Peter but a nameless "one of you" is instructed to fish, "it is possible that an older tradition than Matt. 17^{24ff} is showing through" (1963: 310 n. 3). But variation from the canonical account is typical of early allusions to this Matthean story. See, e.g., AcThom 143, where Thomas praises his Lord as "he who is the truth and does not lie, and paid tribute [*Syr. adds* and] poll-tax for himself and his disciples"; Melito *Pass. Hom.* 622–23 "It is he from whom you extorted money, demanding from him his two-drachma poll-tax."

5:11 *Jesus:* Fam. 2 mss. LPS and AT have "the Lord Jesus"; V has simply "the Lord."
5:13 *he calmed . . . sea:* Fam. 2 "and the waves of the sea became calm" (Duensing-Müller).
5:15 *fish-hook (maqāṭena mašgart 'anqar):* A strange form, combining "hook" and "net" (on the lexical difficulties, see Duensing, 1922: 184); hence Duensing-Müller "the hook, the net."

[20]as we asked and said, "What do these five loaves <mean>?" 5:22 [a]» 1:6
[21]They are a type of our <statement of> faith for baptized
Christians, that is:
[22]In the Father almighty,[a]
in Jesus Christ,
in the Holy Spirit,
and in the holy church,
and in the forgiveness of sins.

5:20 • *What . . . <mean>?* Literally, "What are these five loaves?" There is an identical construction in Josh 4:21, where, exactly following the MT ("What are these stones?"; RSV "What do these stones mean?") the LXX has τί εἰσιν οἱ λίθοι οὗτοι; (see also Josh 4:6). †

5:21 • *type,* or "parable," "symbol" (James), "picture" (Duensing-Mueller): *messālē* is a cognate of *'amsāl* (see notes on 3:9; 18:1; 32:3). In 18:2, where both texts are difficult, the latter is found probably opposite the specific Coptic (Greek) τύπος. Dillmann offers the meanings *typus, exemplum,* et al. ("type, pattern"; *DLLA, s.v. messālē* [col. 175]). †

• *our <statement of> faith ('aminotena):* "Faith" here likely has the force of a technical term—"our [*sc.* apostolic, orthodox] belief." †

• *for (ba'enta):* The very common preposition *ba'enta* is normally translated "about, concerning," and commonly stands for περί + genitive. But other freer uses are found, e.g., Gal 2:9 ὑπὲρ ἐμοῦ "for me" = *ba'enti'aya*; Col 4:8 εἰς αὐτὸ τοῦτο "[I have sent him to you] for this very purpose" (RSV) = *ba'enta zentu gebr*; Heb 2:9 ὑπὲρ πάντων "for everyone" = *ba'enta kʷellu.*

• *baptized Christians:* See apparatus note below. The fam. 1 reading is of considerable significance, because it locates the credal statement as the confession of full members of the Christian community—those initiated into the Christian mysteries. The term "great Christians" is found regularly in Ethiopic versions of older church order literature, in which these distinctions are of course important; discussion and references in Hills, 2008: 62–64.

5:22 • *In the Father, . . . :* With this five-part formula, cf. Hippolytus *Apost. trad.* 21.12–17; 23.8–10; also the preliminary creed at *Apost. trad.* 21.11, in connection with which Dix (1992: lxii–lxiii) quotes the disputed baptismal creed in the (4th-cent.?) Deir Balizeh papyrus:

I believe in God the Father Almighty
And in His only-begotten Son our Lord Jesus Christ
And in the Holy Ghost
and in the resurrection of the flesh
and the Holy Catholic Church.

Holland (1976: 193 n. 3), however, questions the form-critical classification of *Ep. apost.* 5:22: "That this passage is a creed seems to be highly dubious."

5:21 *baptized Christians ('abiy kerestiyān):* So fam. 1; literally, "great [*or* full] Christians," a common idiom for baptized persons, in contrast to the *ne'us kerestiyān,* "the little [*or* young] Christians," i.e., neophytes or catechumens. The fam. 2 reading is *'abiy kerestennā,* "great Christianity." †

5:22 *Jesus Christ:* Fam. 2 adds "our Savior."

Holy Spirit: Fam. 2 adds "the Paraclete."

7:3 [a]Cf. 50:8
[b]» 38:7

6 Our Lord and Savior revealed and showed this to us, and likewise we to you, [2]so that, taking thought for eternal life, you may be established in the grace of the Lord and in our ministry and our preaching. [3]Be strong, not faltering in the certain knowledge of the Lord Jesus Christ, and he will be merciful and gracious, and will save for all eternity.

7 Cerinthus and Simon have come, to go about the world. [2]Now they are enemies of our Lord Jesus Christ, who turn aside those who believe in the true Word and deed, that is, Jesus Christ. [3]So beware, and guard yourselves against them, for in them is affliction and pollution and death,[a] whose end is decay and judgment.[b]

7 Cerinthus and Simon have come, [and go] about the *world* (κοσμος). [2]*Now* (δε) they are enemies of our Lord *Jesus Christ* (ις χς), for they distort the words and the work, that is, *Jesus Christ* (ις χς). [3]So keep yourselves from them, *for* (γαρ) in them is death and a great stain of corruption, whose end is *judgment* (κρισις) and eternal loss.

7:1 • *Cerinthus and Simon* are already identified, in reverse order, in 1:1. These are of course not *pagan* but *Christian* adversaries. For Simon, see already Acts 8:9–24; also the various *Acts of Peter*; the *Acts of Peter and Paul*; and the *Pseudo-Clementines.* In the *Epistula,* he is not given the epithet "magician" or its equivalent. For Cerinthus (*fl.* ca. 100) as docetist, as opponent of St. John, and as proto-Marcionite, see Polycarp *apud* Eusebius *Hist. eccl.* 3.28.6; Irenaeus *Adv. haer.* 1.26; 3.3.4; 3.11.1; Hippolytus *Ref.* 7.33; 10.21. †

• *to go about the world:* Cf. Satan's wandering "to and fro" in Job 1:7; 2 John 7; *Gos. Bart.* 4.52 ἐγὼ ἐν τῷ κόσμῳ ἤμην περιερχόμενος "I [*sc.* Satan] wandered to and fro in the world."

7:3 • *So beware . . . :* Cf. Rom 16:17; Ignatius *Trall.* 7.1 "Beware therefore of such men"; *Smyrn.* 7.2 "It is right to refrain from such men."

• *whose end is judgment* (Copt.), likely for Greek ὧν τὸ τέλος κρίσις (or κατάκριμα); cf. 38:7; 47:6.

6:2 *that you may be established (kama tekunu šururāna):* Fam. 2 *kama tekunu sutufāna* "that you may be associates" (Duensing-Müller).

the Lord: Mss ACNPRTV "our Lord"; ms Q "God."

our preaching(sebkatena): So ms O; all other mss read *sebḥatina* ("our glory"; so Duensing-Müller), possibly understood as "our glorious work [for God]" (see note on 5:4 "glorious work").

6:3 *be merciful (yemēhher):* Or "teach," depending on whether the guttural is read as *h* or *ḥ*, and on whether the scribes in question are observing this distinction. Several fam. 2 mss lack "he will be merciful" (so Duensing-Müller).

8 Look, then, we have not hesitated or delayed concerning the true testimony of our Lord and Savior: [2]what he did as we, being with him, saw for ourselves, and whatever our thoughts within us, he both interpreted and did.	**8** Therefore we have not delayed to write to you concerning the *testimony* (μαρτυρια) of our *Savior Christ* (σωρ χς): [2]what he did, as we followed him, *both* (ετι) in thought and deed.
9 This one of whom we are witnesses we know: he who was crucified in the days of Pontius Pilate and Archelaus the judge,[a] who was crucified	**9** This is he [of whom] we bear witness that he is the Lord, who was *[crucif]ied* (σταυρου) by Pontius Pilate [and A]rchelaus between two

9:1 [a]» 28:2

8:1 • *not delayed to write:* This is an epistolary convention (see MM, *s.v.* ὀκνέω ["to delay" [p. 444b]). For its use in the preface to a theological treatise, see, e.g., Papias *frg.* 2 (*apud* Eusebius *Hist. eccl.* 3.39.3) "I shall not hesitate (οὐκ ὀκνήσω) to set down for you . . . what I have learned and remembered"; Irenaeus *Epid.* 1 "We have not delayed . . . to commune with you a little in writing, . . . to confirm your faith"; *Corp. Herm.* 11.1 "I shall not hesitate to declare (εἰπεῖν οὐκ ὀκνήσω) what I am inspired to say."

8:2 • *interpreted:* The following words, "and did" (*or* "caused"; Duensing-Müller), are read in mss ACLMNOPTV; in the context of the dialogue, this would appear to mean "how he answered our questions" or possibly "gave their interpretation."

9:1–2 • *This one . . . witnesses:* Possibly this phrase belongs at the end of chap. 8: "of whom [*or* of which] we became witnesses." With the entire summary of the events of the passion, cf. Acts 2:22–24; 3:13–15; 5:30–31; 10:36–42; 1 Cor 15:3–5; *Ep. Pet. Phil.* (NHC VII,2) 139.15–21. The following notes supply only the most important additional references; for more detailed comparison with the NT gospels and the *Gospel of Peter*, see Hills 2008: 67–95.

• *in the days of:* This Ethiopic reading and the parallel Coptic ("by," that is, under the jurisdiction of) both reflect the Greek ἐπί + genitive; see BDF §234 (5) "Metaphorically 'over' of authority, control (Attic)"; (8) "Temporally . . . of contemporaneity (classical): ἐπὶ Ἀβιάθαρ ἀρχιερέως Mk 2:26" (pp. 122–23).

• *Archelaus:* Cf. Matt 2:22, where the reference is to Archelaus, son of Herod the Great and Malthace. But possibly this is a reference to Julius Archelaus, son of Helcias; see Josephus *Ant.* 19.354–55; 20.140, 147; *Ap.* 51 (see de Zwaan, 1933: 349). †

• *judge (makʷannen):* The standard Ethiopic term for "judge, administrator, high official," but with no particular royal lineage; but cf. Duensing-Müller "prince."

• *between two thieves:* Schmidt (1919: 37 n. 14) retroverts to ἐν μέσῳ τοῦ ζυγοῦ λῃστῶν; cf. Matt 27:38; Mark 15:27; Luke 23:33; John 19:18; *Gos. Pet.* 4.10.

8:1 *our Lord and Savior:* Mss LMPV "our Lord Jesus Christ."

9:2 [a]Cf. Ac 13:29
10:1 [a]» 9:4
10:2 [a]» 5:1

between two thieves, [2]and with them[a] was taken down from the wood of the cross, and was buried in a place called "the Skull"; [3]to which place went three women: Sarah and Martha and Mary Magdalene. [4]They took ointment to pour upon his body, weeping and grieving over what had happened. [5]But when they reached the tomb and found the stone where it had been rolled away from the tomb, they opened the door but did not find his body.

thieves (ληστης), [2][and] was buried in a *place* (τοπος) called ["the *Skul*]*l* (κρανιον)." [3][Three] women went there: Mary, Martha and Mary [Magd]alene. [4]They took ointment to pour [upon h]is *body* (σωμα), weeping and *grieving* (λυπει) over [what] had happened. [5]*But* (δε) when they reached the *to*[*mb*] (ταφος) and looked inside they did not find the *body* (σωμα).

10 But as they grieved and wept the Lord appeared to them and said to them, "Do not weep. I am he whom you seek. [2]But go, one of you, to your brothers[a] and say to them, 'Come, the teacher is risen from the dead.' "

[3]Mary came and told us.

10 *But as* (ως δε) they *grieved* (λυπει) and wept the Lord appeared to them and said to them, "For whom do you weep? Do not weep. I am he whom you seek. [2]*But* (αλλα) go, one of you, to your brothers and say, 'Come, the teacher is risen from the dead.' "

[3]Martha came and told us.

9:2 • *the Skull:* In the Synoptic Gospels (Matt 27:33; Mark 15:22; Luke 23:33), this is not the place of burial; but see John 19:41.
9:4 • *weeping and grieving:* A recurring motif in the *Epistula*; see 10:1; 15:3; 43:5, 10. Cf. Mark 16:10; *Gos. Pet.* 7.26, 27; 12.52; 14.49.
10:1 • *the Lord appeared:* The resurrected Jesus himself appears; contrast Matt 28:2; Mark 16:5; Luke 24:4.
10:2 • *Come . . . dead:* Schmidt (1919: 39 n.11) retroverts to ὑπάγετε, ὁ διδάσκαλος ἠγέρθη ἀπὸ τῶν νεκρῶν; cf. Matt 28:7.

9:2 *with them:* Mss CN add "was numbered and" (cf. Isa 53:12; Luke 22:37).
9:3 • *Martha:* Coptic ⲧⲁⲙⲁⲣⲑⲁ, literally, "she who belonged to Martha" (Duensing) or "the daughter of Martha" (Müller). Ethiopic mss QR add *wa-Māryā* "and Mary." Hannah (2008: 618–19) judges that the name "Sarah" replaced "Salome" (cf. Mark 16:1) through a transcriptional error by the Ethiopian translator or a later scribe. †
10:2 *the teacher:* Fam. 2 "our teacher" (Duensing-Müller); the epithet recurs in 11:4; 32:1. For the whole phrase here mss ACNT have "Look, our teacher [CN: our Lord] is calling you; he has risen"; cf. John 11:28 ὁ διδάσκαλος . . . φωνεῖ σε.

[4]We said to her, "What do you want with us, O woman? Is it possible for him to live who has died and been buried?" [5]We did not believe her, that our Savior had risen from the dead.

[6]Then she went back to the Lord and said to him, "None of them believed me concerning your resurrection."

[7]He said, "Go, another of you, and tell them again."

[8]Sarah came and likewise reported to us, but we did not believe her. [9]She returned to the Lord and told him, as had Mary.

11 Then the Lord said to Mary and her sisters, "Let us go to them."

[2]And he came and found us fishing, but we doubted and did not believe: [3]he appeared to us as a phantom,[a] and we did not

[4]We said to her, "What do you want with us, *O* (ω) woman? Is it possible for him to live who has died and been buried?" [5]We did not [*bel*]*ieve* (πιστευε) her, that the *Savior* (σωρ) had risen from the dea[d.

[6]*Th*]*en* (τοτε) she went <back> to the Lord and said to him, "None of them *believed* (πιστευε) me, that you are alive."

[7]He said, "Go, another one of you, to them and tell them again."

[8]Mary came and told us again, but we did not *believe* (πιστευε) her. [9]She returned to the Lord and she told him.

11 *Then* (τοτε) the Lord said to Mary and also to her sisters, "Let us go to them."

[2]And he came and found us inside.[a] He called us out. [3]*But* (δε) we thought that it was a *phantom* (φαντασια): we did not

11:2 [a]Cf. Jn 20:19, 26
11:3 [a]Cf. Mt 14:26; Mk 6:49; Lk 24:37

10:4 • *What do you want with us, O woman?* The question echoes the wording of Jesus' famous response to his mother in John 2:4 (τί ἐμοὶ καὶ σοί γύναι;), the first pronoun now being plural.
11:3 • *he appeared to us / we thought it was:* Both the Ethiopic (*masalana*) and the Coptic (ⲁⲛⲁⲛ ⲇⲉ ⲛⲁⲛⲙⲉⲟⲩⲉ) reading likely derive from the same Greek phrase, ἐδόκει ἡμῖν or ἔδοξεν ἡμῖν (see also 13:3); cf. Acts 15:25. In Herm. *Sim.* 3.1 ἐδόκει μοι ("it appeared to me") becomes *yemasselani* (Abbadie, 1860: 51); so also Herm. *Sim.* 9.2:2 ("they seemed to me"); Herm. *Mand.* 8.11 ("does it not seem to you . . ?") and often; but in Herm. *Vis.* 3.7:1 δοκοῦντες ("they think that . . .") is likewise translated *'enza yemasselomu* (Abbadie, 1860: 13).

11:2 *found us inside* (ⲛ̄ϩⲟⲩⲛ) / *fishing* (*'enza negēlleb*): The Ethiopic fam. 1 reading, "fishing," is attractive in light of the post-resurrection stories in John 21:1–8; *Gos. Pet.* 14.60 ("I, Simon Peter, and my brother Andrew took our nets and went to the sea"). The fam. 2 reading *netgallabab*, "veiled" (so Duensing-Müller and most modern translations), is also attractive in the context of an epiphany (see further 12:2). Both verbs have the root idea of a "net" or "covering." †

11:4 [a]» 32:1

[b]Cf. Mt 26:34, 75; Mk 14:30, 72; Lk 22:34, 61; Jn 13:38; 18:27

11:7 [a]Cf. Mt 14:27; Mk 6:50; Lk 24:39

[b]Cf. Jn 20:20, 25, 27

believe that it was our Lord. But it was he. [4]And he spoke to us thus: "Come, do not fear. I am your teacher,[a] whom you, Peter, denied three times before the cock crowed;[b] and now do you deny again?"

[5]But we went to him, pondering and doubting whether it was indeed he. [6]And he said to us, "Why do you doubt and not believe? I am he who told you about my flesh, and my death, and my resurrection. [7]That you may know that it is I:[a] Peter, put your fingers in the nail-wounds in my hands; and you too, Thomas, <put your fingers> in my side;[b] and you too, Andrew, see if my foot treads upon the ground and there is a footprint. [8]For it is written in

believe (πιστευε) that it was the Lord. [4]*Then* (τοτε) [he said] to us, "Come, do not fear. I [. . . am your teacher], whom you, Peter, *den*[*ied*] (αρνα) three times; and now do you *deny* (αρνα) again?"

[5]*But* (δε) we went to him, *doubting* (δισταζε) in [our] hearts whether it could somehow be he. [6]*Then* (τοτε) he said to [us], "Why do you *still doubt* (δισταζε ετι) and not believe? I am he who told you about my *flesh* (σαρξ), my death, and my resurrection. [7]That you may know that it is I: Peter, put your fingers in the nail-wounds in my hands; and you too, Thomas, put your fingers in the *spear-* (λογχη) wounds in my side; *and* (δε) you too, Andrew,

11:4 • *denied . . . deny:* Later, the author will address the issue of apostasy among those who have "confessed and denied" (39:10). On the form ⲣ̄ ⲁⲣⲛⲁ (from ἀρνεῖσθαι), see Layton, 2000: 155 (§192). †
11:5 • *doubting:* The verb διστάζειν occurs in the NT only at Matt 14:31 (see *Ep. apost.* 24:4) and 28:17 (of the resurrection): "some doubted."
11:7 • *That you may know . . . :* With the episode in 11:7–12:3, cf. *2 Apoc. Jas.* (NHC V,4) 56.14–57.19: " 'Behold, I shall reveal to you those <things> that <neither> the heavens nor their archons have known [cf. *Ep. apost.* 12:3]. . . . But now, stretch out your [hand]. Now, take hold of me.' [And] then I stretched out my hands and I did not find him as I thought <he would be>. But afterward I heard him saying, 'Understand and take hold of me.' Then I understood, and I was afraid. And I was exceedingly joyful."

• *Peter, Thomas, Andrew:* The three are named in the same order, immediately after John, as in the list of apostles in 2:1 according to fam. 1 mss.
11:8 • *For it is written in the prophet:* In the NT, with one exception "for it is written" (γέγραπται γάρ) is directly followed by the quotation: Matt 4:6, 10; 26:31; Luke 4:10; Acts 23:5; Rom 12:19; 14:11; 1 Cor 1:19; 3:19; (and cf. 1 Cor 15:45); Gal 3:10; 4:22, 27. The exception is Acts 1:10: ". . . in the book of Psalms."

• *'The foot . . . ground':* An unknown saying, possibly from a lost Jewish apocryphal writing (so Hornschuh, 1965: 78–79 and n. 39). Guerrier (1913: [56] 196 n. 1) compares Dan 14:19 (=Bel 19), where Daniel mocks those who would claim a visit from the pagan god Bel: "Look at the floor, and notice whose footsteps these are (Ἰδὲ δὴ τὸ ἔδαφος καὶ γνῶθι τίνος τὰ ἴχνη ταῦτα, Theod.; LXX Βασιλεῦ, ταῦτα τὰ ἴχνη τίνος ἐστί;)." Similar formulations are found in Job 11:7; Wis 18:17; Luke 24:39. †

the prophet:[a] 'The footprint of a demonic phantom does not fasten upon the ground.'"

12 So we then touched him,[a] <to determine that> that he had truly risen in the flesh; 2then we fell on our faces before him, sought pardon, and entreated him because we had not believed him.

3Then our Lord and Savior said to us, "Arise, and I will reveal to you what is in heaven and what is above heaven, and

look at my feet and see if they do not make contact with the ground. 8*For* (γαρ) it is written in the *prophet* (προφητης): 'The foot of a *demonic phantom* (φαντασια δαιμων) does not fasten upon the ground.'"

12 *So* (δε) we [tou]ched him, that we might know truly whether he [had risen] in the *flesh* (σαρξ), 2and we fell on our [faces] *confessing* (εξομολογει) our sins, that we had been [unbe]lieving.

3*Then* (τοτε) the Lord our *Savior* (σωρ) said, "Ari[se,] and I will reveal to you what is above heaven and what is in heaven

11:8 [a]Cf. 33:4
12:1 [a]» 2:3

12:1 • *we touched him . . . :* Both in general situation and in specific details this account is strikingly similar to the opening of the late fourth- or early fifth-century *Testamentum Domini:* "It came to pass, after our Lord rose from the dead, and appeared to us, and was handled [*literally*, touched] by Thomas and Matthew and John, and we were persuaded that our Master [*literally*, Teacher] was truly risen from the dead, that falling on our faces we blessed the Father of the new world . . . ; and being held in very great fear, we waited prostrate as babes which speak not. But Jesus our Lord, putting His hand on each one of us separately, lifted us up, saying, 'Why hath your heart thus fallen. . . ?'" (*T. Dom.* 1. *proem.;* Cooper-MacLean, 1902: 4). The ascension scene in *Ep. apost.* 51 exhibits similar correspondences; see note on 51:2–4.

• *Truly:* Coptic (though not using the Greek term) and Ethiopic both likely reflect Greek ἀληθῶς, "the watch-word against Docetism" (Lightfoot, 1889–1890, 1981: 2/2. 173 n. 8); but see 40:1 (Coptic), where the actual Greek word is found.
12:2 • *we fell on our faces:* A form-critical signal that the account is an epiphany (more particularly, a commissioning) in biblical and extra-biblical tradition; see, e.g., Ezek 1:28–2:2; Dan 8:15–19; 10:8–12; Matt 17:6–7; *1 Enoch* 14.24–15.2; 60.4–6; *2 Enoch* 22.5–23.7; *Acts Pet. 12 Apost.* (NHC VI,*1*) 9.1–10.13.
12:3 • *Then . . . :* The post-resurrection discourse begins here. "Then" in introductions to speeches seems to be a mark of deliberate dialogue composition; for details, see the Additional Note. †

12:3 *what is in heaven:* Ethiopic fam. 2 "what is on earth" (so Duensing-Müller).

12:4 [a]Cf. Mt 28:18
[b]» 13:2
13:1 [a]Cf. 4:1

your resurrection that is in the kingdom of heaven, [4]concerning which my Father sent me[a] to take up you and those who believe in me."

13 What he revealed to us is this[a] that he said:

"When I was coming from the Father <of> all, as I passed through the heavens, having put on the wisdom of the Father I was clothed with the power of his might. [2]I was in the heavens, as I passed through the angels and archangels in their likeness, and as one of them I passed through the orders and authorities and

and your *rest* (αναπαυσις) which is in the kingdom of heaven. [4]*For* (γαρ) my Father gave me the *power* (εξουσια)[a] to take up you and those who *believe* (πιστευε) in me."

13 *Now* (δε), what he revealed <to us> are these things that he said:
"When (δε) I was to come down from the Father of all and *pass by* (παραγε) the heavens, I put on the *wisdom* (σοφια) of the Father and I put on the *power* (δυναμις) of his might. [2]I was in the heavens, and I *passed by* (παραγε) the *archangels* (αρχαγγελος) and the *angels* (αγγελος) in their likeness, *as if* (ως) I were one of them among

• *your resurrection / your rest:* Cf. *2 Clem.* 5.5; 6.7; and see the apparatus note on the present verse.

• *the kingdom of heaven:* Also in 19:1 (fam. 2 only), 5; 22:2; 42:2, 7 (Ethiopic: "kingdom"); "kingdom of my Father": 19:1; 26:5; 29:6; 32:4; "kingdom" without qualifier: 21:4; 28:5 (Coptic); 29:6; 39:10 (Ethiopic).

12:2 • *confessing their sins:* In the NT, ἐξομολογεῖν -εῖσθαι + "sins" is found only at Matt 3:6; Mark 1:5; Jas 5:16; i.e., not at all in connection with disbelief in the resurrection.

13:1 • *What he revealed . . . :* 13:1–3 and 14:1–7 are quoted in slightly abbreviated form in a *Homily in Honor of Saturday* of Ase Zäʾra Yaʿqob (1434–68 CE) (see Haile, 1982: 192).

---

your resurrection / your rest: Resolution of the text-critical question as to the priority of "resurrection" (Ethiopic *tenšāʾē*) or "rest" (Coptic ⲁⲛⲁⲡⲁⲩⲥⲓⲥ = ἀνάπαυσις) depends on both internal and external evidence. Elsewhere in the *Ep. apost.*, the Coptic / Greek term is found with its proper Ethiopic counterpart *ʿeraft* ("rest": 19:14; 27:1; 28:5) or (once: 26:5) with a cognate verb. Similarly, the Ethiopic NT consistently has *ʿeraft* for ἀνάστασις (Matt 11:29; 12:43; Luke 11:24; Rev 4:8; 14:11). †

13:1 *his might:* Coptic ϫⲓⲛ is unique here and at 17:8 in Achmimic texts known to Till (1928: 277 and n. 2; so also implicitly Crum, *s.v.* [p. 773b,] citing only this passage and two texts in Subachmimic). The common Sahidic noun is ϭⲟⲙ ("strength, power"; ϭⲁⲙ in Achmimic and other dialects; *s.v.* ϭⲟⲙ [p. 815b]).

rulers,[a] having the measure of the wisdom of him who sent me.

3The archangels Michael and Gabriel and Uriel and Raphael followed me to the fifth firmament of heaven, since it seemed to them that I was one of them; I was given power such as this by the Father.

4Then[a] I caused the archangels to be enthralled in <their> voice, and to go to the altar of the Father and do their work of service until I go to him; in this

the *rulers* (αρχη) and *authorities* (εξουσια)—I went through them, having the *wisdom* (σοφια) of him who sent me. 3*But* (δε) Michael, who is the *commander-in-chief* (αρχιστρατηγος) of the *angels* (αγγελος), and Gabriel and Uriel and Raphael—they (δε) followed me down to the fifth *firmament* (στερεωμα), *for* (γαρ) they thought in their hearts that I was one of them; *and* (δε) the Father gave me such *power* (δυναμις) as this. 4On that day I equipped the *archangels* (αρχαγγελος) with a marvelous voice, so that they might go up to the *altar* (θυσιαστηριον) of

13:2 [a]Cf. 28:1
13:4 [a]» 15:9

13:2 • *him who sent me* and *the Father who sent me*, phrases likely deriving from the gospel of John (see especially statements in the mouth of Jesus: John 5:36; 6:57; 7:29; 8:42; 10:36; 11:42; 17:3, 8, 21, 23, 25; also John 1:6; 3:17, 28, 34; 5:38; 6:29), are now formulaic as a virtual title whose uses are distributed rather evenly through the revelation discourse portion of the writing: see *Ep. apost.* 13:5; 17:3, 6; 19:5, 21; 21:1, 3; 26:2, 5 (lacking in the Ethiopic); 28:4; 33:6; 36:5, 6; 39:6; 43:7; 45:8; 51:1; cf. already 3:2; 12:4 (the Coptic differs); 33:6.
13:3 • *commander-in-chief* (ⲁⲣⲭⲓⲥⲧⲣⲁⲧⲏⲅⲟⲥ): For Michael as ἀρχιστράτηγος, see also Dan 8:11; *Jos. Asen.* 14.7(8); *2 Enoch* 22.6; 33.10; *T. Abr.* A 1.4 and passim; *3 Bar.* 11.6, 7, 8; 33.10; *Gk Apoc. Ezra* 4.24; also in 1.4, of Raphael. †

• *it seemed to them / they thought in their hearts:* Both the Ethiopic (*'emasselomu*) and the Coptic (ⲉⲩⲙⲉⲩⲉ ⲅⲁⲣ ⲁⲃⲁⲗ ϩⲛ̄ ⲡⲟⲩϩⲏⲧ) reading likely derive from the same Greek phrase, ἐδόκει αὐτοῖς or ἔδοξεν αὐτοῖς (see also 11:3).

• *that I was one of them:* The archangels do not recognize the descending redeemer; cf. *Asc. Isa.* 10.7–16; Irenaeus *Adv. haer.* 1. 30.12; *Epid.* 84; Clement of Alexandria *Exc. Theod.* 1.26.1; *Gos. Phil.* (NHC II,*3*) 57.28–58.10 "He [revealed himself to the] angels as an angel"; *Treat. Seth* (VII,*2*) 56.20–57.6; *Trim. Prot.* (NHC XIII,*1*) 45.21–29; 49.6–23; *Pist. Soph.* 1.7.

13:3 *Uriel and Raphael:* Ethiopic fam. 2 "Raphael and Uriel" (so Duensing-Müller), which is the order in *Orac. Sib.* 2.215. In *1 Enoch* 9.1 (v.l.) it is Michael, Uriel, Raphael, and Gabriel. †

13:4 *service:* Ethiopic fam 2 "serve the Father" (so Duensing-Müller). With the Coptic "fulfill the service (ὑπηρετεῖν)," cf. 24:6 below; also Sir 50:14; *Hist. Rech.* 16.7.

13:5 [a]» 5:4
[b]» 13:2

way I acted in the likeness of his wisdom. [5]For I became all in all with them, so that when I have fulfilled the Father's merciful will, the glorious work[a] of him who sent me,[b] I might return to him.

14 "You know, don't you, that the angel Gabriel came and brought the good news to Mary?"

[2]We said to him, "Yes, O Lord."

[3]He answered and said to us, "Do you not remember that I told you before that to the angels I became like an angel?"

the Father to *serve* (υπηρετει) and fulfill the *service* (διακονια) until I go to him; this is the way in which I acted by the *wisdom* (σοφια) of the likeness. [5]*For* (γαρ) I became all things in everything so that I might fulfill the Father's *plan of salvation* (οικονομια), the glorious work of him who sent me, and return to him.

14 "*For* (γαρ) you know <don't you> that the *angel* (αγγελος) Gabriel brought the good news to Mary?"

[2]We answered, "Yes, O Lord."

[3]*Then* (τοτε) he answered and said to us, "Do you *not* (μη) remember that I told you, a little while ago, that among the *angels* (αγγελος) I became an *angel* (αγγελος)—<that> I became all things in everything?"[a]

13:4 • *by the wisdom of the likeness,* or "in the image of <his> wisdom" (cf. Ethiopic).

13:5 • *the Father's merciful will:* Ethiopic literally "the will of the mercy of the Father" (so Duensing-Müller). For Ethiopic *meḥrat* ("mercy") = Coptic ⲟⲓⲕⲟⲛⲟⲙⲓⲁ (οἰκονομία) see also 21:2 (Schmidt, 1919: 51 n. 11). †

14:1 • *You know . . . :* With the "annunciation" account in *Ep. apost.* 14:1–7, cf. Luke 1:26–38; and for the special means of transference from above, *Orac. Sib.* 8.456–479; *Gos. Heb.* frg. 1.

• *brought the good news:* The Coptic has ⲉⲓⲛⲉ ⲛ̄ⲡϣⲙ̄ⲛⲟⲩϥⲉ, which is "brought" + ϣⲙ̄ⲛⲟⲩϥⲉ, "good news" (Crum, *s.v.* ϣⲓⲛⲉ [p. 570a]), sometimes for εὐαγγελίζειν; Ethiopic *zēnāwa* (*DLLA*, *s.v.* [col. 1063]) extends from the neutral "report" to the specific "bring good news"; see already 2:1, translated "we announce," but 23:1, "to preach."

14:3 • *He answered:* The use of this phrase is is one of several indications of careful dialogue composition; see the Additional Note on 12:3. †

• *I became . . . everything:* This phrase, in the Coptic only, appears to have been inspired by 1 Cor 9:22.

[4]We said to him, "Yes, O Lord." [5]He said to us, "At that time I appeared to Mary in the form of the angel Gabriel and spoke to her; her heart received me and she believed and laughed. [6]I, the Word, entered her and became flesh;[a] [7]I became my own servant in <my> appearance in the likeness of an angel. [8]I will act in this way after I have gone to the Father.	[4]We said to him, "Yes, O Lord." [5]*Then* (τοτε) he answered and said to us, "*So* (γαρ) on that day, when I took the *form* (μορφη) of the *angel* (αγγελος) Gabriel, I appeared to Mary and spoke to her; her heart received me and she *believed* (πιστευε). [6]I *formed* (πλασσε) myself, entered her womb, and became *flesh* (σαρξ); [7]*because* (επει) for myself I alone was *servant* (διακονος) to Mary in <my> *appearance* (αισθησις) in the likeness of an *angel* (αγγελος). [8]I will do likewise after I have gone to my Father.
15 "But as for you, then, keep the remembrance of my death,[a] that is, the Pass-	**15** "But as for you, remember my death *when* (οταν) the *Passover* (πασχα) takes place.

14:3 [a]Cf. 1Cor 15:28
14:6 [a]Cf. Jn 1:14
15:1 [a]Cf. Lk 22:15;

14:5 • *the form* (*'amsāl* / ⲙⲟⲣⲫⲏ = μορφή): Cf. *Ques. Bart.* 2.15 "When I [Mary] lived in the Temple of God and received my food from the hand of an angel, one day there appeared to me one in the form of an angel"; see also 14:7.

• *laughed:* Cf. Gen 18:12, and numerous early Christian references to Sarah's laughter in Schmidt, 1919: 289–94. Regarding the difference between the versions here, Schmidt (1919: 51 n. 9) suggests a primitive confusion between ἐγέλασε (resulting in the Ethiopic reading) and ἔπλασσε (the Coptic). †

14:7 • *servant* (*lā'k* / ⲇⲓⲁⲕⲟⲛⲟⲥ = διάκονος): Cf. Rom 15:8 χριστὸν διάκονον γεγενῆσθαι; *Pist. Soph.* 1.62. For the son as "servant" see also Herm. *Sim.* 5.5.2, where, however, the noun is δοῦλος, not διάκονος. Also relevant here is Jesus as παῖς ("boy, youth, *servant, slave*"; references in BAGD, *s.v.* 1.γ [pp. 604b–605a]).

• *likeness of an angel:* Cf. 2 Cor 11:4; also *Apoc. Mos.* 17.1, where Satan appears to Eve "in the form of an angel" (ἐν εἴδει ἀγγέλου); also *Apoc. Mos.* 29.15 = *Vit. Adam* 9.1.

15:1 • *But as for you . . . :* With the entire account in chap. 15, cf. Acts 12:1–17; and see Richardson, 1973.

14:5 *to Mary:* Ethiopic fam. 2 mss LP "to the virgin Mary"; QRS "to the holy virgin."

14:8 *after . . . Father:* The punctuation in Ethiopic fam. 1 mss suggests the section break above; but 14:8b may belong with 15:1, as a temporal clause preceding the imperative: "After I have gone to my Father . . . remember my death. . . ."

1Cor 11:24–25

over. [2]Then one of you will be thrown into prison on account of my name, [3]and he will greatly grieve and mourn,[a] for while you keep the Passover he is in prison, saddened that he has not kept the Passover with you. [4]I will send my power in the form of the angel Gabriel: [5]the prison gates will be opened, and he will go forth and come to you, that he may watch and take rest with you. When the cock crows [6]and you have completed my *agape* and my memorial, he will again be taken and thrown into prison as a testimony, [7]until he comes forth and preaches what I have commanded you."

[8]We said to him, "Have you, then, not completed the drink-

[2]*Then* (τοτε) one of you will be thrown into prison on account of my name, [3]and he [will be] in *grief* (λυπη) and sorrow because you keep the *Passover* (πασχα) while he is in prison; <and> being away from you he will *grieve* (λυπει, γαρ) that he does not keep the *Passover* (πασχα) [with] you. [4]But (γαρ) I will send my *power* (δυναμις) in the [like]ness of the *angel* (αγγελος) Gabriel. [5]The prison doors will be opened: he will go forth and come to you, and will keep the night watch with you, remaining with you until the *co*[*ck*] (αλεκτωρ) crows. [6]*But when* (οταν δε) you have completed the memorial for me, and the *agape* (αγαπη), he will *again* (παλιν) be thrown into prison as a testimony, [7]until he comes forth and preaches what I have delivered to you."

[8]We said (δε) to him, "O Lord, *is it* (μη) then *again*

15:4 • *my power (xāyleya* / ⲧⲁⲇⲩⲛⲁⲙⲓⲥ = ἡ δύναμίς μου): Cf. *Gos. Pet.* 5.19.
15:6 • *agape,* that is, "*a love-feast*, a common meal eaten by early Christians in connection with their church services, with the purpose of fostering and expressing brotherly love" (BAGD, *s.v.* ἀγάπη II [p. 6a]); cf. Ignatius *Rom.* 7.3; *Smyrn.* 8.2.
15:8 • *take the cup:* Cf. Matt 20:20–23; 26:26–29; Mark 10:35–40; 14:22–25; Luke 22:15–20; 1 Cor 11:23–25; also *Apoc. Pet.* (Rainer fragment) "Go thou [Peter] to the city that ruleth over the west, and drink the cup which I promised thee"; *Mart. Pol.* 14.2 "that I may share, among the number of your martyrs, in the cup of your Christ"; *Asc. Isa.* 5.13 "For me alone the Lord has mixed the cup."

15:2 *one of you:* So Coptic and Ethiopic ms M; ACKLNOT add "who stand beside me" (Duensing; similarly Müller); cf. Matt 16:28; Mark 9:1; Luke 9:27. Mss BPQRSV add only "who stand [*or* remain]," i.e., without "beside me."
15:5 *angel Gabriel:* Ethiopic fam. 2 "my angel" (so Duensing-Müller).

with my wounds: The Ethiopic would retrovert to μετὰ τῶν τραυμάτων μου; cf. Zech 12:10; Rev 6:9; 19:13; 20:2–4; *Asc. Isa.* 4.14; *Apoc. Pet.* 1.5; *Barn.* 7.9 "with the long scarlet robe"; Hippolytus *Comm. in Dan.* 4.10.4 ἥξει μετὰ τῶν τραυμάτων αὐτοῦ. The Coptic "with those slain on my account" would retrovert to μετὰ τῶν τραυματιῶν μου. †

ing of the Passover? Are we to do it again?"	(παλιν) *necessary* (αναγκη) that we take the *cup* (ποτηριον) and drink?"
[9]He said to us, "Yes, <it is necessary>[a] until I come from the Father with my wounds."[b]	[9]He said to us, "Yes, it is *necessary* (αναγκη γαρ), until the day when I come with those slain on my account."
16 We said to him, "O Lord, what you report and reveal to us is great. [2]So by what power and in what likeness are you to come?"	**16** We said (δε) to him, "O Lord, the things (γαρ) that you have already revealed to us are great. [2]In what kind of power, then, *or* (η) by what manner of *perception* (αισθησις) will you come?"
[3]He said to us, "Truly I say to you, in this way I shall come: as the sun which shines forth, shining seven times[a] brighter than it in glory, [4]borne upon the wings of the clouds[a] in glory, my cross going before me,	[3]He (δε) answered, saying to us, "*Truly* (αμην γαρ) I say to you, I shall *indeed* (γαρ) come as the sun that shines, and shining seven times brighter *than* (παρα) it in my glory; [4]with the wings of the clouds ca[rrying]

15:3 [a]» 9:4
15:9 [a]» 23:1
[b]Cf. 38:2
16:3 [a]Cf. 19:9

15:9 • *until I come . . . :* Cf. 1 Cor 11:26 "As often as you eat this bread and drink the cup, you proclaim the Lord's death *until he comes* (ἄχρι οὗ ἔλθῃ)"; Matt 26:29; Mark 14:25; Luke 22:16, 18. †

16:2 • *power . . . perception:* Cf. Irenaeus *Epid.* 62, commenting on Amos 9:11 (see also Acts 15:16): ". . . that after his death he would rise again, and that he would be in figure man, but in power God, and that he would be judge of the whole world."

16:3–5 • *I shall come . . . :* These verses reflect a widespread biblical and extra-biblical parousia tradition: see Matt 24:27, 30–31; Luke 17:24; *Did.* 16.6–8; Justin *1 Apol.* 51.9; *Dial.* 14.8; *Apoc. Pet.* 1.2–6; 6; *Orac. Sib.* 2.238–244; *Apoc. Elij.* 3.2–4; Ps.-Hippolytus *De consumm.* 36.2–6 (discussion and further references in Hills, 2008: 96–125).

• *shining seven times brighter . . . :* This imagery is found in a wide range of texts and eras; see, e.g., Isa 30:26; Matt 13:43; 17:2; 1QH vii 23–24; 4QEn Aram. frg. g; *1 Enoch* 72.37; 91.16; *2 Enoch* 19.1; 66.7; *Asc. Isa.* 4.14. †

• *Truly, I say to you:* The first of seventeen Amen sayings (16:3; 19:5, 6, 7, 14; 21:1, 8; 24:1; 25:3; 26:1; 28:4; 32:4, 5; 35:4; 41:7; 42:2; 47:8). Except in the Ethiopic of 42:2, the introductory formula consistently has only one "Amen," as in the Synoptic Gospels.

16:3 *seven times:* Ethiopic *tesbeʿito*; mss PQRSV *batesbeʾt* "in (my) incarnation."

16:4 *my cross going before me (qedmēya masqaleya yaḥawwer):* Ethiopic mss AT *meslēya masqaleya yaḥawwer* ("my cross going *with me*"), a reading that possibly reflects an inner-Ethiopic corruption from *mesleya* ("my sign"); cf. the Coptic.

16:4 [b]Cf. Dan 7:13
16:5 [a]Cf. Ac 10:42;

[5]I shall come to earth to judge the living and the dead."[a]

me in glory, the *sign* (σημειον) of [the c]*ross* (σταυρος) before me, [5]I shall come down to the earth to judge the living and the dead."

17 We said to him, "O Lord, after how many years <will this happen>?"

[2]He said to us, "When one hundred and fifty years are fulfilled, between Pentecost and the feast of Unleavened Bread, the coming of my Father will take place."

17 We said (δε) to him, "O Lord, after how many years more will these things happen?"

[2]He said to us, "When the hundredth part and the twentieth part is fulfilled, between *Pentecost* (πεντηκοστη) and the feast of Unleavened Bread, the *coming* (παρουσια) of the Father will take place."

17:1 • *After how many years?* In the Ethiopic but not the Coptic both the question and the answer refer explicitly to "years."
17:2 • *hundredth part and twentieth part. . . :* It has been tempting to conclude from these numbers that the original author intended to specify the year 150 C.E., that is, 30 (the year of the crucifixion and resurrection "in the days of Pontius Pilate," 9:1) + 120 (the predicted return). On this theory, the Ethiopic version reflects a late second-century "revision" of the date, when the parousia failed to take place: 30 + 150 = 180 C.E. There are surveys of the various alternatives to this in Vanovermeire, 1962: 220–39; Hills, 2008: 116 n. 73. Gerlach (1998: 106; following Hornschuh, 1965: 118) rightly holds that this verse cannot be used in support of a particular date of composition. For a fresh approach to the meaning of the Coptic in *Ep. apost.* 17:2, see the Additional Note on 51:1. †

• *the feast of Unleavened Bread:* Coptic ⲁⲧⲥⲉⲉⲣⲉ is the negation (ⲁⲧ-) of ⲥⲉⲉⲣⲉ, "leaven" (Sahidic ⲥⲓⲣ, Crum, *s.v.* [p. 353a]); Crum cites the full phrase here ("TU 43 6" = Schmidt, 1919: Coptic codex p. 6) with reference to Luke 22:1 ἡ ἑορτὴ τῶν ἀζύμων ("the feast of Unleavened Bread"). The Latin fragment has *azyma*. The Ethiopic has *fāsikā* (fam. 2 *fāsikā*), hence Duensing-Müller "between Pentecost and *Passover*"; see already 15:1, 3, 8. But Guerrier has "dans les jours de la *Pentecôte* et de *Pâque*," giving as a footnoted variant the reading of mss AC: "entre le Pentecôte et Pâque" (1913: [59] 199 and n. 5). †

• *the coming of the Father:* Cf. Exod 19:20; 34:5; Num 11:25; Isa 31:4; Mic 1:3; *T. Abr.* A 13.4; *T. Jud.* ἕως παρουσίας τοῦ θεοῦ τῆς δικαιοσύνης. Expectation of the Father's coming is explicitly denied by Didymus the Blind (d. 398) *Eun.* 4 (see *LPGL*, *s.v.* παρουσία 3.c [p. 1044a]).

17:2 *fulfilled:* Ethiopic ms V adds *ba-'iyobēleyo* "at the jubilee"; cf. Lev 25:10, 11 "A jubilee shall that fiftieth year be for you"; *T. Levi* 17.2, 3; patristic references in *LPGL*, *s.v.* Ἰωβηλαῖος (pp. 680–81a), e.g., Ps.-Hippolytus *Frg. 9 in Pss.*, where the jubilee is interpreted as a type of the Christian Pentecost.
17:3 *O Lord:* The Ethiopic reading is supported by the Latin: *Dme* (= *Domine*); and see note on 19:17.

3 We said to him, "O Lord, now you tell us, 'I shall come,' and again you tell us, 'He who sent[a] me will come.'"

4 He said to us, "I am fully in the Father and the Father <is> in me."[a]

5 Then we said to him, "Will you really leave us until your coming? Where shall we find a teacher?"[a]

6 He answered and said to us, "Do you not know that until now I am both here and there with him who sent me?"[a]

7 We said to him, "O Lord, is it possible that you are both here and there?"

8 He said to us, "I am fully in the Father and the Father in me,[a] that is, according to his image and his likeness and his power and his perfection and his light and the perfect Word."

3 *And* (δε) we said to him, "So now, are you telling us, 'I will come'? *How* (πως) then can you say, 'He who sent me will come'?"

4 *Then* (τοτε) he said to us, "I am fully in my Father and my Father is in me

8 according to the likeness of *form* (μορφη) and power and perfection and light; and in perfect measure of voice I am the *Word* (λογος).

2Tm 4:1; 1Pt 4:5

17:3 [a]» 13:2

17:4 [a]Cf. 19:11; 31:11; Jn 10:38; 14:10, 20; 17:21, 23

17:5 [a]Cf. Th 12a: 34.25–27; *Apoc. Elij.* 5.12

17:6 [a]» 13:2

17:3 • *How then can you say...?* See the similar challenge at 41:5 "Why do you now tell us...?"
17:4 • *I am fully in the Father...:* The statement stops short of what is found in *2 Treat. Seth* 59.17–18 "Therefore I did the will of the Father, who is I." Cf. AcJohn 100 με ὅλον παρὰ τῷ πατρὶ καὶ τὸν πατέρα παρ' ἐμοί ("I am wholly with the Father and the Father with me"); the preposition in John 1:1 ("*with* God") is not παρά but πρός. See also the notes on 19:11, 16.
17:7 • *both here and there:* The saying touches on a central question in early Christian thought: the double presence of the divine "above" and "below." See, e.g., *Dial. Sav.* (NHC III,5) 136.10–15; Clement of Alexandria *Exc. Theod.* 1.4.2; Melito *Pass. Hom.* frg. 14; Hippolytus *C. Noetum* 4.11; *Gos. Bart.* 1.31–32.

17:8 *perfect Word:* For "the perfect Word" Ethiopic fam. 2 has "I am the Word" (see Coptic); cf. John 1:1. The Coptic has both "voice" (ϩⲣⲁⲩ) and "word" (ⲗⲟⲅⲟⲥ = λόγος); what in the older recension is two phrases seems to have been conflated in the Ethiopic, possibly because in the latter case the same word (*qāl*) is used for both.

17:8 [a]» 17:4

18:4 [a]» 51:2

[b]Cf. 19:1, 18; 26:5; 31:4; 41:4; 42:7; Mt 5:45, 48; Mk 11:25, 26; Lk 10:21

18:5 [a]Cf. Jn 13:34; 15:12, 17; 1Jn 2:8; 2Jn 5; *2 Clem.* 9.6

18 That is, when he was crucified, died, and arose to say this, [2]the work that was done in the flesh—his being put to death and his ascension—was the perfection of the number and of the wonders and their type: [3]"You will see in me all perfection, for the salvation that comes through me, [4]and <you will see me> as I go[a] to the Father in heaven.[b] [5]But look, now, I give you a new commandment,[a] that you love one another and obey each other, and let there be continual peace among you. [6]Love your enemies,[a] and what you do not wish done to you, that do to no one else.

18 "I became for him the work that I am [. . . . .] perfect according to the *type* (τυπος); [2]I came into being in [the] ogdoad, which is the *Lord's Day* (κυριακη). [3]*And* (δε) you will see all perfection in the salvation that has come to me, [4]and you will see me as I go to heaven, to my Father who is in heaven. [5]*But* (αλλα) look, now, I give you a new *commandment* (εντολη), that you love one another and . . . . . .

18:2 • *[the] ogdoad, which is the Lord's Day:* The Coptic ⲙⲁϩ ϩⲙⲟⲩⲛ is the number eight (Achmimic; see Crum, *s.v.* ϣⲙⲟⲩⲛ [p. 566b]) with the prefix of ordinals, ⲙⲁϩ- (Achmimic and Subachmimic; Sahidic ⲙⲉϩ- ; *s.v.* ⲙⲟⲩϩ [p. 210a]). Its likely Greek antecedent is therefore ὀγδοάς, which is left untranslated above because of its significance as a technical term in some early Christian circles. †

• *type:* The correlation between the Coptic and Ethiopic is not completely clear. But it seems most likely that τύπος is parallel to *'amsāl*, and this is a correspondence of some theological consequence; see notes on 3:9; 32:3.

18:5 • *new commandment:* Here the word is clearly singular both in form and meaning; but see the note on 24:5.

• *obey each other:* The same complex of ideas appears in Herm. *Vis.* 3.5.1 πάντοτε ἑαυτοῖς συνεφώνησαν καὶ ἐν ἑαυτοῖς εἰρήνην ἔσχον καὶ ἀλλήλων ἤκουον "they [*sc.* apostles, bishops, teachers, and deacons] always agreed among themselves, and had peace among themselves, and listened to [*or* obeyed] one another."

18:6 • *what you do not wish done to you . . . :* The so-called Golden Rule (see also 31:3) is found elsewhere in Jewish and early Christian antiquity, in both positive and (as here) negative forms: Tob 4:15; Acts 15:20D (= Western text); 15:29D; *Did.* 1.2; Aristides *Apol.* 15.6; *Const. apost.* 1.1.7; 3.15.3; Syriac *Didasc.* 1 (Connolly, 1929: 6–7 and nn.).

18:1–2 *when he was crucified:* The Ethiopic is presumably in indirect discourse, over against the Coptic.

19 "Preach and teach this to those who believe in me, and preach the kingdom[a] of my Father. 2 Such power as my Father has given to me[a] I will give to you, so that you may bring near to my heavenly Father his children. 3 Preach, and they will believe; it is you who are to bring the children into heaven."

4 We said to him, "O Lord, what you have told us is possible for you, but as for us, how can we do it?"[a]

5 He said to us, "Truly I say to you,[a] preach and teach, as I will be with you[b]—for I delight to be with you, so that you may be heirs[c] of the kingdom of heaven[d] of him who sent me.[e] 6 Truly I say to you,[a] you will be my brothers[b] and companions, for my Father delights[c] in you and in those who through you believe in me. 7 Truly I say to you,[a] so great a joy as this has my Father prepared, such that the angels and powers have desired to behold and see it, but the greatness of my Father will not permit them to see it."

8 We said to him, "O Lord, how can what you tell us be so?"

9 He said to us, "You will see a light which shines brighter[a] than any light—he who is more perfect than perfection: 10 the Son perfected in the Father as light, for the Father is perfect whom death and resurrection make perfect; perfection excelled by perfection itself. 11 I am fully the right hand of the	9 [He said to u]s, "You will *indeed* (γαρ) see a li[ght . . . .] greater than that which shines [. 10 . . .] perfection perfected in [*perfecti*]*on* (τελειον) [. . . 11 *Bu*]t (αλλα) I am fully the [right hand] of the Fa[ther . . . .] than I, who am perfection."

18:6 [a]Cf. Mt 5:44; Lk 6:27; *2 Clem.* 13.4
19:1 [a]» 12:3
19:2 [a]Cf. Mt 28:18
19:4 [a]Cf. *Ap. Jas.* (NHC I,*2*) 6.22–25
19:5 [a]» 16:3
[b]Cf. Mt 28:20
[c]Cf. Rm 8:17; Tt 3:7; Jas 2:5
[d]» 12:3
[e]» 13:2
19:6 [a]» 16:3
[b]» 5:1
[c]Cf. 21:3

19:7 • *prepared . . . see it:* The preparation of a state or place (cf. John 14:2) which heavenly powers wish to experience or inhabit is a motif widely attested; see, e.g., *2 Enoch* 24.3; 40.3; 1 Pet 1:12; Irenaeus *Adv. haer.* 5.36.3; Clement of Alexandria *Div.* 23.3; *Exc. Theod.* 4.86.3; Hippolytus *Ref.* 5.26.16; *Comm. in Dan.* 4.59.2.
19:11 • *right hand of the Father:* Cf. AcThom A 48 "Jesus, right hand of the Father" (*NTApoc*[2] 2. 469 n. *); further references in *LPGL*, *s.v.* δεξιός B.1 (p. 338a). †

19:1 *in me:* Mss QRS "in my name."
preach the kingdom: Fam. 2 adds "of heaven"; cf. Luke 9:2.
19:2 *Such power . . . ,* or *and how my Father has given me power.* Translation depends on whether *za-kama* stands for, e.g., a form of τοιοῦτος -αύτη -οῦτον, a correlative adjective; or for, e.g., ὅπως, the adverb, or likewise πῶς, an interrogative adverb (putatively, in an indirect question) here virtually equivalent to ὅτι (BAGD, *s.v.* πῶς 2a [p. 732b]).
19:3 *the children:* Fam. 2 "his children" (so Duensing-Müller).
19:7 *my Father prepared:* Mss BKQRS "God"; and see note on *prepared . . . see.*
greatness . . . see it: So mss BKMOSV; LB* (and probably AT, which are corrupt) "they will not be allowed to see the greatness of my Father" (Duensing-Müller); CN lack both phrases, presumably through haplography ("to see . . . [to see]").
19:8 *how can what you tell us be so?* Fam. 2 "what kind <of thing> is this that you tell us?" (Duensing-Müller).

19:7 [a]» 16:3
19:9 [a]Cf. 16:3
19:12 [a]Cf. 29:5

Father, in him who brings perfection."

[12]We said to him, "In all things you have become our salvation and life in telling us[a] of such a hope."

[13]He said to us, "Have confidence and be assured. [14]Truly I say to you,[a] a rest[b] such as this will be yours, where there is no eating or drinking, no mourning or singing, no earthly garment and no perishing. [15]You will have no part in the creation below, which defiles, but in what does not perish, which is my Father's. [16]As I am always in the Father, so also are you in me."

[17]Again we said to him, "In what form? That of an angel or that of flesh?"

[12]We said (δε) [to him, "O Lor]d, in all [things] you have become for us [salvation and] lif[e], proclaiming such [hope (ελπις)] to us."

[13]He said to us, "Have con[fidence and] be peaceful in heart. [14]*Truly* (αμην) I say to you, your *rest* (αναπαυσις) will be [such as th]is, in the place (γαρ) where there is no eating *nor* (ουτε) drinking *no*[*r* (ουτε) . . .] *nor* (ουτε) *mo*[*urn*] *ing* (λυπει) *nor* (ουτε) perishing of those who are in [it. [15]As for you] (γαρ), you do not *have fellowship* (κοινωνει) [. . . . .] you will receive the [. . . . .] which is in him, yo[ur . . . .] in me."

[17]*Again* (παλιν) we [said to him, "In what likeness?] *Will it* (ειτε) be like the *angels or* (αγγελος η) [in] the [*flesh* (σαρξ)?"

19:12 • *We said to him:* Ethiopic fam. 2 "And we twelve said to him" (so Duensing-Müller), apparently contradicting the list of (eleven) apostles in 2:1.
19:16 • *I am always in the Father:* See *Teach. Silv.* (NHC VII,*4*) 115.3–10, quoted in the note on 19:11; also, of the "perfect" in *Gos. Tr.* (NHC I,*3*) 42.25–30: "they themselves are the truth; and the Father is within them and they are in the Father, being perfect, being undivided in the truly good one"; *2 Treat. Seth* (NHC VII,*2*) 49.32–50.1 "It is I who am in you (pl.), and you are in me, just as the Father is in you in innocence."
19:17 • *Again . . . :* "Again" in introductions to speeches seems to be a mark of deliberate dialogue composition; for details, see the Additional Note on 12:3. †

19:15 *my Father's:* All Ethiopic mss have *'ella* [MN: *'enta*] *'i-temāssenu* [CN: *'i-temāssen*], "you who will not perish." This phrase, lacking in the Coptic, appears to be a dittography or a gloss, possibly resulting from a primitive confusion between a form of Greek κοινωνεῖν ("to share, participate": the specific verb transliterated in the Coptic version's "have fellowship") and κοινοῦν ("to make common, defile": hence the presumably erroneous Ethiopic readings). †

[18]He answered and said to us, "On this account I have put on your flesh, in which I was born, was killed and was buried and arose through my heavenly Father,[a] that what was said by David the prophet[b] might be fulfilled, concerning my death and my resurrection:	[18]He answ]ered and said to us, "On [this account] I myself took [your] *flesh* (σαρξ), in which [I was born] and was *crucified* (σταυρου) and arose through my Father who is [in heaven], in order that the *proph[ecy]* (προφητια) of David the *prophet* (προφητης) might be fulfilled, conc[erning] what he [. . . .] both of my death and of my *resurrection* (αναστασις), saying:
[19(Ps 3:1)]O Lord, how numerous they have become who afflict me! Many have risen up against me;	[19 (Ps 3:1)]O Lord, they have become numerous who [afflict] me! Many have risen up against me;
[(2)]Many say to my soul, 'There is no salvation with his God.'	[(2)][Ma]ny say to my *so[ul]* (ψυχη), 'He has no [salvation] from God.'
[(3)]But you, O Lord, are my stronghold, my glory and the light of my head.	[(3)][*But* (δε) you, O Lord, are] my deliverer, [you are my glory and he who lifts up] my head.
[(4)]With my voice I cried aloud to the Lord, and he heard me from his holy mountain.	[(4)]With my v[oice I cried to] the Lord, and he heard me.
[(5)]I lay down and slept; I arose, for God raised me up.	[(5)]I lay down and slept; I arose, for you are the Lord, my deliverer.
[(6)]And I will not be afraid of thousands of people who surround me and rise up against me.	[(6)]I will not be afraid among ten thousand *people* (λαος) who oppose me round about.
[(7)]Arise, O Lord my God, and save me! For you smite	[(7)]Arise, O Lord; save me, my God! For you have smitten all

19:14 [a]» 16:3
[b]» 12:3
19:18 [a]» 18:4

19:18 • *O Lord, . . . :* For Psalm 3 as a proof-text for the resurrection, especially 3:5, see, e.g., *1 Clem.* 26.2; Justin *1 Apol.* 38.5; *Dial.* 97.1; Irenaeus *Adv. haer.* 4.33.13; *Epid.* 73; Clement of Alexandria *Strom.* 5.105. †

19:19(2) *salvation from God:* With this Achmimic phrase ⲟⲩϫⲉï ⲛⲁϩⲣⲙ̄ ⲡⲛⲟⲩⲧⲉ ("salvation in the presence of / before God") Till (1928: §178bα [p. 207 and n. 10]) compares Prov 12:2 ⲟⲩϩⲙⲁⲧ ⲛ̄ⲛⲁϩⲣⲙ̄ ⲙ̄ⲡⲛⲟⲩⲧⲉ = χάριν παρὰ κυρίου LXX. A similar expression occurs in 19:19(8).

[b]Cf. 43:4; Lk 24: 44–

all those who are my enemies without cause; and you break the teeth of sinners.

(8)Salvation is of God, and your blessing is upon your people!

20If all that was spoken by the prophets has come to pass, has happened and been fulfilled in me—for I spoke through them—how much more, then, will what I myself make known to you truly and really take place, 21so that he who sent[a] me may be glorified by you and by those who believe in me."

who are my enemies without cause, and you have broken the teeth of the sinners.

(8)Salvation is of the Lord, and his desire is for his *people* (λαος)!

20*Now* (δε), if all the words that were spoken by the *prophets* (προφητης) have been fulfilled in me—*for* (γαρ) I was in them—*how much more* (ποσω μαλλον), then, will what I tell you *really* (οντως) take place, 21so that he who sent me may be glorified by you [and by] those who [*bel*]*ieve* (πιστευε) in me."

20 When he had said this to us, we said to him, "O Lord, in all things you have shown us mercy and have saved us—you have revealed all things to us; yet one thing we would ask, if you will permit us."

2He answered and said to us, "I know that you hear and

20 When (δε) he had said these things [to us, we said to him], "O Lord, in all things you have had mercy on us and saved us—you have revealed all things to us; *yet* <still> (ετι) we wish to inquire of you, if you will permit us."

2He answered and said to us, "I know *indeed* (γαρ) that

19:20 • *fulfilled in me:* For "in me," Moule (1977: 68) suggests the meaning "in my case."

• *how much more . . . really:* πόσῳ μᾶλλον in the NT only nine times: Matt 7:11; 10:25; Luke 11:13; 12:24, 28; Rom 11:12, 24; Phlm 16; Heb 9:14; ὄντως ten times: Mark 11:32; Luke 23:47; 24:34; John 8:36; 1 Cor 14:25; Gal 3:21; 1 Tim 5:3, 5, 16; 6:19.

20:1 • *When he had said this to us:* For similar summary statements, see 22:1; 25:4; 40:5; 51:1; in the NT, Matt 7:28; 11:1; 13:53; 19:1; 26:1.

20:2 • *your heart will be stirred:* The Coptic is literally "you will carry and your heart is pleased" (Duensing); hence Müller is correct idiomatically: "your heart is pleased." The underlying Greek expression is φέρειν ("to carry") + ἡ καρδία ("heart") (see Crum, *s.v.* ⲧⲱⲧ [p. 438b]); cf. e.g., Exod 35:21 LXX ἕκαστος ὧν ἔφερεν ἡ καρδία "every one whose heart stirred him"; similarly Exod 35:26; 36:2.

19:20 *If . . . how much more . . . :* In the Ethiopic, *za . . . 'efo . . .*, "a rather rare construction" in which the *'efo* of the second clause is usually followed by *fadfāda* ("very much") or *'enka* ("so, then") or, as here, both (Lambdin, 1978: §51.3 [p. 232]; cf. Matt 6:30).

listen eagerly. [3]Ask me, then, concerning what you wish—look, you will both ask and remember. Listen: I am pleased to converse with you.

21 "Truly I say to you,[a] just as the Father raised me from the dead,[b] so too you will be raised in the flesh and be taken up above the heavens, to the place of which I have already told you, which he who sent me[c] has prepared.[d] [2]On this account I have completed all mercy: [3]though unbegotten I was born of humankind; though without flesh I put on flesh and grew up,[a] so that you who are born in flesh might in rebirth attain the resurrection in your flesh, a garment that will not perish,[b] with all who hope and believe in him who sent me;[c] for my Father has so delighted[d] in you. [4]And to those for whom I wish it, I shall give life, the promise of the kingdom."[a]

your heart will be stirred when you hear me. [3]*So* (δε) ask me concerning what<ever> you wish, and I will *gladly* (καλως) tell you.

21 "*Truly* (αμην γαρ) I say to you, just as my Father raised me from the dead, in this way you too will arise and be taken up to heaven, to the place of which I have already told you, the place which he who sent me has prepared for you. [2]In this way I will fully complete the *plan of salvation* (οικονομια): [3]though unbegotten I was born of humankind; though without *flesh* (σαρξ) I *have borne fle*[*sh* (φορει, σαρξ) for] to this end I have come, so that you [. . .

46; Th 52a: 42.13–15; *Acts Pil.* 4.3

19:21 [a]» 13:2

21:1 [a]» 16:3; Jn 5:21; *2 Clem.* 9.5

[b]Cf. Ac 13:30

[c]» 13:2

[d]» Cf. Jn 14:2; 1Cor 2:9

21:3 [a]» 3:13

[b]Cf. 1Cor 15:53

[c]» 13:2

20:3 • *Ask me:* Cf. *Soph. Jes. Chr.* (NHC III,*4*) 113.1–2 "If you ask me about anything, I will tell you."
21:2 • *complete the plan of salvation:* Cf. Aristides *Apol.* 15.2 (Greek fragments) "And he, having completed [God's] plan of salvation (τελέσας τὴν θαυμαστὴν αὐτοῦ οἰκονομίαν), through the cross tasted death by (his own) free will, according to the great plan of salvation (κατ' οἰκονομίαν μεγάλην)" (Goodspeed, 1914: 19 n. 9); also AcPaul (Coptic fragment) ". . . and accomplish thy plan (οικονομια) which thou hast appointed for me" (*NTApoc*[2] 2. 389). On the Ethiopic reading "mercy" for the Coptic "plan of salvation," see 13:5.
21:3 • *though unbegotten I was born:* For patristic texts and discussion of this and the following theological antithesis, see Lightfoot, 1889–1889, 1981: 2/2. 90–94 (on Ignatius *Eph.* 7.2); also *Eugnostos* (NHC III,*3*) 71.18–24 = *Soph. Jes. Chr.* (NHC III,*4*) 94.13–21; *Teach. Silv.* (NHC VII,*4*) 101.33–102.5; *Melch.* (NHC IX,*1*) 5.1–11.

21:4 *life* is lacking in Ethiopic fam. 2.

[d]Cf. 19:6
21:4 [a]» 12:3
21:8 [a]» 16:3

[5]Then we said to him, "What you speak of and promise is great."

[6]He answered and said to us, "Do you believe that all that I have told you will happen?"

[7]We answered and said to him, "Yes, O Lord."

[8]He said to us, "Truly I say to you,[a] I have received all authority from my Father, that I may deliver those in darkness into light, those in corruptibility into incorruptibility, those in error into truth, and those in death into life: [9]that those in captivity be set free, for what is impossible with humankind in possible with God.[a] [10]I am

[7]. . . and said to him,] "Ye[s, O Lord."

[8]*Then* (τοτε) he said to us, "*Truly* (αμην) I] say to [you, I have received all *authority* (εξουσια)] from [my Father, that I may deliver those who] are in [d]arkness [into light . . .

21:6 • *Do you believe . . .?* Though all Ethiopic mss have the imperative *'emanu*, the context (especially the "Yes" in both recensions, 21:7) suggests the indicative (*ta'ammenu*) with or without the interrogative particle *-nu*. But the ambiguous Greek πιστεύετε (2 pers. plur. pres. *indic.* and *impv.* act.) is rendered twice with the same imperatival form in the Ethiopic of John 14:1 ("Believe / Do you believe?"); see also 26:5; 45:2. †

21:8 • *that I may deliver . . . :* Cf. Acts 26:17; 1 Pet 2:9. For similar salvific statements in "from . . . to" combination, see Irenaeus *Epid.* 55 "He is our Counsellor . . . giving counsel to leave off our ignorance and receive knowledge, and to go forth from error and come to truth, and to cast forth corruptibility and receive incorruptibility"; Clement of Alexandria *Prot.* 10.93.1 "Let us therefore repent, and pass from ignorance to knowledge, from foolishness to wisdom, from licentiousness to self-restraint, from unrighteousness to righteousness, from godlessness to God"; Ethiopic *A.C.O.* "Prayer of Early Morning": "from darkness into light, from corruption into incorruptibility, and from ignorance into the knowledge of the truth" (Horner, 1904: 222).

• *into truth:* Ethiopic *ṣedq* has a broad range of meanings, including "justice" and "righteousness" as well as "truth." The present translation is guided by the state that precedes it: "from error. . . ."

21:10 • *I am the hope . . . :* This and the following epithets are strongly reminiscent of phrases in extant early liturgies; see, e.g., *Liturgy of St. Mark* (Brightman, 1896: 127; ANF 7. 555b); the "Prayer for those who have Fallen Asleep" in the Ethiopic version of the *Apostolic Church Order* (Horner, 1904: 229).

21:8 *all authority* (*kʷello šelṭāna*): The Coptic (Greek) reconstruction ⲉⲝⲟⲩⲥⲓⲁ ⲛⲓⲙ (for πᾶσα ἐξουσία) is very probable; see previous instances of Ethiopic *šelṭān* where the parallel Coptic text is sound. The statement is reminiscent of Matt 28:18, except that for Matthew's theological passive (ἐδόθη μοι, "has been given to me") this author identifies the subject, perhaps under the influence of John 5:22 "The Father . . . has given all judgment (τὴν κρίσιν πᾶσαν) to the Son." †

21:10 *the destitute (xeṭu'an):* Literally, "those in need"; mss ACNTV "the poor."

the hope of the hopeless, the helper of the helpless, the possession of the destitute, the physician of the sick, the resurrection of the dead."

22 When he had said this to us[a] we said to him, "O Lord, is it true that the flesh is to be judged with the soul <and spirit>? [2]Or will one, the spirit, rest in the kingdom of heaven[a] and the other be eternally punished while still living?"

[3]He said to us, "How long[a] do you ask and seek?"

23 Again we said to him, "O Lord, since you have commanded us to preach, to proclaim, and to teach, it is necessary <that we ask>; [2]so that having heard accurately from you we may become effective preachers, and may teach them, and they may believe in you. [3]For this reason we ask you."

22 When (δε) he had said these things to us we said to] him, ["O Lord, ... will the] *flesh* (σαρξ) [be judged with the *soul* (ψυχη) and the *spirit* (πνα) ? [2]And will one], then, [rest in the kingdom of heaven,] (and) the other [(be) eternally *punished* (κολαζε) while still li]ving?"

[3]He said (δε) to us, "Until what d[a]y do you ask and inquire?"

23 *Again* (παλιν) we said to him, "It is *necessary* (αναγκη γαρ) that we we ask of you, since you command us to preach; [2]so that we may learn correctly from you and become effective preachers, and that those who are taught by us may *believe* (πιστευε) in you. [3]This is why we repeatedly question you."

21:9 [a]Cf. Mt 19:26; Mk 10:27; Lk 18:27

22:1 [a]» 20:1

23:1 • *effective:* Coptic ⲣ̄ ϣⲉⲩ, "to be useful, prosperous, virtuous," e.g., for χρηστός, εὖ πράσσειν (Crum, *s.v.* [p. 599b]); Ethiopic *xēr* expresses "good" or "excellent" in any appropriate sense (*DLLA, s.v.* [col. 610b]: "plerumque ἀγαθός vel χρηστός"). See also 41:7.

23:1 *it is necessary:* For ἀνάγκη with γάρ, see also 15:9; in the NT, Matt 18:7; 1 Cor 9:16.

22:2 [a]» 12:3
22:3 [a]» 15:9
24:1 [a]» 16:3
24:4 [a]Cf. Mt 6:30; 8:26; 14:31; 16:8; Lk 12:28
[b]» 15:9
24:5 [a]Cf. Jn 14:15, 21; 15:10

24 He answered and said to us, "Truly I say to you,[a] the flesh of every person will arise alive with his soul and spirit."

[2]We said to him, "O Lord, is it possible that what is dissolved and perished should revive? [3]It is not as if we disbelieve that we ask, nor that you are unable to do it, but we truly believe that what you say has happened and will happen."

[4]He became angry and said to us, "O you of little faith,[a] how long[b] do you ask me? Nevertheless, ask <and I will tell you> without grudging <what> you wish to hear. [5]Keep, then, my commandments,[a] and do what I tell you, without hesitation and without shame. [6]Serve

24 He answered us, saying, "*Truly* (αμην) I say to you, the *resurrection* (αναστασις) of the *flesh* (σαρξ) will take place while the *soul* (ψυχη) and the *spirit* (πνα) are in it."

[2]We said to him, "O Lord, *is it* (μη) possible for what is dissolved and pe[ri]shed to be revived? [3]It is *not as* (ουχ ως) *unbelievers* (απιστος) that we ask, *or* (η) <as if> you cannot do <this>, *but* (αλλα) we *truly believe* (οντως πιστευε) that what you say will happen."

[4][And he was an]gry with us, saying, "*O* (ω) you of little *fa<ith>* (-πιστις), until what day do you ask? *But* (αλλα) ask me what<ever> you wish and I will tell you without *grudging* (-φθονει). [5]*Only* (μονον) keep my *commandments* (εντολη) and do what I tell you; show

24:1 • *the flesh of every person will arise:* Cf. *2 Clem.* 9.1 "Let none of you say that this flesh is not judged and does not rise again"; for the tripartite anthropology of flesh / soul / spirit, see already 1 Thess 5:23.
24:4 • *without grudging* (ογωн̄р̄φθονει): Cf. 42:4; Justin *1 Apol.* 6.2 "giving without grudging, as we have been taught (ὡς ἐδιδάχθημεν, ἀφθόνως δίδοντες)"; Hippolytus *De antichr.* 29 ταῦτά σοι . . . μεταδίδομεν ἀφθόνως. †
24:5 • *Only keep . . . :* мονον with the imperative here and at 42:9 (see note).
• *my commandments* or *my commandment* (*te'zāzeya*): Ethiopic *te'zāz* ("commandment") has a regular plural form, *te'zāzāt*, not found here. But the singular is also used collectively (translating ἐντολαί in, e.g., Num 15:40; Sir 45:5; 32:2; 35:24; *Asc. Isa.* 1.7; Eph 2:16; 1 John 2:3, 4) (*DLLA*, *s.v.* *'azzaza* [col. 794]). For this collective use opposite Coptic plurals, see also *Ep. apost.* 26:2, 5; 27:3, 4; 29:1; 39:11; 42:6; 44:1; 46:1; and, in light of these precedents, presumably also where the Ethiopic stands alone: 36:5;, 49:8; 50:9, 10. Note also the "new commandment" in 18:5.

24:4 *without . . . :* Coptic ογωн̄ (in 24:4 and three times in 24:6) is rare in Achmimic; according to Till (1928: 205 n. 15) it is almost confined to the *Ep. apost.*

24:5, 6 *without shame:* The Coptic text has a two-line dittography here; the text is repeated from 25:1–2.

without partiality in the strait, right, and narrow way.[a] [7]In this will my Father rejoice concerning you in all things."	partiality to no one lest I turn my favor from you; [6]*but* (αλλα) without hesitation, without shame, and without partiality *serve* (διακονει) in the straight, narrow and confined way. [7]In this way [my] Father will rejoice concerning you."
25 Again we said to him, "O Lord, look, with much questioning we enrage you."	**25** *Again* (παλιν) we said to him, "O Lord, *by now* (ηδη γαρ) we are ashamed that we repeatedly *burden* (βαρει) you with such questioning."
[2]But he said to us, "I know that you question me in faith and with all your heart; I rejoice with you. [3]Truly I say to you,[a] I am glad, and my Father in me rejoices, that you enquire and ask in this way; your boldness makes me rejoice and gives to yourselves life."	[2]*Th*[*en* (τοτε) he ans]wered and said to us, "I know (γαρ) that you question me in *faith* (πιστις) and with all your heart; therefore I rejoice on account of [you]. [3]*Truly* (αμην γαρ) I say to you, I am [glad], and my Father who is in me, that [you] question me; your boldness (δε) [makes me] rejoice and gives to yourselv[es life]."
[4]When he had said this to us[a] we were joyful. [5]We said to him, "O Lord, in all things you have been merciful to us and given us life; for all that we ask you, you tell us."	[4]When he had said (δε) this to us we [*rejoiced* (ευφρανε) that] we had asked him. [5]We said to him, ["O Lord, in all things] you give us life and show [us] mercy; so will you now tell us what we ask?"

24:6 [a]Cf. Mt 7:13–14; Lk 13:24
25:3 [a]» 16:3
25:4 [a]» 20:1

25:3 • *your boldness*, in both versions a negative expression, literally "your lack of shame"(тетн̄мн̄татϣіпе; *'i-xāfirotekemu*).

25:1 *by now:* The combination ἤδη γάρ is found in the NT only at John 9:22; 1 Tim 5:15 (cf. Acts 4:3; 2 Thess 2:7; 2 Tim 4:6).
25:4 *we were joyful:* Ethiopic fam. 2 adds "for he had spoken to us in gentleness" (so Duensing-Müller). This addition is likely inspired by *Asc. Isa.* 7.6 "And I rejoiced because he [*sc.* the angel] spoke to me with kindness" (Charles, 1900: 104; OTP 2. 165–66). †

25:8 [a]Cf. Mt 10:26; Lk 12:2; Th 5: 33.10–14; POxy 654.4

26:1 [a]» 16:3

[b]» 15:9

[c]Cf. 29:4; Ps 62:12; Prv 24:12; Sir 16:12; Mt 16:27; Rm 2:6; 1Pt 1:7

[d]Cf. 2Cor 5:10

6 Then he said to us, "What is it that falls? The flesh or the spirit?"

7 We said to him, "The flesh."

8 He said to us, "Now, what has fallen will arise, and what is sick will recover,[a] so that in this my Father may be glorified. 9 As he has done to me, so will I <do> for all of you who believe in me.

6 [Th]*en* (τοτε) he said to us, "What is it [that per]ishes? The *flesh* (σαρξ) [. .] is in the *spirit* (πνα)?"

7 We said to him, "The *flesh* (σαρξ) per[ishes."

8 *Then* (τοτε)] he said to us, "*Thus* (αρα) what has fallen will [arise], and what is lost will be found, and what is si[ck will] recover, so that in this way the glory of my Father may be [revea]led. 9 As he [has do]ne for me, so too will I do for all of you who believe (πιστευε).

26 "Truly I say to you,[a] the flesh will arise alive with the soul and the spirit, that[b] they may confess and be judged justly according to the works they have done,[c] whether good or bad,[d] 2 so that there may be

26 "*Truly* (αμην δε) I say to you, the *flesh* (σαρξ) will arise with the *soul* (ψυχη) [and the *spirit* (πνα)], so that on that [day their *de]fence* (απολογια) may take place concerning what they have done, *whether*

25:8 • *what has fallen will arise:* The phrase may derive from Jer 8:4 "When men fall, do they not rise again? If one turns away, does he not return?" (LXX μὴ ὁ πίπτων οὐκ ἀνίσταται; ἢ ὁ ἀποστρέφων οὐκ ἐπιστρέφει;). On this and similar proverbial statements used in early Christian arguments about the resurrection, see van Eijk, 1971. The extra phrase, "what is lost will be found," in the Coptic text is an example of what Bultmann has referred to as "analogous formulation" (1963: 85–87); but whether or not the phrase was an early part of the text it is impossible to decide. †

26:1 • *that they may be judged:* A similar collocation of terms occurs in the introduction to the longest extant fragment of the *Apocalypse of Ezekiel* in Epiphanius *Adv. haer*. 64.70.5–6: "[Ezekiel] refers to the righteous judgment, in which soul and body share."

26:2 • *selection (xeryata* / ⲉⲕⲗⲟⲅⲏ = ἐκλογή): The term, which can express the biblical idea of "election" (as of a chosen people), is also found elsewhere in connection with divine judgment; e.g., in *1 Enoch* 45.3; *Ps. Sol.* 9.4; 2 Pet 1.10. The Ethiopic addition, "and demonstration," is reminiscent of *T. Mos.* 5.1 "When the times of exposure (*tempora arguendi*) come near and punishment arises" (Charles, 1897: 70; OTP 1. 929).

• *believers ('ella 'amnu* / ⲛ̄ⲛ̄ⲡⲓⲥⲧⲟⲥ): For "believers" = "Christians," see, e.g., Acts 12:3D; 1 Tim 4:3, 12; Ignatius *Eph.* 21.2; *Magn.* 5.2; Origen *Hom* 18.8 *in Jer*.

• *the commandments:* The Ethiopic may also be translated "the commandment"; see note on 24:5.

a selection and demonstration of those who believe and have done the commandments of my Father who sent me.[a]

[3]Then the just judgment[a] will take place. [4]For thus my Father wills, and he said to me, 'My son,[a] on the day[b] of judgment, neither fear the rich nor pity the poor, but according to the sins of each one deliver him to eternal punishment.'[c] [5]As for those who have loved me and have kept my commandment,[a] to them I will give rest[c] in life[d] in the kingdom[e] of my Father[f] who is in heaven.[g] [6]Look, <they will> see what he has given me: [7]he has given me the power <that I may do> what I wish and what I have desired for those to whom I have given my promise.

(ειτε) good *or* (ειτε) bad, [2]so that there may be [a *se*]*lection* (εκλογη) of *believers* (πιστος), those who have done the *com*[*mandments* (εντολη) of my] Father who sent me. [3]Thus the *judgment* (κρισις) will take place severely. [4]*For* (γαρ) my Father said to me, 'My son, on the day (γαρ) of *judgment* (κρισις) you will *ne*[*ither* (ουτε) fear] the rich *nor* (ουτε) pit[y the] poor, *but according to* (αλλα κατα) the sin of each one you will [*del*]*iver* (παραδιδου) him to eternal *punishment* (κολασις).' [5]*But* (δε) as for my beloved ones, who have done the *commandments* (εντολη) of [my Fa]ther who sent me,[b] I will give them *rest* (αναπαυσις) of life in the kingdom of my [Father who is in] heaven; [6]and they will see what he has *gra*[*nted*] (χαριζε) me: [7]he has given me *power* (εξουσια) so [that I may] do what I wish, and that what I have promised and willed to give, I may [*grant* (χαριζε)] them.

26:2 [a]» 13:2
26:3 [a]Cf. 2Ths 1:5
26:4 [a]Cf. Mt 3:17; 17:5; Mk 1:11; 9:7; Lk 3:22; 9:35
[b]» 15:9
[c]Cf. Mt 25:46
26:5 [a] Cf. Jn 14:15
[b]» 13:2
[c]» 12:3
[d]Cf. 28:3
[e]» 12:3; cf. *2 Clem.* 5.5
[f]Cf. 29:6; Mt 26:29
[g]» 18:4

26:4 • *For thus my Father wills:* This phrase, only in the Ethiopic, seems to echo Matt 11:26 = Luke 10:21 ὅτι οὕτως εὐδοκία ἐγένετο ἔμπροσθέν σου.
26:5 • *loved me and kept my commandment:* The Ethiopic may also be translated "commandments" (see note on 24:5); but here the (albeit secondary) influence of John 14:15 would seem decisive in favor of the singular.

26:6 *<they will> see:* The Ethiopic indicative *yerē"eyu* (see Coptic), restored from the imperative *re'yu*; cf. 21:6; 45:2.

27:1 [a]Cf. 3:9; 28:3; 31:10
[b]» 12:3
27:3 [a]Cf. 1Jn 2:4

27 "For on this account I descended to the place of Abraham, Isaac, and Jacob, to your fathers and the prophets,[a] and preached to them, that they may come forth from the rest[b] which is below into heaven. [2]I have given them the right hand of the baptism of life, and pardon and deliverance from all evil, as <I have given it> to you and, from now on, to those who believe in me. [3]But whoever believes yet does not do my commandments,[a] although he has confessed my name he benefits not at all. [4]He

27 "*For* (γαρ) on this account I descended to [the place of] Lazarus and preached [to . . . . . . and] to the *prophets* (προφητης), that they might come forth from the *rest* (αναπαυσις) which is below and go up to that which [is above . . . [2]. . . .] them the right hand [of the *baptism* (βαπτισμα)] of life and forgiveness and deli[verance from] every [evi]l, just as I have done for you and for [those who] *believe* (πιστευε) in me. [3]*But* (δε) if someone *believes* (πιστευε) [in me yet] does not do my *com-*

27:1 • *I descended . . . :* A *descensus in inferos* (note: here to the "lower regions," not *infernos*, "the inferno") is widely related in early Christian literature; see, e.g., 1 Pet 3:19 (though the precise meaning is uncertain); Ignatius *Magn.* 9.2; Herm. *Sim.* 9.16; *Gos. Pet.* 41–42; Justin *Dial.* 72.4; Irenaeus *Adv. haer.* 4.27.2; *Dem.* 78; among more recent discoveries, *Teach. Silv.* (NHC VII,*4*) 103.34–104.14; *Testim. Truth* (NHC IX,*3*) 32.33–33.2; *Trim. Prot.* (NHC XIII,*1*) 36.4–5. Further references and discussion in Attridge, 1990; Pérès, 1993.

• *[the place of] Lazarus:* In both its NT contexts, the name Lazarus is associated with death and rebirth (Luke 16:19–31; John 11:1–44; 12:1). The Coptic reading, if correct (cf. 9:3), suggests as an original Greek text εἰς τὸν τόπον τοῦ Λαζάρου—not a standard circumlocution for Hades. This exact wording does occur, however, with reference to "Bethany" (home town of Lazarus) in Eusebius *Onomast. s.v.* Βηθανία· δείκνυται εἰς ἔτι καὶ νῦν ὁ Λαζάρου τόπος (Klostermann, 1904: 58).

• *Abraham, Isaac, and Jacob:* Cf. 4 Macc 13:17 "For if we [*sc.* seven brothers] die, Abraham and Isaac and Jacob will welcome us, and all the fathers will praise us"; Matt 22:32; Mark 12:26; Luke 20:37; *Apoc. Pet.* 16.1; *Gos. Bart.* 1.9 "I went to the underworld to bring Adam and all the patriarchs, Abraham, Isaac, and Jacob." †

27:3 • *my commandments*, or, in the Ethiopic, "my commandment," as also in the next verse; but see note on 24:5.

27:1 *descended to:* Ethiopic fam. 2 adds "and have spoken with" (so Duensing-Müller).

your fathers and the prophets: The Ethiopic manuscript traditions are united in this reading. Between "preach" and "prophets" the Coptic is very fragmentary; the two barely legible letters -ⲕⲁ- allow the reconstruction ⲛ̄ⲛ̄ⲇⲓ]ⲕ̣ⲁ̣[ⲓⲟⲥ ⲙⲛ̄ "to the righteous and." Cf. Matt 10:41; 13:17; *Trip. Tract.* (NHC I,*5*) 111.8–9, 32–33; Cyril of Jerusalem *Catech.* 4.11 "he descended to the lower regions, so that there too he might redeem *the righteous* (τοὺς δικαίους)."

27:2 *baptism of life:* Between "right hand" and "of life" the Coptic is entirely lacking; but the complete phrase appears in both versions in 42:3.

has run <his> course in vain;[a] his end will be destruction[b] and punishment in great pain, for he has transgressed my commandments.

mandments (εντολη), although he has *con*[*fessed*] (ομολογει) my name he *benefits* (ωφελει) not at all. [4]He has [run] <his> course in vain; as for such (γαρ) [as these, their end] will be in destruction and [ruin, for they have] *transgressed* (παρανομει) my *commandments* (εντολη).

28 "But to you I have granted to become children of God, and to be cleansed from all evil and from every power of judgment;[a] and so I will do also to those who believe in me through you—[2]as I have told you and promised you—that they may come forth from prison and be freed from chains and from the spears and from the fierce fire."

[3]We said to him, "O Lord, in all things you have made us rejoice and given us rest[a] in faith and truth: for you have preached to our fathers and to the prophets.[b]"

28 "[*But* (δε) much more], children of life, have I rescued [you] from every *evil* (κακον) and from [the *power* (εξουσια) of] the *rulers* (αρχων), (you) and everyone who *bel*[*ieves* (πιστευε) in] me through you. [2]What I have promised (γαρ) [you I] will also give to them, so that they may come [forth from] prison and the chains of the *rulers* (αρχων) and the fierce fire."

[3]We [said] to him, "O Lord, you have given rest (γαρ) of [life to us] and you have given [. . . .] in mighty works for [. . . . of] *faith* (πιστις); so now will you preach these things to [us,

27:4 [a]Cf. Gal 2:2; Phl 2:16
[b]» 7:3; 38:7
28:1 [a]Cf. 13:2
28:3 [a]Cf. 26:5
[b]» 27:1

28:1 *children of life:* Ethiopic fam. 2 mss have "children of light in God" (so Duensing-Müller); mss CN "children of light and children of God." The Coptic reading, "children of life," is possibly a periphrasis for "children of God" (cf. John 1:12; 1 John 5:20; *Diogn.* 9.6). †

I rescued you (Coptic ⲁⲓ̈ⲥⲱⲧⲉ ⲙ̄ⲙⲱⲧⲛⲉ) or *to be cleansed* (Ethiopic *tenṣeḥu*), the difference possibly due to some overlap of meaning in, e.g., ἐκκαθαίρειν, ἐξαιρεῖσθαι.

28:2 *from spears ('em-kʷennāt):* This unanimous Ethiopic reading makes reasonable sense in context. But in light of the Coptic, it is possibly corrupt for the consonantally very similar *'em-makʷānent* ("from the judges" or "from the *rulers*"); this is the plural of the word used to describe Archelaus in 9:1 (see note). The whole phrase, from "chains" to "fire," is reminiscent of the place of punishment as described in *Gos. Phil.* (NHC II,*1*) 68.30 "An apostolic man in a vision saw some people shut up in a house of fire and bound with fiery [chains]."

28:3 *the prophets:* Coptic "our fathers" restored on the basis of lacuna length, the Ethiopic reading, and the use of the phrase in 27:1. All Ethiopic mss except AT add "and so also to us and to everyone."

28:4 [a]» 16:3
[b]» 13:2
28:5 [a]Cf. Jn 14:2
[b]» 12:3
29:1 [a]Cf. 1Cor 4:6
[b]Cf. Dt 12:32; Prv 30:6; Eccl 3:14; 12:12-13; Sir 42:21; Rv 22:18-19; *1En.* 104.10-11; *2En.* 48.7-8
[c]Cf. 50:8
[d]Cf. Mt 18:6; Lk 17:2

4 He said to us, "Truly I say to you,[a] you, and those who believe, and those who are yet to believe in him who sent me,[b] I will lead up to heaven, 5 to the place which my Father has prepared[a] for the elect—he will grant the rest[b] that he has promised, and eternal life.

sinc]*e* (επει) you have preached to [our fathers] and the *prophets* (προφητης)?"

4 *Then* (τοτε) he said to us, "Truly (αμην γαρ) I say to you, everyone who will *believe* (πιστευε) in me a[nd who has] *believed* (πιστευε) in him who sent me I will [lead] up to heaven, 5 to the place which my Father [has prepared] for the elect; and I will give you the choice kingdom,[a] in *rest* (αναπαυσις) and eternal life.

29 "But those who have transgressed my commandments and teach another <teaching>, taking away and adding,[b] considering <only> their own glory,[c] turning aside those who believe in me rightly: I shall deliver them to ruin."[d]

2 We said to him, "O Lord, will there be another teaching, and affliction?"

29 "*But* (δε) those who have *transgressed* (παρανομει) [my *command*]*ments* (εντολη) and have taught another teaching [beyond] what is written,[a] and adding [. . . own . . .], teaching with other words [those who *be*]*lieve* (πιστευε) in me rightly; if [they are made to f]all because of <them>, such as these [will be brought to] eternal *punishment* (κολασις)."

2 We said (δε) [to him], "O Lord, *will there* (μη) be the teaching of oth[ers], beyond what you have told us?"

29:1 • *my commandments*, or (in the Ethiopic) "my commandment"; see note on 24:5.
29:2 • *another teaching:* The Ethiopic noun, both here and in the very similar 50:8, is *temhert*, conventionally translated "teaching." †

28:5 *the elect:* Ethiopic ms C "his elect"; O "for the holy ones / saints (*qeddusān*)." BKLMOPSV add "and the elect of the elect" (so Duensing-Müller: "and most elect"); cf. 2 Sam 22:27 LXX (= Ps 17:26 LXX); Mark 13:20 ("elect, whom he chose"); Clement of Alexandria *Div.* 36.

choice kingdom (ⲧⲙⲛ̄ⲧⲣ̄ⲣⲟ ⲉⲧⲥⲁⲧⲡ): The Coptic is a Qualitative form ("choice, chosen"; Crum, *s.v.* ⲥⲱⲧⲡ [p. 365a] "Qual, a. "*chosen,* exquisite"). Similar in meaning to a Greek perfect passive participle or, here, to the familiar adjective ἐκλεκτή, it is clearly attached to the noun "kingdom," not to the disciples. †

[3]He said to us, "<Yes,> so that those who do good and evil may be manifest. [4]Then the just judgment will take place according to the works that they have done;[a] and they will be delivered to destruction."	[3][He said to] us, "It is *indeed* (γαρ) necessary that it come about, *in order that* (ινα) [those who do] good and evil [be manifest]. [4]This is the way in which the *judgment* (κρισις) of those who do these things will be revealed: *according to* (κατα) their works they will be judged and *delivered* (παραδιδου) to death."
[5]We said to him, "We are blessed, because we see you[a] and hear you as you tell us this, and our eyes have seen such mighty works as you have done."	[5]*Again* (παλιν) we said to him, "O Lord, we are *blessed* (μακαριος), [because we see] you and hear you as you [preach] such [things to us], for our eyes have seen these mighty works that you have done."
[6]He answered and said to us, "Much more blessed will they be who do not see yet believe, for they will be called children of the kingdom,[a] perfect[b] in the perfect one, to whom I shall be eternal life in the kingdom[c] of my Father."[d]	[6]He ans[wered and said] to us, "Much more *blessed* (μακαριος γαρ) are they who have not seen yet have *believed*, (πιστευε), for such as these will be called children of the kingdom, a[nd they] will be *perfect* (τελειος) [in] the *perfect* (τελειος) one, and I shall be [eternal life] to them in the kingdom of my Father."

29:4 [a]» 26:1
29:5 [a]Cf. 3:13; Ps 47:8; Mt 13:16–17; Lk 10:23–24
29:6 [a] » 12:3; cf. Mt 8:12; 13:38
[b]Cf. Mt 5:48
[c]» 12:3
[d]Cf. 26:5

29:3 • *<Yes> / It is necessary:* Warnings about the necessity or inevitability of false teaching in the last days are widely attested. See, e.g., 4 Ezra 14:35; Luke 17:1; 1 Cor 11:19; 1 John 2:19; Justin *Dial.* 35.3; Syriac *Didasc.* 23 "There shall be heresies and schisms"; *Ps.-Clem. Hom.* 2.17; 16:21.
29:6 • *much more blessed . . . :* Cf. John 20:29; discussion and further references in Cameron, 2005: 48–54.

29:3 *in order that:* ϊⲛⲁ for ἵνα here and at 44:4 (so Schmidt, 1919). But Chaîne is skeptical: both occurrences are in corrupt contexts; and in the latter (so Chaîne), the form is to be restored as a Coptic 2d or 3d future (1933: §876 [p. 403]).
29:5 *as you tell us:* Ethiopic *nagara* is generally "to tell, narrate, report," rather than "to preach, proclaim." Hence the translation in 19:12: the Ethiopic *za-kama-ze tasfā tenaggerana* ("telling us of such a hope") despite the parallel Coptic ⲉⲕ] ⲧⲁϣⲉⲁⲉⲓϣ ⲛⲉⲛ ⲛ̄[ⲧϩⲉⲗⲡⲓⲥ ⲧⲉ]ⲓ̈ ⲛϯⲙⲓⲛ[ⲉ ("proclaiming such hope to us"). Here Till's conjecture (1928: §141g [p. 165 and n. 12]), based on that earlier verse, is followed.

29:7 [a]» 15:9
[b]Cf. Jn 13:1; 16:10, 17
30:1 [a]Cf. Mt 28:19; Mk 16:15
[b]Cf. Mt 19:28; Lk 22:30; Rv 21:12
[c]Cf. 2:2
[d]Cf. Jn 9:35 v.l.; 1Jn 3:10, 13
30:2 [a] Cf. Is 53:1; Jn 12:38
[b]Cf. Ac 2:22; 2Cor 12:12; 2Ths 2:9; Hb 2:4
30:4 [a]Cf. Jn 14:27; 16:33
[b]Cf. Jn 20:22

7 Again we said to him, "O Lord, how is it possible to believe that you will leave us, as you said a time[a] is coming and an hour, when you are to go to your Father?"[b]

30 He answered and said to us, "Go and preach[a] to the twelve tribes of Israel,[b] and to the Gentiles, and to the land of Israel to the East and the West, to the North and South,[c] and many will believe in the Son of God."[d]

2 We said to him, "O Lord, who will believe us,[a] who will listen to us, and how will we be able to do, to teach, and to tell the wonders,[b] the signs, and the mighty works that you have done?"

3 He answered and said to us, "Go and preach about the mercy of my Father; what my Father has done through me so I too will do through you, in that I shall be with you; 4 and I will give you my peace,[a] and power from my spirit,[b] so that

7 *Again* (παλιν) [we said to him], "How can it be *believed* (πιστευε) [that you] will leave us, as you tell us, 'A day is coming, and an hour, when I shall go up to my Father'?"

30 He said (δε) to us, "Go and preach to the twelve *tribes* (φυλη); and preach also to the *Gentiles* (εθνος) and the whole land of *Israel* (ιηλ) [from East] to West and from <South to> North; a multitude will *be*[*lieve* (πιστευε) in the] Son of God."

2 We said (δε) to him, "O Lord, who will *believe* (πιστευε) us, *or* (η) [who will] listen to us [. . . .] teach [. . . . the wonders and the signs [that you] have done, and the [marvels?"

3 *T*]*hen* (τοτε) he answered and said to us, "Go and preach the mer[cy of my] Father; what he has done through me [I will do] through you, in that I am with you; 4 and I shall give you my *peace* (ειρηνη), and from the *spirit* (πνα) I shall give you

30:1 • *East, . . . :* Cf. Mark 16:8 (the continuation in L Ψ 099 0112); Luke 13:29.

30:1 *the land of Israel:* In light of the context, this reading is possibly corrupt from "the whole earth" (Schmidt, 1919: 95 n. 13).
30:3 *mercy:* Before "mercy" Ethiopic fam. 2 has "the coming and" (so Duensing-Müller, in parentheses), a gloss originating either in the transmission of the Ethiopic (the two words are similar: "his coming" = *meṣ'atu*; "his mercy" = *meḥratu*) or in a Greek antecedent ("coming" = ἔλευσις; "mercy" = ἔλεος).

they may believe. [5]To them also will this power be given and bequeathed, that they may give it to the Gentiles.

power that you may *prophesy* (προφητευε) eternal life to them. [5]To them also (δε) will I give my *power* (δυναμις), that they may teach the rest of the *Gentiles* (εθνος).

31 "Look, you will meet a man whose name is Saul—which interpreted means Paul—who is a Jew, circumcised according to the
command of the Law.[a] [2]He will hear my voice from heaven in terror and with fear and trembling; his eyes will be darkened,[a] and by
your hand be sealed with spittle. [3]Do everything for him as others have done for you.[a] [4]Raise up this man, and immediately his
eyes will be opened and he will glorify God, my heavenly Father.[a]
[5]He will be strong among the nations;[a] he will preach, and he will
teach many, and they will be delighted to hear him and many will
be saved. [6]Then he will be hated and delivered into the hand of the
enemy, and he will testify to me before transitory kings.[a] [7]Upon him

31:1 [a]Cf. Ac 13:9; 21:39; 22:3; Phl 3:5
31:2 [a]Cf. Ac 9:4; 22:7; 26:14
31:3 [a]» 18:6
31:4 [a]» 18:4
31:5 [a]Cf. 30:5
31:6 [a]Cf. Ps 119:46

30:5 • *the other Gentiles,* or *nations:* Both the Coptic ⲛ̄ϩⲉⲑⲛⲟⲥ and the Ethiopic *'aḥzāb* retain the ambiguity of Greek ἔθνη as "Gentiles, nations" (see also 31:5). The context favors the former translation, though Coptic ⲥⲉⲉⲡⲉ ("the rest of" or "the remainder" [Crum, *s.v.* (p. 351b), with references]; absent from the Ethiopic) is admittedly awkward here, before Paul's mission is introduced. But perhaps there is an allusion to Rom 1:13 "that I may reap some harvest among you as well as *among the rest of the Gentiles* (ἐν τοῖς λοιποῖς ἔθνεσιν)"; ⲥⲉⲉⲡⲉ translates λοιπός in, e.g., Jer 15:9.
31:2 • *by your hand:* The agency is presumably important: what in the book of Acts is done by Ananias (9:12, 17) is here the prerogative of the apostolic group.
31:7 • *Upon him . . . :* The sense seems to be that it is Paul's vocation or destiny to give perfect testimony.

31:2 *with spittle* (*ba-tefa'*): So fam. 1 and most fam. 2 mss. Guerrier, following ms L, which lacks the phrase, takes "sealed" in the fuller sense: "signed (with the sign of the cross)." He suggests that "with spittle" is an addition derived from John 9:6 (Guerrier, 1913: [73] 213 n. 1). There is a variant in mss PSV, presumably the result of simple scribal error: *ba-tesfā*, "in (*or* with) hope."
31:3 *Do everything . . . :* The text and translation of this and the following verse are uncertain. The oldest witness, ms O, is followed: only ms O has the third person plural verb *gabru* ("others *have done*"). Duensing-Müller, following fam. 1 mss, give "And do all to him as I have done to you. Deliver (?) (him?) to others" (Müller eliminates the parentheses and question marks); cf. 42:9 "Only do what I say to you, as I too have done." †
31:6 *the enemy:* Mss CN "his enemies"; AT "sinful people" (cf. Matt 26:45; Mark 14:41). For "the enemy" as a supernatural opponent, see, e.g., *T. Dan* 6:3; Matt 13:28 (though in the parable the phrase is ἐχθρὸς ἄνθρωπος); Luke 10:19.

transitory (xalāfeyān), that is, not the "immortal king" who is God. Ms M *mawāteyān* "mortal"; LPV *mawā'eyān* "victorious"; AT "mortal and victorious"; S "victorious and transitory." Cf. Acts 9:15; *1 Clem.* 5.5–7 "Through jealousy and strife Paul . . . when he had reached the limits of the West . . . gave his testimony before the rulers. . . ."

31:8 [a]Cf. Ac 26:17; Gal 1:16; 2:8–9
31:9 [a]Cf. Rm 15:19
31:10 [a]» 27:1
31:11 [a]» 17:4
31:12 [a]» 1:4
32:1 [a]Cf. Ac 26:6; Eph 3:6; 2Pt 1:1

will be the perfection of my testimony, in that he who persecuted and hated me, he it is who will believe in me and will preach and teach. [8]Among my elect he will be a chosen vessel[a] and a wall that does not fall. [9]Through the last of the last the preaching to the Gentiles will be completed,[a] according to the will of my Father. [10]Therefore, what you have learned in the scriptures—that your fathers the prophets[a] spoke concerning me and <that> through me it has been fulfilled—they truly spoke of this as well, and it is fulfilled; so you too, then, become their guide. [11]And everything that I have told you and which you have written concerning me, that I am the Word of the Father and the Father is in me, so you, too, become through this man, as befits you. [12]Teach, and remember[a] what has been said in the scriptures and fulfilled concerning me; then the Gentiles will have salvation."

32 We said to him, "Teacher, do we have one hope[a] of inheritance with them?"

[2]He answered and said to us, "Are the fingers of the hand alike,

31:8 • *wall . . . fall:* Cf. Jer 1:18; 15:20; 1QH vi 26–27; vii 8–9 "Thou hast made me like a strong tower, a high wall, . . . and all my ramparts are a tried wall which shall not sway"; Acts 9:15; Ps.-Titus *Epistle* 21 "Paul, chosen vessel and the impregnable wall among the disciples" (*NTApoc*[2] 2. 62 and n. 57, with attention to texts in the ascetic tradition). †

31:9 • *the last of the last* (*'axārihu la-'axāreyān*) possibly stands for an original superlative form, but the meaning is in any case virtually identical to Paul's "last of all" in 1 Cor 4:9 (*daxarta*, for ἐσχάτους in apposition to "apostles"); cf. also 1 Cor 15:8–9.

31:12 • *then . . . salvation:* Cf. Acts 13:47; 28:28. Duensing-Müller understand Paul as the subject: "then he will be for the salvation of the Gentiles."

32:1 • *Teacher:* This address, read by all Ethiopic mss, is unique in the dialogue portion of the writing; but see the emphasis on the Lord as risen *teacher* in 10:2; 11:4.

32:2 • *Are the fingers of the hand alike . . . ?* Guerrier (1913: [74] 214 n. 3) remarked that the proverb, "All the fingers are not equal," was alive in Arabic in his day; but it is very widely found (cf. the Latin proverb, *manus digiti coaequales non sunt, omnes tamen usui*). The *topos* of "same origin, same fruit" is found widely in antiquity, e.g., Isa 5:4; Matt 7:16 "Are grapes gathered from thorns, or figs from

---

31:10 *scriptures, . . . that:* Ethiopic ms M lacks *kama* ("that"), and therefore likely understands the phrase to mean "in the scriptures [*or* writings] of your fathers the prophets."

your fathers: Mss BKQ "our fathers."

concerning me: Mss AT "concerning you" (cf. 35:4).

31:11 *you have written:* It is not clear whether the author means the NT scriptures or the *Ep. apost.* itself; the two christological phrases immediately following are near quotations of 17:4, 8, i.e., part of what the disciples have just now "written." Fam. 2 and three other mss have "and which I have written to you concerning myself," a reading perhaps congenial to the Ethiopian tradition in light of a passage in the Ethiopic (but not the extant Latin) version of the *Acts of Peter* (part of the compendious *Maṣḥafa Gadla Ḥawāreyāt*): "And when I [= Peter] had received into my hand the eight books which our Lord had written with his own hand, . . ." (*Acts St. Pet.* 1; Budge: 1. 386 [text]; 2. 389 [translation]).

or the heads of corn in the field? Do fruit-bearing trees give the same fruit? Do they not give fruit according to their kind?"

[3]We said to him, "O Lord, are you speaking again[a] in parables to us?"

[4]He said to us, "Do not be troubled.[a] Truly I say to you,[b] you are my brothers[c] and companions in the kingdom[d] of my Father, for so it has pleased him.[e] [5]Truly I say to you,[a] I shall give this hope also to those whom you have taught and who have believed in me."

33 We said to him again, "O Lord, when shall we meet this man, and when will you go to your Father and ours, to our God and Lord?"

[2]He answered and said to us, "This man will come from the land of Cilicia[a] to Damascus[b] in Syria, that he may ravage the church which you are to create—that is, I through you. [3]What I say will be accomplished quickly: [4]He will be strong in this faith, and the word of the prophet will be fulfilled,[a] which says, [5]'Look, from the land of Syria I am beginning to call new Jerusalem,[a] and Zion I shall call to myself and she will be taken captive'; [6]and she who was barren,[a] having no children, will be fruitful, and will be called the daughter of my Father, and my bride; for so it has pleased[b] him who sent me.[c] [7]I shall turn that man aside, that he not carry out his evil intention, and this will be my Father's glorious work.[a] [8]For after I have gone, when I am with with my Father, I shall speak with him from heaven,[a] and everything about him that I have told you beforehand will take place."

34 We said to him again, "O Lord, how much you have told us and announced to us—you have revealed great unspoken things[a]

32:3 [a]Cf. Mt 13:10; 22:1
32:4 [a]Cf. Jn 14:1, 27
[b]» 16:3
[c]» 5:1
[d]» 12:3
[e]Cf. 33:6; Mt 11:26; Lk 10:21; 12:32
32:5 [a]» 16:3
33:2 [a]Cf. Ac 21:39; 22:3; 23:34
[b]Cf. Ac 9:2–3; 22:5–6, 10–11; 26:12, 20
33:4 [a]Cf. 11:8; Jn 12:38
33:5 [a]Cf. Rv 3:12; 21:2
33:6 [a]Cf. Is 54:1; Gal 4:27
[b]» 32:4
[c]» 13:2
33:7 [a]» 5:4
33:8 [a]Cf. Ac 9:4; 22:6–7; 26:14
34:1 [a]Cf. Jer 33:3

thistles?" (cf. Luke 6:43–44); Thom 45 (40.31–41.6); Ignatius *Eph.* 14.2; *Apoc. Pet.* (NHC VII,3) 76.4–8; Seneca *Ep.* 87; Epictetus *Disc.* 2.20; Plutarch *Mor.* 472F.
32:3 • *in parables* (*ba-messālē*): See notes on 3:9 ("the patriarchs and prophets spoke in parables") and 5:21 (introducing the creedal statement).
33:5 • *'Look . . .'*: On this saying, see Schneider, 1969.
33:6 • *and my bride:* The conjunction *wa-* can bear the meaning "but" (so Duensing-Müller). But since "daughter" has a metaphorical rather than a metaphysical reference, the logic of the imagery suggests "and" with the meaning "also" or even "hence." In Rev 21:9 "the Bride, the wife of the Lamb" is "the holy city Jerusalem, coming down out of heaven from God" (21:10). †

32:4 *brothers in . . . Father:* Fam. 2 "in the kingdom of heaven with my Father" (Duensing-Müller). Cf. *Acts Pet. 12 Apost.* (NHC VI,1) 2.32–3.12; *Interp. Know.* (NHC IX,1) 9.30–32.
for so it has pleased him: Mss CN omit.
33:1 *our God and Lord:* Cf. John 20:28; mss ACNT "our Savior."

34:8 [a]Cf. Rv 6:13; 8:10; 9:1
[b]Cf. Rv 8:7; 11:19; 16:21
34:9 [a]Cf. *Orac. Sib.* 5.512–531
[b]Cf. Rv 8:5; 11:19; 16:18
34:10 [a]Cf. Rv 11:13; 16:19

to us, and in all things you have given us rest and have shown us
mercy. [2]For after your resurrection you have revealed everything to
us so that we might truly be saved. [3]But you told us that signs and
wonders in heaven and on earth will take place before the end of
the world comes. So teach us, that we may know."

[4]He said to us, "I will teach you not only what will happen among
you, but <also> among those whom you teach and who believe, and
among those who hear this man and believe in me. [5]It will happen
in those years and those days."

[6]We said to him again, "O Lord, what is it that will happen?"

[7]He said to us, "At that time believers and unbelievers will see a
trumpet from heaven, and the sight of great stars visible by day; [8]a
dragon reaching from heaven to earth, stars like fire falling,[a] and a
great hail[b] of fierce fire; [9]the sun and moon fighting each other,[a] the
ceaseless terror of thunder and lightning, thunderclap and earthquake together;[b] [10]cities falling,[a] and people dying in their ruins;
endless drought for want of rain, severe and prolonged plague; so
much death, and so sudden, that there will be no grave for the dead.
[11]Children and parents will be carried away on one bed; parents will
not turn to their children, nor will children turn to their parents,
or relatives to their relatives; [12]and those remaining, who are left
in despair, will arise and see those who left them when they were

34:3 • *But you told us that:* From this point until the end of chap. 36 the *Epistula* is indebted to to the *Testament of our Savior Jesus Christ in Galilee* or its principal source, an apocalypse apparently also used by the author of the *Testamentum Domini* (see Funk, 1901). The *Testament in Galilee* is found in all Ethiopic mss containing the *Ep. apost.*, and was perhaps understood as a preface to it; Guerrier (1913: [37–47] 177–87) includes its eleven chapters in his enumeration of chapters in the *Epistula*.
34:10 • *no grave for the dead* suggests both the scale of the catastrophe and the shame of having no proper burial; see 2 Kgs 9:10; Ps 79:3; Jer 22:19; *Ps. Sol.* 2.27.
34:13 • *from one is taken, and to another is given,* or "they will take from one and give to another" (Duensing-Müller); the translation depends on whether the third person plural forms are understood as personal or impersonal. In the latter case, the construction can be a periphrasis for the activity of God. In the NT gospels, see, e.g., Matt 7:1–2, 7; 25:29; Luke 6:37–38;11:9 ; 19:26.

33:4 *He will be strong:* Only mss CN read "strong." After "that is" in 33:2 the text may be translated "I who speak through you; and I shall come quickly in that faith, so that the word of the prophet may be fulfilled, which says, ..." The lack of punctuation after "quickly" in twelve of the fourteen MSS perhaps supports this translation.
the prophet: Mss ACNT "the prophets," perhaps in tacit acknowledgment that what follows is not a word-for-word quotation from a single OT "prophet"; there is a similar case in the variant readings at Mark 1:2.
33:5 *call to myself,* or "I will subdue" (Duensing-Müller).
34:7 *a trumpet:* Mss AT "at the blowing [*or* sounding] of a trumpet."

carried away. [13]For the plague is full of hostility and affliction, of jealousy and murder; from one is taken, and to another is given; [14]and what comes afterward is worse than this.

35 "Then my Father will become enraged at people's wickedness, because their guilt is great and the abomination of the pollution upon them is vast in the corruption of their life."

[2]We said to him, "O Lord, what, then, of those who set their hope on you?"

[3]He answered and said to us, "How long are you still dull of heart?[a] [4]Truly I say to you,[a] as the prophet David spoke concerning me[b] and those who are mine, so too he [*sc.* the Father] wills concerning those who believe in me. [5]But in the world there will be deceivers and enemies of righteousness; and the prophecy of David will come to pass, which says: [6]'Their feet are quick to shed blood and their tongue weaves deceit'; and 'the venom of asps is on their lips'; [7]and 'I see you as you go about with a thief, and set your portion with an adulterer';[a] [8]and further, 'As you sit there you speak against your brother, and set up a stumbling block for the son of your mother.'[a] What do you think? 'Shall I be like you?'[b] [9]Now then, see what the prophet has said concerning everything, so that all that has been said beforehand may be fulfilled."

36 We said to him again, "O Lord, will the Gentiles then not say, 'Where is their God?' "[a]

[2]He answered and said to us, "In this the elect will be revealed, that having been afflicted with torment such as this they come forth."

[3]We said to him, "So will their departure from this world take place through the plague that has afflicted them?"

[4]He said to us, "No, but when they are subjected to such affliction as this it will be a test for them, whether they have faith.[a] [5]If they remember this word of mine and keep my commandments

35:3 [a]Cf. Lk 24:25
35:4 [a]» 16:3
[b]Cf. 31:10
35:7 [a]Cf. Ps 50:18
35:8 [a]Cf. Ps 50:20
[b]Cf. Ps 50:21
36:1 [a]Cf. Ps 79:10; 115:2; Joel 2:17
36:4 [a]Cf. Jas 1:3; 1Pet 1:7

35:5 • *enemies of righteousness,* or "those who hate the truth"; cf. Acts 13:10.
36:3 • *their departure:* Cf. Wis 3:2 "their departure (ἐξόδος) was thought to be an affliction."
36:5 • *my commandments*, the noun being understood collectively, as often earlier; see note on 24:5.

35:4 *concerning me:* Fam. 2 "concerning you" (cf. 31:10).
35:6 *on their lips:* Fam. 2 "under their lips."
35:7 *with a thief:* Mss BKQR "like a thief" (cf. 36:7).
36:5 *their life,* or "their waiting" (Duensing-Müller); Ethiopic *nebrat* "session, condition, state; dwelling."

36:5 [a]» 13:2
36:6 [a]» 13:2
36:7 [a]Cf. 35:7
36:8 [a]Cf. 48:3; 1Pt 4:14
[b]Cf. *Jub.* 23.21
36:11 [a]» 5:4
37:2 [a]» 15:9
37:3 [a]Cf. Lk 21:10–12

they will arise; their <remaining> life will last <only> a few days,
that he who sent me[a] may be glorified, and I with him. 6For he sent
me[a] to you that I might tell this to you, and that you tell Israel and
the Gentiles, so that they <too> might hear, and be saved, and believe in me, and <thus> survive the affliction of the plague. 7But
whoever survives such mortal affliction will be taken and kept in
prison, under judgment as if <he were> a thief."[a]

8We said to him, "O Lord, will they be <treated> like unbelievers,[a] and will you judge equally those who have survived the plague?"[b]

9He said to us, "Even if they believe in my name, those who have done what is sinful have behaved like unbelievers."

10We said to him again, "O Lord, in that case, have those who survive no life?"

11He answered and said to us, "Whoever has done my Father's glorious work,[a] his dwelling is with my Father."

37 We said to him, "O Lord, teach us what will happen after this."

2He said to us, "In those years and days[a] there will be war upon war: the four corners of the world will be shaken and at war with each other. 3Then a
continual tumult of clouds and darkness, and persecution of those who believe in me and of the elect.[a] 4Then schism, strife,
and a wicked way of life among those—even among those who believe in my name—who follow evil and teach a vain

37. . . . . .

2". . . those days . . . . there will be *war* (πολεμος) . . . . the lights will be . . . .

3. . . and the *air* (αηρ) wi[ll . . . .

4. . . . . . .

. . . .in va]in, and te[aching . . . . . a multitude . . . . them.

• *few days:* Cf. Wis 3:5 "Having been disciplined a little, they will receive great good, because God has tested them."
36:6 • *survive,* or "escape" (Duensing-Müller); but Ethiopic *waṣ'a* ("to go or come forth, emerge, depart from") connotes avoidance or rescue only weakly if at all (see Hills, 1992: 592 n. 38).

37:2 *In those . . . :* Schmidt prints his reconstruction of these fragmentary chapters apart from the main text (see 1919: 119–21).

teaching. [5]People will follow them and give allegiance to their riches, to their rituals, to their drunkenness, and to their bribes; and there will be partiality among them.

[5]People . . . them . . . . . .

and their partiality . . . . . .]

38 "But those who wish to see the face of God the Father, who show no partiality toward rich sinners, and who do not fear those who err, but correct them—[2]they, the wounded, will be with the Father; just as those who correct their neighbors will be saved, that is, a son of wisdom[a] through faith. [3]But if he has not become a son of wisdom he will hate and persecute and not turn to his brother, but will ignore and reject him. [4]But those who walk in truth and in the knowledge of faith in me, who have wisdom and knowledge and perseverance for the truth though they are despised as they strive for poverty, and endure it—[5]their reward is great,[a] since they are reproached, tormented, persecuted, destitute; and people are arrogant against them as they hunger and thirst. [6]But

38 "*But* (δε) [those who] wish to [. . . . . .] these will [not show partiality . . . . . . the] sinn[ers . . . . reprove their nei]ghbors, [he will be . . . a son] of *wisdom* (σοφια), since he [believes (πιστευε) . . .]. [3]*But* (δε) if [he is not] the son of *wisdom* (σοφια) . . . he will hate his neighbor, will turn against him and [*negl*]*ect* (απορει) him. [4]But those who *live their lives* (πολιτευεσθαι) in truth and in the knowledge of *faith* (πιστις), having *love* (αγαπη) for me—*for* (γαρ) they have *endured* (υπομεινε) *mistreatment* (υβρις)—people will despise them, since they walk in poverty and *endure* (υπομινε) those who hate them [and] reproach them. [5]They have been [tormented], destitute; people are arrogant against them as they walk in hunger and thirst. [6]*But because* (αλλα επει) they

38:2 [a]Cf. Lk 7:35

38:5 [a]Cf. Mt 5:12; Lk 6:23

38:2 • *wounded (qʷesulāna):* Cf. 15:9, where Jesus foretells his coming "with my wounds." Here in 38:2 Guerrier (1919: [80] 220) emends the text to *qʷeṣṣulāna* ("crowned"), but with no manuscript support; cf. but *Barn.* 7.9 "the one that is accursed is crowned"; Herm. *Sim.* 8.3.6; 8.4.6.

37:5 *their rituals (ḥermatomu):* Mss LPSV read *ḥertemennāhomu* "their depravity" (Duensing-Müller); in Phil 1:28 the same form translates αὐτοῖς . . . ἀπωλείας ("their destruction" [RSV]).

38:6 *in heaven (ba-samāyāt):* Ethiopic mss CN *kama ʾenta samʿāt* "as martyrs" (cf. 50:4).

38:6 [a]Cf. Rm 2:7
[b]Cf. 1Ths 4:17
38:7 [a]Cf. 7:3; 27:4; 47:6; Rm 6:21; Phl 3:19
39:2 [a]Cf. Ac 24:15
39:3 [a]» 15:9
[b]Cf. 3:6

because they have endured
they will be blessed in heaven:[a]
they will be with me forever.[b]
7 But woe to those who hate
and despise them, whose end is
destruction."[a]

39 We said to him, "O Lord,
will this <really> happen to
them?"

2 He answered and said to
us, "How will the just judgment
take place—of the sinners or of
the righteous?"[a]

3 We said to him, "O Lord,
on that day[a] will they not say
to you, 'You presided over righteousness and sin, and separated light and darkness,[b] evil
and good'?"

have *endured* (υπομεινε) for
the *blessed*ness (μακαριος) of
heaven they will be with me
forever. 7 *But woe* (ουαι δε) to
those who walk in arrogance
and boasting, for their end is
destruction."

39 We said (δε) to him, "O
Lord, this is your concern, that
you do not allow us to come
upon them."
2 He answered (δε) and said
to us, "In what way will the
judgment (κρισις) take place—of
the *righteous* (η δικαιος) *or* (η)
of the *unrighteous* (αδικος)?"
3 We said (δε) to him, "O
Lord, on that (γαρ) day they
will say to you, 'You did
not pursue *righ[teousness]*
(δικαιοσυνη) and *unrighteousness* (αδικια), light and darkness, *evil* (κακον) and *good*
(αγαθον).' "

38:7 • *But woe to:* οὐαὶ δέ, this combination in the NT only at Matt 23:14; 24:19; 26:24; Mark 13:17; 14:21; Luke 17:1 T.R.

• *whose end is destruction:* The phrase is likely derived from Phil 3:19 ὧν τὸ τέλος ἀπώλεια. The likelihood is increased by the presence of the next part of that verse in 47:6 (see note).

39:3 *will they not . . . ?* The negative ("not") is misplaced in either the Ethiopic or the Coptic recension. (There is a similar case in the Ethiopic *Apoc. Pet.* 1.6 "The coming of the Son of Man will [not] be manifest.") The logic of the argument would support the Ethiopic as best representing the original, which was probably a sentence beginning with οὐ introducing a question expecting the answer yes. Jesus is asked, in effect, "You (the Lord) created these distinctions between righteous and unrighteous, so are you not responsible for them?" †

presided over ('amlākka): By conjecture, the causative (II,1; CG) form of Ethiopic *malaka* ("to occupy, rule"; cf. Sir 38:33 "pass judgment"; *DLLA*, *s.v.* [col. 150]). †

separated (falaṭka): Mss LMV *faṭarka* "you created."

[4]He said to us, "Adam was given the power to choose[a] which of the two he wished. [5]He chose the light, stretched out his hand[a] and took it; and he left the darkness and it was far from him. [6]Likewise it is that every person has the capacity to believe in the light[a] which is life, the Father who sent me.[b] [7]Whoever believes in me will live if he has done the works of light. [8]But if he confesses that he is <of the> light but does <the works> of darkness,[a] he can say nothing in his defense, nor will he be able to lift his face and look at the Son, who I am. [9]I will say to him, 'You sought and you found,[a] you asked and you received.[b] For what do you con-

[4]*Then* (τοτε) he said, "I will answer them, saying, 'Adam was given the *power* (εξουσια) to choose one of the two. [5]He chose the light and put his hand upon it; *and* (δε) he left the darkness and cast it from him.' [6]In this way every person has the *capacity* (εξουσια) to *believe* (πιστευε) in the light, which is life and which is the Father who sent me. [7]Everyone (δε) who *believes* (πιστευε) and does the works of light will have life in them. [8]*But* (δε) if someone *confesses* (ομολογει) that he belongs to the light but does the works of darkness, one such as this has no *defense* (απολογια) to make, *nor* (ουτε) will he be able to lift his face to [look at the] Son of God, who I [am]. [9]I will say (γαρ) to him, 'When you sought you found, and when you *asked* (αιτει) you

39:4 [a]Cf. Dt 30:15, 19; Sir 15:17; *T. Asher* 1.3–6

39:5 [a]Cf. 5:2

39:6 [a]Cf. *2 Bar.* 54.15–16; Jn 12:36

[b]» 13:2

39:8 [a]Cf. Is 29:15; *T. Naph.* 2.10; Rm 13:12; Eph 5:11

39:9 [a]Cf. Mt 7:7, 8; Lk 11:9, 10

[b]Cf. Mt 5:42; Lk 6:30; Jn 16:24; Jas 1:5; 1Jn 5:16

39:4–5 • *Adam was given the power . . . :* There is a remarkable precedent to these verses in Sir 15:14–17: "It was [God] who created man in the beginning, and he left him in the power of his own inclination (LXX ἐν χειρὶ διαβουλίου αὐτοῦ). If you will, you can keep the commandments, and to act faithfully is a matter of your own choice. He has placed before you fire and water: stretch out your hand (ἐκτενεῖς τὴν χεῖρά σου) for whichever you wish. Before a man are life and death, and whichever he chooses (εὐδοκήσῃ) will be given to him." †
39:7 • *Everyone . . . in them:* The switch from the singular ("everyone") to the plural ("in them"), jarring in English, accurately reflects the Coptic. For a similar case in the NT, see Jas 2:15–16: "If *a brother or sister* (ἀδελφὸς ἢ ἀδελφή) is ill-clad . . . and one of you says *to them* [αὐτοῖς] . . . ."

39:5 *it was far from him (reḥqa 'emmenēhu):* Mss AT *wadqa 'emmenēhu* "it fell from him"; fam. 2 *reḥqa 'emmenēhā* "he withdrew from it [fem.]." Possibly the Ethiopic verbal form is corrupt from *'arḥaqa* "he removed <it>" (cf. Coptic).
39:8 *does <the works> of darkness:* Fam. 2 "dwells in the darkness"; cf. John 12:46; 1 John 2:9, 11.

39:10 [a]» 12:3
39:11 [a]» 28:1
39:12 [a]Cf. 3:10; Jn 1:14
40:1 [a]» 12:1
40:2 [a]Cf. Jas 5:16

demn me? 10 Why did you leave me and the kingdom?[a] You have <both> confessed me and denied me!'

11 "Now then, see that everyone has the ability to live and to die: whoever does and keeps my commandments will be a son of light,[a] that is, of the Father <who is> in me—those who keep and do my commandments. 12 On this account I came down from heaven: I, the Word, became flesh[a] and died, teaching and admonishing, 13 so that those who are to be saved might be saved, and the lost forever lost, punished by fire in flesh and soul."

40 We said to him, "O Lord, truly[a] we are sad about them."

2 He said to us, "You do well, for likewise are the righteous concerned about sinners and pray[a] and entreat God the Father and ask him."

received. For what do you *condemn* (καταγινωσκε) me, *O* (ω) man? 10 Why did you leave me and *deny* (αρνα) me? Why did you *confess* (ομολογει) me and <yet> *deny* (αρνα) me?'

11 "*So then* (αρα ουν), everyone has the *power* (εξουσια) to live and to die: so whoever keeps my *commandments* (εντολη) will be a son of light, that is, of the Father who is in me. 12 On account of (δε) those who pervert my words I came down from heaven: I am the *Word* (λογος); I became *flesh* (σαρξ), suffering and teaching 13 that those who are called will be saved and those who are lost, lost forever, [tormented] alive and *punished* (κολαζε) in [their *f*]*lesh* (σαρξ) and their *soul* (ψυχη)."

40 We said (δε) to him, "O Lord, *truly* (αληθως) we are concerned about them."

2 He said (δε) to us, "You do *well, for* (καλως γαρ) the *righteous* (δικαιος γαρ) are concerned about sinners and pray for them, entreating my Father."

39:10 • *you have both confessed <me> and denied:* Cf. 11:4; Titus 1:16 θεὸν ὁμολογοῦσιν εἰδέναι τοῖς δὲ ἔργοις ἀρνοῦνται ("They [*sc.* the corrupt and unbelieving] profess to know God, but they deny him by their works"); the pairing of ὁμολογεῖν with ἀρνεῖσθαι occurs also in Matt 10:31–32; Luke 12:8–9; John 1:20; 1 John 2:22–23.
39:11 • *my commandments:* See note on 24:5.

39:11 *so then* (ⲁⲣⲁ ⲟⲩⲛ), taken here as reproducing the Greek inferential particle ἄρα + the adverb οὖν (so, e.g., Rom 5:18; 7:3, 25; 8:12; 9:16, 18; 14:12, 19; Gal 6:10; Eph 2:19; 1 Thess 5:6; 2 Thess 2:15). †
of the Father <who is> in me: Ethiopic fam. 2 "of my Father" (so Duensing-Müller).

[3]We said to him, "O Lord, does no one then entreat you?"

[4]He said to us, "Yes, I too hear the prayers of the righteous for them."

[5]We said to him, "O Lord, all this you have taught us,[a] and you have had mercy on us and given us life; [6]and we shall preach to those who are worthy and will have a reward with you."

41 He said to us, "Go and preach, and be effective servants and laborers."

[2]We said to him, "O Lord, you <are> our father."

[3]He said to us, "Are all fathers, all servants, all teachers?"[a]

[4]We said to him, "O Lord, is it not you who said to us, 'Do not call <anyone> father on earth, or teacher, for one is your Father and your teacher,

[3]*Again* (παλιν) we said to him, "O Lord, why does no one ask of you?"

[4]He said (δε) to us, "Yes, I will hear the prayer of the *righteous* (δικαιος) that they make for them."

[5]*And* (δε) when he said this to us, we said to him, "O Lord, in all things (γαρ) you have taught us and had mercy on us and saved us, [6]so that we may *preach* (κηρυσσε) to those who are worthy to be saved and obtain a reward with you."

41 He answered (δε) and said to us, "Go and prea[ch, and] you will be [effective] *laborers* (εργατης) and *servants* (διακονος)."

[2]We said (δε) to him, "It is you who will preach through us."

[3]*Then* (τοτε) he answered us, saying, "Do not all be fathers *nor* (ουδε) all teachers."

[4]We said to him, "O Lord, it is you who said to us, 'Do not call <anyone> father on earth, *for* (γαρ) one is your Father, who is in heaven, and your

40:5 [a]» 20:1

41:3 [a]Cf. Mt 23:8–10; 1Cor 12:29; *Interp. Know.* (NHC IX,*1*) 9.27–29

41:1 • *effective*, or "good, useful"; so also in 41:7. See note on 23:1.
• *laborers:* Ethiopic *gabbār* and Coptic ⲛ̄ϩⲉⲣⲅⲁⲧⲏⲥ both translate Greek ἐργάται; cf. Matt 9:37; Luke 10:2; *1 Clem.* 34.1; *Thom. Cont.* (NHC II,*7*) 138.34 "How shall we be called 'laborers'?" †

40:3 *does no one then entreat you?* In the Coptic, the present translation follows the suggestion of Wajnberg (in Schmidt, 1919: 128 n. 7), that the manuscript's ϣⲓⲡⲉ ("to be ashamed": hence Duensing-Müller's "why is no one afraid of you?") is corrupt for ϣⲓⲛⲉ ("to seek, ask"). †

41:1 *servants:* Ethiopic ms V adds *maṣwāteyāna wa-* "almsgivers and."

41:4 [a]» 18:4
41:7 [a]» 16:3
42:2 [a]» 16:3
[b]» 12:3
42:3 [a]» 27:2

who is in heaven'?[a] [5]And now do you tell us that we shall be fathers of many children and teachers and servants?"

[6]He answered and said to us, "You have spoken well. [7]Truly I say to you,[a] all who hear you and believe in me will receive the light of the seal that is in my hand, and through me you will be fathers and effective teachers."

42 We said to him, "O Lord, how is this possible, that <these> three be in one?"

[2]He said to us, "Truly, truly I say to you,[a] you will be called fathers, because with love and mercy you have revealed to them the things of the kingdom of heaven;[b] [3]by my hand they will receive the baptism of life[a] and forgiveness of sins;

teacher.' [5]Why then do you now tell us, 'You will be fathers of many children and *servants* (διακονος) and teachers'?"

[6]He answered (δε) and said to us, "<It is> *just as* (κατα) you have said. [7]*For truly* (αμην γαρ) I say to you, whoever hears you and *believes* (πιστευε) in me will [receive from] you the light of the *seal* (σφραγις) [through me], and *baptism* (βαπτισμα) through me; you will b[e fath] ers and *servants* (διακονος) and teachers."

42 We said (δε) to him, "In what way, then, is each one of us to be these three?"

[2]He said (δε) to us, "*Truly* (αμην) I say to you, you will *indeed* (μεν) be called fathers *because* (επει) with willing hearts and *love* (αγαπη) you have revealed to them the things of the kingdom of heaven; [3]and you will be called *servants* (διακονος), because through you they will receive by my

41:5 • *now do you tell us . . . ?* See the similar challenge at 17:3.
41:7 • *effective*, literally, "useful"; so also in 41:1.
42:2 • *you will indeed be called:* The Coptic has μέν, conventionally translated "on the one hand" and anticipating a counterpart in δέ, "on the other hand." Here, no δέ follows—an unexpected circumstance in a writing that has numerous uses of δέ, including many redundancies.

• *fathers:* Cf. 1QH vii 20 "Thou hast made me a father to the sons of grace"; 1 Cor 4:15.

41:6 *you have spoken correctly:* Ethiopic *'artā'kemu behila* is not merely "speaking well" (see 45:1) but "speaking rightly, properly." This might approximate to καλῶς ἐλαλήσατε (cf. John 4:17; 13:13); but the Coptic, reading κατά, suggests the sense καθὼς ἐλαλήσατε (cf. Esth 6:10 and v.l.).
42:2 *the things of the kingdom of heaven:* For the Ethiopic, Duensing-Müller give "what is (in) heaven"; but all mss agree with the Coptic (cf. Acts 1:3).
42:3 *by my hand:* The Ethiopic lacks the phrase "and you will be called servants, because." A likely reason is the regulation preserved, e.g., in *Const. apost.* 3.11.1; 8.46.11, that deacons (διάκονοι) may not baptize. This proscription likely post-dates the original composition of the *Epistula*, and also the making of the Coptic translation of it; alternatively, it reflects local custom. †

[4]and <you will be called> teachers because you have delivered my word to them without contentiousness.[a] [5]You corrected them, and they turned back in that for which you reproved them.[a] [6]You did not revere their riches, nor flatter <them to their> face, but you kept the commandments of my Father and did them. [7]You <will> have a reward[a] with my heavenly Father,[b] and they will have forgiveness of sins and eternal life and fellowship in the kingdom."[b]

[8]We said to him, "O Lord, if they had ten thousand tongues they would not be able to give thanks to you as is fitting."

[9]He answered and said to us, "Do what I have told you, as I have done to you;[a]

hand the *baptism* (βαπτισμα) of life and forgiveness of their sins; [4]and you will be called teachers because you have given them the *word* (λογος) without *grudging* (-φθονει). [5]You *admonished* (νουθετει) them, and when you reproved them they turned back. [6]You did not revere their riches [and] their <outward> face, *but* (αλλα) you kept [the *commandmen*]*ts* (εντολη) of my Father and did them. [7]You will have a great reward with my Father who is in heaven, and they will have forgiveness of sins and eternal life; and they will *have fellowship* (κοινωνει) in the kingdom of heaven."

[8]We said to him, "O Lord, *even if* (καν) each one of us had ten thousand tongues to speak with, we would not be able to *give thanks* (ευχαριστει) to you, promising us things of this kind."

[9]*Then* (τοτε) he answered, saying to us, "*Only* (μονον) do what I say to you, as I too have done;

42:4 [a]Cf. 24:4
42:5 [a]Cf. Ezek 33:8-9
42:7 [a]Cf. Mt 5:12; 6:1; 10:41–42; Lk 6:23
[b]» 18:4
[b]» 12:3
42:9 [a]» 31:3

42:6 • *the commandments:* See note on 24:5.
42:8 • *ten thousand tongues:* The rhetorical image of the desire for many tongues goes back to Homer *Iliad* 2.489 ("Not if ten tongues were mine, ten mouths to speak") and reappears frequently in ancient authors, e.g., in Ovid *Fasti* 2.119–21; Vergil *Aeneid* 6.625–27; Valerius Flaccus *Argonautica* 6.36; Theophilus *Ad Autolycum* 2.12. †
42:9 • *Only do . . . :* ΜΟΝΟΝ with the imperative here and at 24:5; as the speech of Jesus in the NT gospels only in Mark 5:36 = Luke 8:50 "Do not fear, only believe."

42:6 *their riches* (*be'lomu*): This Ethiopic reading is confirmed by the Coptic. Guerrier prints the consonantally similar reading of fam. 2 mss LPV *'ebēlomu* ("I said to them"); cf. ms M *'ebelomu* ("I will say to them").

42:7 *fellowship in the kingdom:* At the end of the verse, Ethiopic ms N uniquely adds "and <you will be called> servants, for you have completed (*or* perfected, beautified) all things through your teaching."

43:1 [a]Cf. GPh 85.32–33
43:5 [a]» 9:4
[b]Cf. Is 22:22

43 "and be like the wise maidens, who shone and did not sleep but went out with their lamps[a] to meet <their> lord, the bridegroom, and went with him into the bridechamber. [2]But the foolish, who talked with them, were not able to stay awake but fell asleep."

[3]We said to him, "O Lord, who are the wise and who are the foolish?"

[4]He said to us, "The wise are these five, of whom the prophet said, 'They are the daughters of God.' Hear their names."

[5]But we were distressed and sad and wept[a] for those who were shut out.[b]

[6]He said to us, "The five

43 "and you will be like the wise *maidens* (παρθενος), who stayed awake and did not sleep, *but* (αλλα) [went] out to <their> lord, to the bridechamber. [2]*But* (δε) [the foolish] were not able to stay awake, *but* (αλλα) [fell a]sleep."

[3]We said (δε) to him, "O Lord, who are the wise and who are the foolish?"

[4]He said to us, "<There are> five wise and five foolish—*for* (γαρ) it is these of whom the prophet (προφητης) said, 'They are the children of God.' Hear, then, their names."

[5]*But* (δε) we wept and were troubled about those who had fallen asleep.

[6]He said to us, "*Now* (γαρ),

43:1 • *be like the wise maidens:* Unlike Matt 25:1–12, where it is "the kingdom of heaven" that is compared, here it is "you," the apostolic group and, by extension, the continuing church. On the Gnostic and anti-Gnostic dimensions of this section, see Staats, 1969.
43:4 • *daughters of God:* The Ethiopic texts has the distinct plural, *'awāled*, of *walatt*, "daughter." "Children of God" as a prophetic (David? see 19:18) utterance suggests an allusion to Ps 81(82):6 LXX "You are gods, sons of the Most High (υἱοὶ ὑψίστου), all of you"; cf. Rom 8:14.
43:5 • *they wept . . . :* Cf. Aristides *Apol.* 15.11 "If they (*sc.* Christians) see that one of their number has died in his iniquity . . . , over this one they weep bitterly and sigh" (Goodspeed, 1914: 21).
43:6 • *the five:* Cf. already Plato *Prot.* 349B, where the "five names" of virtues are σοφία καὶ σωφρονσύνη καὶ ἀνδρεία καὶ δικαιοσύνη καὶ ὁσιότης ("wisdom, temperance, courage, justice, and holiness"). Comparable lists are found frequently in early Christian literature, e.g., 2 Cor 6:6–7; Gal 5:22–23; 1 Tim 6:11; 2 Pet 1:5–7. †

43:6 *joy / grace:* The Coptic reading, χάρις ("grace"), is secure, and the Ethiopic *feššeḥā*, regularly for χαρά ("joy"), is a unanimous reading. Confusion between the terms is common; indeed, "it seems that χάρις is not always clearly distinguished in meaning from χαρά" (BAGD, *s.v.* χάρις [p. 877a]). See the variations in, e.g., *1 Enoch* 5.7 "light, *joy / grace* and peace" (Ethiopic *feššeḥā*; Greek χάρις); Tob 7:18 χάριν (BA), χαράν (S); Sir 30:16 χαράν (BA), χάριν (S*). †

wise are Faith and Love, Joy, Peace and Hope. 7 If those who believe in me have these, they will be the guides of those who believe in me and in him who sent me.[a] 8 I am the Lord <and> I am the bridegroom; they have received me and entered the house of the bridegroom with me and have reclined with the bridegroom and rejoiced. 9 But the five foolish slept, and when they awoke they came to the house of the bridegroom and knocked at the door, for they were shut out; 10 and they wept[a] because they were shut out."	the five wise are *Faith* (πιστις) and *Love* (αγαπη) and *Grace* (χαρις), *Peace* (ιρηνη) and *Hope* (ελπις). 7 Among those who *believe* (πιστευε), those who (δε) have these will be the guides of those who *believe* (πιστευε) in me and in him who sent me. 8 I (γαρ) am the Lord and I am the bridegroom whom they have received; and they have entered the house of the [bridegroom] and have reclined with me in the bride[chamber and rejoiced]. 9 *But* (δε) the five foolish, [having] fallen asleep, awoke, came to the door of the bridechamber and knocked; *for* (γαρ) they had been shut out. 10 *Then* (τοτε) they wept and *mourned* (πενθει) because it was not opened for them."
11 We said to him, "O Lord, as for their wise sisters who are in the house, do they not open <the door> for them and are they not sad about them?"	11 We said (δε) to him, "O Lord, as for their wise sisters who were inside, in the house of the bridegroom, did they remain without opening <the door> for them, and did they not *grieve* (λυπει) over them *or* (η) entreat the bridegroom to open for them?"
12 He said to us, "Yes, they are sad about them and entreat the bridegroom; but they are not yet able to obtain <anything> for them."	12 He answered, saying to us, "They have not yet been able to obtain grace for them."
13 We said to him, "O Lord, when,[a] then, will they go in because of their sisters?"	13 We said to him, "O Lord, on what day, then, will they go in because of their sisters?"

43:7 [a]» 13:2
43:10 [a]» 9:4
43:13 [a]» 15:9

43:12 • *to obtain grace*: Neither χάρις (see 43:6) not the cognate verb χαρίζεσθαι is present; but in the compound ϫι ϩⲙⲁⲧ the noun ϩⲙⲁⲧ regularly translates χάρις (references in Crum, *s.v.* ϩⲙⲟⲧ [pp. 681a, 682a]).

[14]He said to us, "Whoever is shut out is shut out."	[14]*T*[*hen*] (τοτε) he said to us, "Whoever [is shut out] is shut out."
[15]We said to him, "O Lord, is this word certain? Who, then, are the foolish?"	[15]We said (δε) to him, "O Lord, is this wo[rd . . . . . .]? Who, then, are the foolish?"
[16]He said to us, "Hear <their names>: Knowledge, Understanding, Obedience, Patience, Mercy. [17]These slept in those who have believed and confess me.	[16]He said to us, "Hear their names: *Knowledge* (γνωσις) and Understanding, Obedience, Patience, and Mercy. [17]These it is (γαρ) who have slept in those who have *believed* (πιστευε) and *confessed* (ομολογει) me.
44 "And since they do not do my commandments, those who slept [2]will be outside the kingdom and the fold of the	**44** "*But* (δε) my *commandments* (εντολη) were not done by those who slept; [2]*for* (γαρ) they will remain outside the

43:15 • *this word* (πιϣε[ϫε, *ze-nagar*), or possibly "saying," if the reference is to the previous verse as a set phrase perhaps understood as a dominical saying, though apparently conflicting with Matt 7:7; Luke 11:9 ("knock, and it will be opened to you").
43:16 • *Knowledge, . . . :* Acknowledging the uncertainty of retroversion, Schmidt (1919: 141 n. 11; 380) suggests γνῶσις, σύνεσις (*or* φρόνησις, ἐπιστήμη), ὑπακοή, μακροθυμία (*or* ὑπομονή), ἐλεημοσύνη (*or* ἔλεος). Tertullian reports that the Valentinians apply "the differences between the bodily senses and the intellectual faculties . . . to the parable of the ten virgins" (ANF 3. 198a). Even more striking is the list in Macarius Aegyptius *De elev.* 4.7, where "the five reasoning senses of the soul" are identified as "understanding, knowledge, discernment, endurance, mercy" (σύνεσις, γνῶσις, διάκρισις, ὑπομονή, ἔλεος; PG 34. 893a; discussion in Staats, 1969). †
44:1 • *my commandments:* See note on 24:5.
44:2 • *fold of the shepherd:* At this point the revelation noticeably switches from imagery familiar from the parable of the Wise and Foolish Maidens (Matt 25:1–12) to that associated especially with the Good Shepherd discourse (John 10:1–18). The author appears not to *quote* either text, and it is of course possible that they were known to him only indirectly.

43:16 *Knowledge . . . :* Ethiopic ms V expands the list, in effect combining the names of the wise and foolish: "Faith, Knowledge, Joy, Understanding, Peace, Obedience, Hope, Patience, Love, Mercy."
44:2 *for they will remain* (ϲεναϭογ γαρ): The Greek antecedent is presumably μενοῦσι γάρ. But in the absence of accents in the early Christian period, the same Greek verb is also the present tense form (μένουσι). If this is what was originally written, a rather clearer meaning emerges: "they *remain*," which explains how it is that the commandments have not been kept. †

shepherd. [3]And whoever stays outside the fold the wolf[a] will eat, and although he heard <the word?> he will die: much pain and affliction [4]and lack of patience will come upon him, and though severely afflicted and lacerated and torn by long and terrible punishment, he will not be able to die quickly."

kingdom and the *fold* (αυλη) of the [shepher]d and his sheep. [3]And whoever [remains (δε)] outside the sheep[*fold*] (αυλη) the wolves will eat, and he will [. . .], dying in great suffering; [4]he will [have] no [res]t or *patience* (υπομονη), but [will] be severely (?) afflicted, *in order that* (ινα) he [may . . . . . .; he will be *punished* (κολαζε)] with great [*punishments* (κολασις), and will b]e in *torment* (βασανος)."

44:3 [a]Cf. Mt 7:15; 10:16; Jn 10:12; Ac 20:29

45

We said to him, "O Lord, you have revealed all things to us well."[a]

[2]He said to us, "Know and understand these words."

[3]We said to him, "O Lord, there are these five who are to enter your kingdom; and the five who are shut out, they will be outside your kingdom. [4]But those who stayed awake, and entered with the Lord and the bridegroom, do not rejoice at those who slept."

45

[We (δε) said to him], "O Lord, you have revealed all things t[o us] *well* (καλως)."

[2]*Then* (τοτε) he answered, [say]ing to us, "You do not *understand* (νοιε) these words?"

[3]We said to him, "Yes, O Lord: through these five they will enter your kingdom. [4]*Nevertheless* (μεντοιγε) those who rejoiced and were with you, the Lord and the bridegroom, do not rejoice at those who slept."

45:1 [a]Cf. 41:6

45:1 • *revealed . . . well:* Cf. *Disc.* 8–9 (NHC VI,6) 52.20–22 "O my father [Hermes Trismegistus], you have spoken every word well to me."
45:4 • *Nevertheless:* Coptic ⲙⲉⲛⲧⲟⲓⲅⲉ = μέντοιγε, worthy of note as a compound particle relatively unusual in Greek of any era (Denniston, 1954: 405), and not present in the NT or the apostolic fathers; once in the LXX (Ps 38[39]:6; also Job 18:5 Sym.; Jer 36[43]:25 Sym.). LSJ, *s.v.* μέν B.II.4.c (p. 1102b): "in later Gk. μέντοιγε always stands first in the sentence."

44:4 *in order that:* See note on 29:3.
45:2 *Know and understand:* The Ethiopic has the imperative, the Coptic the indicative (as a question); see note on 21:6. With Coptic ⲧⲉⲧⲛ̄ⲣⲛⲟⲓ̈ⲉ ⲉⲛ cf. Mark 8:17 οὔπω νοεῖτε οὐδὲ συνίετε;

45:8 [a]» 13:2
46:1 [a]Cf. 2Chr 19:7
[b]Cf. Jer 9:23

[5]He said to us, "They will rejoice that they have entered with the Lord, but they will be sad on account of those who slept, because they are their sisters; [6]for these ten are the daughters of God the Father."	[5]He said to us, "They do *indeed* (μεν) rejoice that they have entered with the bride[groom], the Lord, but they *grieve* (λυπει) on account of those who s[lept], because they are their sisters; [6]*for* (γαρ) the ten are the daughters of God the Father."
[7]We said to him, "O Lord, it is of your greatness that you give grace to their sisters."	[7][*Then* (τοτε)] we said to him, "[O Lor]d, [. . . . .]."
[8]He said to us, "This thing is not yours but his who sent me,[a] and I agree with him.	[8]He said to us, "[. . . . .] *but* (αλλα) his who sent me, a[nd I myse]lf *agree* (συνευδοκει) with him.
46 "But as for you, preach and teach truly and rightly, revering and fearing no one,[a] but especially the rich, among whom are found those who do not do my commandments but revel in their riches."[b]	**46** "*But* (δε) as for you, go, preach and teach uprightly and *well* (καλως), revering no one and fearing no one, especially (δε) the rich, *for* (γαρ) they do not do my *commandments* (εντολη) *but* (αλλα) revel in their riches."
[2]We said to him, "O Lord, is it only the rich?"	[2]We (δε) said to him, "O Lord, is it [onl]y the rich?"

46:1 • *my commandments:* See note on 24:5.

• *revel in their riches:* The phrase is virtually a formula in early Christian polemic; see Herm. *Vis.* 1.1.8 "those who have evil designs in their hearts . . . and *glory in their wealth* (καὶ γαυριῶντες ἐν τῷ πλούτῳ αὐτῶν)"; 3.9.6 "See to it then, *you who rejoice in your wealth* (ὑμεῖς οἱ γαυριώμενοι ἐν τῷ πλούτῳ ὑμῶν), that the destitute may not groan"; Polycarp *Phil.* 6.1; *Acts Pet. 12 Apost.* (NHC VI,*1*) 11.26–12.14 "The rich men . . . who reveled in their wealth and pride—do not dine in [their] houses."

45:7 *it is of your greatness:* Schmidt (1919: 145 n. 6) proposes to restore the Coptic thus: "you it is who [gives grace to them for their sisters' sake]."

46:2 *is it . . . ?* Ethiopic fam. 2 has "do you speak to us . . . ?" (so Duensing-Muller).

[3]He said to us, "As for one who is not rich, if he gives and does <not> refuse him who has nothing, he will thus be called by people a <bene>factor.

47 "But if someone falls bearing his burden, that is, the sin that he has committed against his neighbor, let his neighbor reprove him in return for what he has done for his neighbor.[a] [2]If he has reproved his neighbor and he returns, he will be saved, and the one who reproved him will find eternal life. [3]But if that one, whom he helped, sees him who helped him sinning and flatters him, he will thus be judged with a severe judgment; [4]for 'A blind man who leads a blind man, both will fall into a pit.' [5]Likewise, then, the hypocrite who shows partiality, and the one who is flattered, to whom he shows partiality, will both be judged with the one judgment,

[3]He answered, saying [to us, "If there is one] who is not rich, (but) has a little *property* (βιος) and gives to those in want [and the poor], people will call him [a bene]factor.

47 "*But* (δε) if someone falls beneath <his burden>, because of the sins that he has [committed, let] his neighbor reprove him *in return for* (αντι) [the good that] he has done his neighbor. [2][If he,] his neighbor, has [repro]ved him and he returns, he will be saved, <and> the one who reproved him will receive a reward and live fo[r ever]. [3]*For* (γαρ) if someone in want sees the one who has helped him sinning and does not reprove him, he will be judged with a severe *judgment* (κριμα): [4]'A blind man (δε) leading a blind man, b[oth] fall in[to a] pit.' [5]And whoever shows partiality [will be like] the two, *just as* (κατα) the *pro*[*phet* (προφητης) said], [6]'*Woe*

47:1 [a]Cf. *T. Gad* 6.3

46:3 • *benefactor* ([ⲣⲉϥⲣ̄ⲡⲉⲧ]ⲛⲁⲛⲟⲩϥ, *gabārē*): Probably for Greek εὐεργέτης (see Crum, *s.v.* ⲛⲁⲛⲟⲩ- [p. 227b]). The unanimous Ethiopic reading *gabārē* means simply "doer." Guerrier suggests that a copyist has accidentally omitted the word that would commonly complete the sense "*well*-doer": *šannāyt*. †
47:2 • *he will be saved:* Both recensions avoid the ambiguity of Jas 5:20 as to *who* is saved by the believer's act of reconciliation.
47:4 • *'A blind man . . . ':* Cf. Matt 15:14; Luke 6:39 (as a question); Thom 34 (39.18–20); discussion in Hills, 1990a. Strikingly, in a series of proverbial sayings Jerome (*Ep.* 7.5) quotes together both "A blind man leads the blind into a pit" and "Men's family god is their belly" (see *Ep. apost.* 47:6).

47:6 [a]Cf. Ex 23:7; Is 5:23; 1QH xiv 20-22; xv 24
[b]Cf. 7:3; 27:4; 38:7; 3Macc 7:11; Rm 16:18
47:8 [a]» 16:3
[b]» 15:9
48:3 [a]Cf. 36:8

as the prophet said, 6 “Woe to hypocrites who justify sinners for the sake of gifts,[a] those whose god is their belly.’[b] 7 Do you see how the judgment <comes about>? 8 Truly I say to you,[a] on that day[b] I shall neither fear the rich nor have mercy on the poor.

(ουαει) to those who show partiality and ac[quit the *impious* (ασεβης)] for the sake of *gifts* (δωρον), those whose god is their belly.’ 7 See, then, that a *judgment* (κρισις) [. . . . . .]. 8 *For truly* (αμην γαρ) I say [to you, on] that day I shall *neither* (ουτε) fear [the r]ich *nor* (ουτε) have mercy on the [poor].

48 “If there is someone whom with your own eyes you have seen sinning, rebuke him between the two of you. If he listens to you, you have won him back. 2 But if he does not listen to you, obtain two or as many as three <others and> rebuke your brother. 3 If he does not listen to you, then let him be to you as a Gentile[a] and a tax collector.

48 “If you see a sinner, re[prove him] between you and him <alone>. 2 *But* (δε) if he does not listen to you, take with you up to three others and instruct your brother. 3 If he *again* (παλιν) does not listen to you, let him be to you as [. . .

49 “If you <merely> hear a report <of something>, do not testify against your brother; do not slander, and do not love to hear slan-

47:6 • ‘*whose god is their belly*’: Likely reproducing Paul’s criticism of his opponents in Phil 3:19 ὧν ὁ θεὸς ἡ κοιλία. The previous phrase in that verse is apparently quoted in *Ep. apost.* 38:7. Hornschuh (1966: 18) suggests an ultimate derivation from a prophetic pseudepigraphon cited by Paul himself. †
48:1–3• *If you see a sinner, . . . :* With this style of communal regulation, cf. Matt 18:15–17; Luke 17:3; Gal 6:1–2; Jas 5:19–20; *T. Gad* 6.3–7; *Did.* 15.3; also 1QS v 25–26; CD ix 1–3.
48:3 • *let him be to you:* As in Matt 18:17, “you” is singular. The Coptic text breaks off here; Schmidt (1919: 151 n. 14) reasonably conjectures the continuation ⲛ̄ⲟⲩϩⲉⲑⲛⲓⲕⲟⲥ ⲙⲛ̄ ⲟⲩⲧⲉⲗⲱⲛⲏⲥ.

47:6 *gifts:* Ethiopic *menšā’*, “gift,” here in a collective sense. The word is rare; *DLLA* (*s.v. naš’a* [col. 639]) cites only this passage for it (“Kid. f. [= *Maṣḥafa Kidān* folio] 41”), as meaning *munus, donum* (but “ut videtur” — “so it seems”).

der. [2]For thus it is written, 'Let not your ear heed anything against your brother.'[a] [3]But if you have <actually> seen <him sinning>, then chastise him, rebuke him, and turn him back."

[4]We said to him, "O Lord, in all things you have taught us and exhorted us. [5]But, O Lord, must there be division, dissention, jealousy, chaos, hatred, and affliction among believers, who ought in their own midst to trust in the preaching of your name? [6]For you indeed said, 'Let them chastise one another and show no favor to those who sin, who hate the one who corrects them.' "

[7]He answered and said to us, "But why, then, is the judgment to take place? [8]So that the wheat may be put into its barns, and the chaff be thrown into the fire[a]—those who in this way hate the one who loves me and chastises those who do not do my commandments.

50 "Taking counsel together against them they will indeed hate, persecute, despise, ridicule, and speak falsely against those who love me, [2]though they were chastising them that they might be saved. [3]They will hate and alienate and ignore those who chastise, correct, and exhort them; they will ignore even those who wish to do good to them. [4]But those who have persevered in this way will be as martyrs[a] with the Father, for they have had zeal for righteousness and they have no zeal for destructive jealousy."

[5]And we said to him, "O Lord, will the like of this also happen among us?"

[6]He said to us, "Do not fear. It is not among many <that this will happen>, but among few."

[7]We said to him, "Tell us how."

[8]He said to us, "There will come another teaching,[a] and dissention: seeking their own glory[b] and promoting and teaching a worthless teaching—for there is a deadly offence in it—[9]they shall turn

49:2 [a]Cf. Sir 7:12; 19:4–6; Jas 4:11
49:8 [a]Cf. Mt 3:12; 13:30; Lk 3:17
50:4 [a]Cf. 38:6
50:8 [a]» 29:2
[b]Cf. 29:1; Jn 7:18

49:2 • *'Let not your ear heed . . . ':* Cf. Herm. *Mand.* 2.2 "Speak evil of no one, and do not listen gladly to him who speaks evil." Ehrhardt (1964: 375 n. 2) suggests a derivation from Prov 20:19 Theod. (lacking in LXX): ἀποκαλύπτων μυστήριον πορεύεται δόλῳ, καὶ ἀπατῶντι χείλη αὐτοῦ μὴ συναναμίσγου (Field, 1875: 2. 352); MT "He who goes about gossiping reveals secrets; therefore do not associate with one who speaks foolishly" (cf. Vg); cf. also *T. Gad* 4.3 "If a brother makes a false step, immediately [hatred] wants to spread the tale to everyone, and is eager to have him condemned for it, punished, and executed." Duensing-Muller include 49:3 in the quotation.

49:8 • *my commandments:* The singular form is here taken collectively; see note on 24:5.

50:8 • *deadly offence:* The phrase, and perhaps the entire verse, suggests an *inclusio* with the *Epistula's* warning in 1:2 and 7:1–3 about the teaching of Simon and Cerinthus, which produces "death and a great stain of corruption." †

51:1 [a]» 20:1
[b]» 13:2
51:2 [a]Cf. 18:4; Lk 24:50–51; Jn 20:17; Ac 1:9–11

away from my commandments even those who believe in me, and
try to bring them out of eternal life. 10But woe to those who falsify
this my word and commandment, and also to those who give heed
to them and withdraw from the life<-giving> teaching; they will be
eternally punished with them."

51 When he had said this and completed the discourse with us,[a]
he spoke again to us: "Look, after three days and three hours he
who sent me will come[b] so that I may go with him."
2 And as as he spoke there was thunder and lightning and an
earthquake; the heavens opened and a bright cloud came and took
him away.[a] 3<There was> the sound of many angels rejoicing and
giving praise, saying, "Gather us, O priest, in glorious light."
4And when he had drawn near to the firmament of heaven,
we heard him say, "Depart in peace in the name of our Lord Jesus
Christ."

50:9 • *my commandments*, the singular term here (as in the next verse) taken collectively; see note on 24:5.
51:1 • *after three days and three hours . . . :* If this is a prediction of the ascension, it is likely in knowing contradiction of Luke 24:50–51 (also the day of resurrection?) and Acts 1:3 ("forty days"). Now, since "he who sent me" is the Father, this statement in 51:1 is presumably to be correlated with 17:2 (" . . . will the coming of the Father take place"), unless some more satisfactory alternative can be discovered. In either case, the chief exegetical question is whether the movement referred to in the phrase "so that I may go with him" is the same as the Lord's departure in 51:2. †
51:2 • *And as (wa-ba-kama) . . . :* Ethiopic *wa-* is the weakest conjunction, almost always to be translated "and" or left untranslated. Like Greek καί, it can on occasion mean "but" or "then," just as *wa-* can sometimes translate δέ and other terms (see *LCDG*, *s.v.* [p. 158b]); *DLLA*, *s.v.* [col. 880]; for δέ, e.g., in Matt 2:1, 3; cf. BAGD, *s.v.* καί I.2.g, 6 [pp. 392b, 393a]). Certainly, it would be convenient from

---

51:3 *<There was>:* Mss CN "we heard" (see 51:4).
in glorious light (ba-berhāna sebḥat), or *in the light of glory*, is the reading of mss ALMOP. Mss QR "in your glorious light"; BCKNSTV "in his glorious light." Cf. Bar 5:9 (also a conclusion, after God's "gathering" of Israel in 5:5): "God will lead Israel with joy in the light of his glory (τῷ φωτὶ τῆς δόξης αὐτοῦ) with the mercy and righteousness that come from him." The rarity of the expression is perhaps due to its being perceived as involving redundancy.
51:4 *he had drawn near (qarba)*: Mss ACNT have *qarbu*: "they had drawn near," presumably with reference to Jesus and the angels.
in the name . . . Jesus Christ: It is admittedly awkward to have Jesus himself say this, but all manuscripts except two (mss PV) have only the punctuation that separates words, not sentences, before "in the name. . . ." As seen earlier, Ethiopic punctuation marks, though themselves quite unambiguous as orthographic signs, cannot always be relied on; the scribe may or may not have had a full understanding of what he was copying. In this case, at least "Jesus Christ" in the mouth of Jesus has a biblical precedent in John 17:3. Mss MP lack "Christ"; ms V lacks the entire phrase. All mss except O, which is followed here, have colophons, typically beginning "The Testament of our Lord is ended," including blessings or personal remarks of the scribe. †

a linguistic or logical perspective to translate "But . . ." here: "*But, as it happened, . . .*" It is extremely improbable, however, that an author or later copyist would rely on so subtle an adversative expression at this climactic moment. And to this author it would surely be unacceptable *theologically* to have Jesus thus portrayed as ignorant of the time of his departure (see the previous verse).

• *as he spoke . . . :* Cf. *Acts. Pil.* 14.1 "While Jesus was still speaking to his disciples, we saw him taken up into heaven"; and especially *T. Dom.* 2.27 "And falling down we worshipped Him, saying, Glory to Thee, O Jesus, Name of light, who didst give us the teaching of Thy commandments, so that we may be like unto Thee, we and all those who hear Thee. And when he spoke to us and taught and commanded us, and showed many loosings and miracles, He was taken up from us, giving us tranquility [*or* peace]" (Cooper-MacLean, 1902: 138).

51:3 • *Gather us* (*'astagābe'ana*), or possibly *Keep us together,* if referring to the unity desired between heavenly and earthly realms; also possible as a final plea for unity (understood as freedom from heresy) within the Christian community. But given its position in the writing, it is more likely the reprise of a biblical refrain with eschatological implications: 1 Chron 16:35 "Deliver us, O God of our salvation, and *gather* and save *us* (ἐξελοῦ ἡμᾶς) from among the nations, that we may give thanks to thy holy name, and glory in thy praise"; Ps 106(LXX 105):47 "Save us, O Lord our God, and *gather us* (ἐπισυνάγαγε ἡμᾶς) from among the nations, that we may give thanks to thy holy name and glory in thy praise"; Tob 13:5 "[God] *will gather us* (συνάξει ἡμᾶς) from all the nations among whom you have been scattered"; 2 Macc 2:7, 18 "God . . . *will gather us* (ἐπισυνάξει [ἡμᾶς]) from everywhere under heaven into his holy place"; Matt 24:31 "[the angels] *will gather* (ἐπισυνάξουσιν, *yāstagābe'omu*) the elect"; also *Did.* 9.4 "As this broken bread was scattered . . . but was brought together (συναχθέν) and became one, so let thy Church *be gathered* (συναχθήτω) together from the ends of the earth . . . "; 10.5 "Remember, Lord, thy Church, . . . and *gather it together* (σύναξον αὐτήν) in its holiness from the four winds to thy kingdom which thou hast prepared for it"; *Mart. Pol.* 22.3 "that the Lord Jesus Christ may *gather me* (κἀμὲ συναγάγῃ) together with his elect into his heavenly kingdom."

• *priest:* The summons to Christ as "priest" recalls the angelic worship in 13:4, to be continued "until I go to him [*sc.* the Father]." For Christ as "priest" (ἱερεύς) see, e.g., Heb 5:6 (cf. "high priest," in Heb 2:17; 3:1; 5:5, 10; et al.); Justin *Dial.* 118.2.

51:4 • *Depart in peace:* A common biblical farewell; in the singular: 1 Sam 1:17; 29:7; 2 Sam 15:9; 2 Kgs 5:19; Judg 8:35; Mark 5:34; Luke 7:50; 8:48; plural: Judg 18:6; Acts 16:36; Jas 2:16.

ADDITIONAL NOTES

1:1 *book:* With the words in the title, Vanovermeire (1962: 20) compares Rev 1:1 (ἀποκάλυψις Ἰησοῦ Χριστοῦ . . .) in proposing the translation "The Book which Jesus Christ Revealed to His Disciples." This proposal rightly recognizes that the first phrase of the *Ep. apost.* is also its "title," as, for example, in the *Gos. Truth* (NHC I,*3*) 16.31 and, with slight modification, the *Gos. Eg.* (NHC III,*2*) 40.12. Commonly, a colophon repeats this information.

for all <people>: The regular Ethiopic for ἡ καθολικὴ ἐκκλησία ("the catholic church") is *'enta lāʿla kʷellu bēta kerestiyān*, literally, "the Church which is over all" (*DLLA*, *s.v. kalala* [col. 815]); for the "catholic" faith the transliteration *katolikā* (or *kotolikā*) is also found (ibid., *s.v.* [col. 851]; *LCGD*, *s.v.* [p. 154a]).

false apostles: See also Justin *Dial.* 35.3 "Many false messiahs and false apostles will arise, and they will deceive many believers" (ἀναστήσονται πολλοὶ ψευδόχριστοι καὶ ψευδαπόστολοι, καὶ πολλοὺς τῶν πιστῶν πλανήσουσιν; Goodspeed, 1914: 130); cf. Matt 24:11; Mark 13:22. Likewise, in several respects reminiscent of *Ep. apost.* 1:1 is *Didasc.* 23 (Syriac, Latin): "When we had divided the world into twelve parts, and were gone forth among the Gentiles into all the world to preach the word, then Satan set about and stirred up the People to send after us false apostles (Lat. *pseudapostolos*) for the undoing of the word" (Connolly, 1929: 200–201); the Latin term *pseudapostolus* occurs already in, e.g., Tertullian *Praescr.* 4; *De res.* 24.

1:2 *deceit:* To be entrapped and hence to be "killed by deceit" is an idea found in, e.g., Exod 21:14; Deut 27:24 (LXX ἀποκτεῖναι δόλῳ); Matt 26:4; Mark 14:1 (the Jewish leaders plot πῶς αὐτὸν [= τὸν Ἰησοῦν] ἐν δόλῳ . . . ἀποκτείνωσιν). As for the distinction between *ḥabl and ḥebl*, OT textual criticism supplies a comparable phenomenon. In LXX 2 Kgdms 22:6; Ps 17(18):5, 6, in the memorable phrases ὠδῖνες θανάτου and ὠδῖνες ᾅδου ("the *bonds* of death, Hades") the noun ὠδίς (LSJ, *s.v.* I. [p. 2030b] "pangs or throes of childbirth, travail") appears "due to confusion of Heb. *ḥēbel* 'pang' with *ḥĕbel* 'cord' " (*s.v.* II. [p. 2031a]; see further BDB, *s.v. ḥebel* I. "cord, territory, band" [p. 286b]; II. "destruction" [p. 287b]). In the case of 2 Kgdms 22:6, the Greek variant in L† (Lucianic recension) has σχοίνια, "ropes, cords" (see Acts 27:32, immediately below).

Lightfoot (1889–1890, 1981: 2/3. 194) reports a similar confusion of terms in the Armenian recension of Pseudo-Ignatius. In Ps.-Ignatius *Phil.* 4.1, where the Greek has "[Satan] pointed [Judas] to a *rope* to hang himself with," "rope" or "noose" (βρόχος), which in the Syriac intermediary version will have been *ḥablā'* (PSCSD, *s.v.*, "cord, rope, line, noose" [p. 124a]; e.g., in the Peshitta at John 2:15 and Acts 27:32 for σχοινίον; in Cor 7:35, βρόχος is found as *maḥnuwqi'tā'*, "strangling, noose": PSCSD, *s.v.* [p. 265a]), was presumably read by the Armenian translator as *ḥᵊbālā'* (PSCSD, *s.v.*, "corruption, hurt, harm" [p. 124b]).

1:5 *We greet you:* On the placement of the greeting (ἀσπάζομαι) formula, see Schoedel, 1985: 103: "In this period it had begun to appear not only at the end but also at the beginning of letters just after the salutation."

sons and daughters: It is a curious coincidence that the sole NT use of the combination "sons and daughters," in 2 Cor 6:18, is as here followed almost immediately by the epithet "almighty" (παντοκράτωρ), otherwise found in the NT only in the book of Revelation.

1:6 *God:* "God almighty" (so mss AB*CKNOV), without "the Father," is distinctive of the creed of Marcellus of Ancyra (d. ca. 374; see Kelly, 1972: 103–4).

almighty: The present translation of *'axāzē kʷllu 'ālam* (following James, 1924: 487) reflects the judgment that the Greek underlying this Ethiopic expression is παντοκράτωρ (Lat. *omnipotens*), for which the conventional ET is "almighty." The term is of considerable significance in the early church, especially in creedal formulas. It is noteworthy that Wajnberg (in Schmidt, 1919: 26, 27, 32) rejects "der Allmächtiger" (= παντοκράτωρ) in favor of the fuller, more literal, "der Herrscher der [ganzen] Welt" (1:6; 3:2) and "der Herrscher des Weltalls" (5:22); similarly, the full phrase in the Ethiopic *Didasc.* 1, ultimately derived from ὁ παντοκράτωρ πατήρ in *Const. Apost.* 1.1.1 (Funk, 1905: 5) is rendered "Ruler of the whole world" by Platt (1834: 2) and Harden (1920: 2). As it happens, the Greek word (occurring more than 200 times in the LXX; 10 times in the NT, all but one [2 Cor 6:18—see note on "sons and daughters" in *Ep. apost.* 1:5] in Revelation) is rendered in a remarkable variety of ways in Ge'ez:

(1) *za-kʷello yemallek* ("[the one] who rules all things"), in the majority of places in the LXX and all but one in Revelation (1:8; 4:9; 11:17; 15:3; 16:7, 14; 19:6, 15; 21:22); the exception is Rev 4:8 (see [6], below);

(2) *ze-yenaggeš la-kʷellu* or *za-yenaggeš lā'la kʷellu* ("[the one] who reigns over all"), e.g., in Jer 32(39):14, 18(19); 40:11; Bar 31:1, 4 (further references in *DLLA, s.v. nagša* [col. 689]);

(3) *kahālē kʷellu* ("all-powerful"), e.g., in Wis 7:23; 11:24 (*DLLA, s.v. kehla* [col. 813]);

(4) *za-kʷello ye'exxez* ("[the one] who controls [*or* holds] all things"), especially frequent in the church order literature, e.g., more than thirty times in the Ethiopic *Apostolic Church Order;* and the cognate phrase *'axāzē kʷellu*, e.g., twice in *A.C.O.* (Eth.) 35 (Horner, 1904: text 22 [ET 153]), and parallels in *A.C.O.* (Copt.) 46.11, 18 (ⲡⲡⲁⲛⲧⲟⲕⲣⲁⲧⲱⲣ; Lagarde, 1862: 256–57; Horner, 1904: 317, 319) and Hippolytus *Apost. trad.* 21.11b; 23.8; cf. also *T. Dom.* (Eth.) 49, 50 (Beylot, 1984: 120, 125) = *T. Dom.* (Syr.) 2.7, 8 (Cooper-MacLean, 1902: 123, 125). Cf. the title δέσποτα τῶν ὅλων (after παντοκράτορ) in the liturgy at *Const. apost.* 8.9.8 (Funk, 1905: 486); similarly the *Liturgy of St. Mark* (Brightman, 1896: 114, 121, 123, and often);

(5) *saddāy* (Greek Σαδδαΐ), e.g., in Ezek 10:5 (*DLLA, s.v.* [col. 396]);

(6) *'amlāka 'amālekt* ("God of gods"), e.g., in Rev 4:8 (a partial quotation of Amos 3:14; 4:13 LXX), which for κύριος ὁ θεὸς ὁ παντοκράτωρ has *'egzi'abḥēr 'amlāka 'amlāk* ("God [*or* Lord], God of gods").

The following considerations seem to be decisive in favor of the translation "almighty" and its probable derivation from παντοκράτωρ: (a) the phrase in *Ep. apost.* 1:6 is very close to usage (4) above; (b) the threefold use of the phrase (1:5; 3:2; 5:22) suggests not an ad hoc title but a fixed expression; and (c) the third occurrence is in a creedal statement, the like of which commonly have παντοκράτωρ (*omnipotens*) in extant early Christian texts.

2:1 *We . . . : Ep. apost.* 2:1 is the earliest extant reference to Peter and Cephas as two separate persons (so Ehrman, 1990).

3:1 *we know this:* The declaration "we know this," and the insistence on apostolic witness, are reminiscent of the creedal statement produced by "the blessed presbyters" of Smyrna and quoted in Hippolytus *C. Noet.* 1.7 (Butterworth, 1977: 44–45):

> We too have knowledge of (οἴδαμεν) a single God—in the true way.
> We have knowledge of Christ.
> We know that the Son suffered as in fact he suffered, died as in fact he died;
> and rose up again on the third day and is at the right hand of the Father,
> and is coming to judge living and dead.
> And these things that we state are what we learnt (καὶ ταῦτα λέγομεν ἃ ἐμάθομεν).

The various elements of the hymnic material in 3:2–13 are found widely in Jewish and Christian literature; in the latter, see, e.g., *1 Clem.* 20.1–12; *Const. apost.* 8.12.6–27.

3:9 *parables:* Cf. Justin *Dial.* 90.2 ὅσα εἶπον καὶ ἐποίησαν οἱ προφῆται, . . . παραβολαῖς καὶ τύποις ἀπεκάλυψαν; Clement of Alexandria *Prot.* 1.10.1 τὰ προφητικὰ αἰνίγματα; *Keryg. Pet.* 6 (*apud* Clement of Alexandria *Strom.* 6.15.128) "But we opened the books of the prophets which we had, which partly in parables, partly in enigmas (ἃ μὲν διὰ παραβολῶν, ἃ δὲ δι' αἰνιγμάτων), partly in certainty and in clear words name Christ Jesus"; Hippolytus *De antichr.* 29 διὰ παραβολῶν καὶ αἰνιγμάτων.

3:13 ... *who was to be killed:* Since *yetqattel* (here: "he was to be killed") and *ta'awqa* ("he was made known") are such dissimilar forms, inner-Ethiopic corruption is unlikely. Possibly, therefore, a Greek antecedent was misread, e.g., a form of φονεύειν ("to kill") read as if a form of φαίνειν ("to reveal, show forth"); or of φθείρειν ("to destroy") as if from ἐκφέρειν ("to bring forth").

grew up: In a passage often quoted, Ignatius *Trall.* 9 similarly emphasizes Jesus' humanity: "who was of the family of David, and of Mary, who was truly born, both ate and drank, was truly persecuted under Pontius Pilate, was truly crucified and died . . . "; the extant Ethiopic extracts from *Trall.* 9.1–2 add "truly grew up" (*'emuna lehqa)* before "ate and drank"; so also the parallel Arabic fragments (Cureton, 1849: 261; Lightfoot, 1889–1890, 1981: 2/3. 304, 306).

5:1 *brothers:* Here the "brothers" are the narrators of Jesus' deeds; therefore in 5:1 either "brothers" means simply "brothers" (in some literal or metaphorical sense other than "followers" or "apostles") or the author has inadequately conformed a source to the perspective of the writing as a whole. There is a similar question in John 2:11–12. There, with support from *Ep. apost.* 5 Bultmann suggests that "the fact that some authorities [i.e., mss] omit the μαθηταί ['disciples'] in v. 12, while others mention them *before* the ἀδελφοί ['brothers'] shows that they were not originally mentioned in the text; they were added later, since they were missed after (v. 2 and) v. 11. Indeed it is likely that they [i.e., the disciples] were not even mentioned [in the source] in v. 2, but that they have replaced here the ἀδελφοί who originally were mentioned alone" (1971: 114 and n. 6).

5:2 *paralytic:* By contrast, of the fourteen occurrences of χωλός, none is translated *maḍāg*[w]*e'*; nine have *ḥankās* ("lame, crippled"), three have *seburān* ("broken down, crippled"), one has the literal rendering *ḍewwusa 'egarihu* ("weak, crippled in his feet"; Acts 3:2), and in Acts 14:8 χωλός is omitted with the majority text.

5:20 *what . . . <mean>?* In light of the putative etiological significance of the Joshua narrative ("they are there to this day," Josh 4:9), there may be an echo in *Ep. apost.* 5 of the stones / bread typology found in, e.g., Matt 4:3; 7:9; Luke 4:3; 11:11. In any case, the five loaves of the feeding are elsewhere interpreted allegorically, e.g., in Clement of Alexandria *Strom.* 6.94.1–5. It is possible that in the construction of the list the miracle of the loaves *and fish* was consciously linked with its predecessor, about the coin in the *fish's* mouth. On the frequency of the number five in the scriptures, against gnostic numerology, see Irenaeus *Adv. haer.* 2.24.4.

5:21 *type:* Also instructive here is Herm. *Sim.* 2.2 "These two trees . . . are put as a type (εἰς τύπον; *messālēhomu*) for the servants of God" (Abbadie, 1860: 50). Similarly, in 1 Cor 10:11 *'amsāl* reflects τυπικῶς (the Ethiopic possibly reading τύποι with [A]DFG et al.).

our <statement of> faith: The phrase ἡ πίστις ἡμῶν occurs in the NT, though probably in a non-technical sense, e.g., in Rom 1:12; Heb 12:2; 1 John 5:4; also *Barn.* 1.6; 2.2; *Ps.-Clem. Hom.* 15.3.1. In post-Pauline NT writings, Bultmann claims of πίστις that "it is becoming a historical term, so to speak, a term for becoming or being Christian or also for Christianity in the sense of the content of its belief" (1951–55: 2. 211). Hence for Irenaeus "our faith" (*fides nostra*), grounded in the testimony of "the prophets, the apostles, and all the disciples" (*Adv. haer.* 3.24.1), stands opposed to all gnostic speculation.

baptized Christians: To make better sense of Guerrier's text (i.e., fam. 2: "great Christianity"), Wajnberg (in Schmidt, 1919: 32 n. 3) suggested reading *'abiy* ("great") in its construct form, creating a genitive grammatical relationship: "the *Great One* [i.e., God] of Christianity / Christians" (so James, 1924: 487). For "Great One" (μέγας) as a title or epithet used of God, see *1 Enoch* 9.3; 14.2, 20; 104.1; *Orac. Sib.* 2.243.

7:1 *Cerinthus and Simon:* Elsewhere not Cerinthus but "Cleobius" is paired with Simon, e.g., in Hegesippus *apud* Eusebius *Hist. eccl.* 4.22.5; *3 Cor.* 1.2–3, in which the Corinthians make this plea to Paul: "Two men are come to Corinth, named Simon and Cleobius, who pervert the faith of many through pernicious words, which thou [*sc.* Paul] shalt put to the test"; Syriac *Didasc.* 23 "When we had divided the whole world into twelve parts . . . , then Satan set about and stirred up the People to send after us false apostles for the undoing of the word. And he sent out from the People one whose name was Cleobius, and joined him to Simon, and others also after them" (Connolly, 1929: 200 and n. 21); to Cleobius, *Const. apost.* 6.7.1 adds "Dositheus, *Cerinthus* (Κήρινθος; but note v.l. κορίνθιος) and Marcus and Menander and Basilides and Saturnilus" (Funk, 1905: 319). The variant κορίνθιος may in part be the result of itacism between the vowels ε and ο; in *Ep. apost.* 7:1 the Coptic scribe similarly gives the name not as ⲕⲉⲣⲓⲛⲑⲟⲥ but as ⲕⲟⲣⲓⲛⲑⲟⲥ (the first word of the Coptic text, in Schmidt, 1919: 1*).

It is noteworthy that Simon's simony, that is, his attempt to buy the gift of the Holy Spirit (Acts 8:14–24), is not alluded to in the *Epistula*, though (a) *Ep. apost.* 37:5–38:1, which warns of the rich and their bribes, would have been a suitable place for Simon as an example of the alleged behavior of the rich; and (b) the church orders (*Didascalia*, *Constitutions of the Apostles*) include and even embellish the account in Acts 8.

As noted earlier, in *Ep. apost.* 1:1 and 7:1 Simon is not given the title or epithet "Magician (Magus)," "Sorcerer," or the like. Even the NT book of Acts does not specifically identify him in this way, instead reporting that προϋπῆρχεν . . . μαγεύων (8:9, RSV "he had previously practised magic")—as if the title no longer applied ("previously"). Coincidentally, in one of the Ethiopic colophons, Simon (now mentioned along with Arius!) is referred to with this conventional title; see Additional Note on 51:4, below.

9:1 *Archelaus:* An Archelaus reappears as a royal opponent of the apostle Philip in *Acts Phil.* 2.15 (Bovon, et al., 1999: 1. 54–55; ANF 8. 505a); see also the late *Par. Pil.* 3 (Tischendorf, 1876: 450); *Vind. Salv.* 12 (ibid.: 476). According to the Armenian recension of the *History of James* 20, Archelaus named his son Herod: "Now this Herod was the son of Archelaus the king; and Archelaus was the son of Herod, who cruelly massacred the infants" (Leloir, 1986–92: 1. 282; cf. *Ps.-Abd.* 8; 20). Similarly, in its compendium of materials about the apostle Paul, the Ethiopic *Maṣḥafa Gadla Ḥawāreyāt* (*Contendings of the Apostles*) also identifies Archelaus as Herod's *father*: "Arestos [said], '. . . He [Paul] is a disciple of Jesus Christ, whom Herod, the son of Archelaus, slew in the days of Pontius Pilate'" (*Hist. Cont. St. Paul* 5; Budge, 1935: 1.461 [text]; 2. 458 [translation]).

9:3 *Martha:* The awkward phrase "she who belonged to" suggests an original Greek "genitive of origin or relationship" (BDF §162 [pp. 89–90]), a classical usage typically identifying one of the following: (1) a man by his father; (2) the same, with additional definite article; (3) a mother by her son; (4) a wife by her husband; (5) slaves in the possession of a family—i.e., not including daughter and mother (see also "Genitive of Possession or Belonging," in Smyth, 1956: 314–15 [§§1297–1305]), especially §1301: "child to parent, wife to husband, and of inferior to superior." Alternatively, it is possible that the possessive article ⲧⲁ- in ⲙⲁⲣⲓⲁ ⲧⲁⲙⲁⲣⲑⲁ ⲁⲟⲩ . . . is the vestige of a τὲ . . . καί construction in the underlying Greek: Μαρία τε καὶ Μάρθα . . . (cf. Luke 2:16 τήν τε Μαριὰμ καὶ τὸν Ἰωσήφ καὶ τὸ βρέφος).

11:2 *found us fishing:* The fam. 1 form *negēlleb*, though very well supported (mss AB*CKNOQRT), is non-standard, as if from a II,1 (or D, that is, "doubled" medial root consonant) verb *gallaba*, not attested in *DLLA* or *LCDG*. We would expect *negalleb*, which is read by ms S alone. But even this form is uncertain. Dillmann's only cited knowledge of it is this passage in ms S (cited as "Kid. f. [= *Maṣḥafa Kidān* folio] 34"), quoted after an Arabic cognate and with the (Latin) definition *piscari* ("to fish"; *DLLA*, *s.v. galaba* [col. 1138]; see also *LCDG*, *s.v.* [p. 201] "to catch fish, capture"). No other references are given (an unusual state of affairs in Dillmann's well-documented lexicon), and the possibility of the fam. 1 reading being the result of later influence from the Arabic must be reckoned with. In addition, *galaba* (or *gallaba*) is not the more usual Geʿez word for "fishing," which is *ʾašgara* (*DLLA*, *s.v.* [col. 266]), as in Matt 17:27; Mark 1:16; Luke 5:10; John 21:3.

Fam. 2 mss B**LMV—including, therefore, Guerrier's basic manuscript, L—have *netgallabab*, "(we being) veiled," from *galbaba* (*DLLA*, *s.v.* [col. 1139]; *LCDG*, *s.v.* [p. 201b]). Guerrier translates "blinded" (*aveugler*), but footnotes the more literal "veiled" ("nous couvrir d'un voile"). The fam. 2 reading suggests this epiphanic moment: the disciples hide themselves from the divine presence, as in the Coptic they are "within." Similarly, in *1 Enoch* 13.9, Enoch finds the Watchers "gathered together as they mourned . . . *with their faces covered* (*ʾenza gelbubān* *gaṣṣomu*, for περικεκαλυμμένην τὴν ὄψιν)" (Charles, 1906: 34–35). But also possible is inner-Ethiopic corruption, perhaps from *ba-Galilā*, "in Galilee"; cf. Matt 26:32; 28:7; Mark 14:28; 16:7; John 21:1.

11:8 'the foot . . . ground': See also Ignatius Smyrn. 3.2 "Take, handle me and see that I am not a phantom without a body (δαιμόνιον ἀσώματον)"; AcJohn 93 "I often wished, as I walked with him, to see if his footprint appeared (ἴχνος αὐτοῦ . . . εἰ φαίνεται) on the ground—for I saw him raising himself from the earth—and I never saw it"; *Acts Pil.* 15.6; Tertullian *Adv. Marc.* 4.8; *De an.* 5 (quoting Lucretius *De rerum nat.* 1.304); Commodian *Carm. apol.* 559–568, especially line 564: "A shade does not make a mark" (*Vestigium umbra non facit—umbra* likely for σκιά, which is a "shadow," as in the Vg of Matt 4:16; Mark 4:32; Luke 1:79; but also "shade of one dead, phantom"; LSJ, s.v. 3 [p. 1609b]). Outside the Jewish and Christian traditions, Philostratus *Her.* 13.2 "As he ran, you could not see a footprint (ἴχνος), nor did his foot make any mark upon the ground (οὐδ' ἂν ἐνσημήναιτό τι τῇ γῇ ὁ ποῦς)" (Lannoy, 1977: 14). In Greek drama, a decisive moment is often the unexpected "recognition" (ἀναγνώρισις) of one character by another, and this recognition can come in several ways, including footprints and wounds of the living or departed; see Aristotle *Poet.* 11.4–8; 16.1–5; Aeschylus *Cheoph.* 197–202; Plato *Gorg.* 524c.

In the late *Nativity of Mary*, at the annunciation to Anna (wife of Joachim) that she is to be the mother of Mary, "an angel of the Lord" (3.1 *angelus domini*) appears and says, "Fear not, Anna, nor think that it is a phantom (*phantasma*) which thou seest" (4.1; Tischendorf, 1876: 114–15; ANF 8. 384b–85a).

12:3 *Then . . . :* In at least three respects, within the dialogue portion of the writing (12:3–50:10) the wording of the introductions to speeches of the Lord and of the disciples probably reflects the deliberate choice of the author or final editor of the *Epistula*. The three words and phrases are as follows:

(1) *Then:* In all fifteen places where the Coptic has ⲧⲟⲧⲉ in the introduction to a speech, it is a speech of the Lord (12:3; 14:3, 5; 17:4; 21:8 [restored]; 25:2, 6, 8 [restored]; 28:4; 30:3; 39:4; 41:3; 42:9; 43:14 [restored]; 45:2). Within a lacuna in 45:7, Schmidt (1919: 23*) supplies ⲧⲟⲧⲉ before "we said" where the Ethiopic lacks "Then"; Schmidt, of course, developed his principal Coptic text (1919: 1*–65*) without knowledge of the Ethiopic. In 17:5 and 21:5, where the Coptic text is lost, the Ethiopic has *wa-'emze* ("and then") before speeches of the disciples.

(2) *[He] answered:* ⲟⲩⲱϣⲃⲉ ("to answer, reply") occurs sixteen times in the extant Coptic (14:2, 3, 5; 16:3; 20:3; 25:2; 29:6; 30:3; 39:2; 41:1, 3, 6; 42:9; 43:12; 45:2; 46:3), with one exception always preceding the verb "to say" and always in the mouth of the Lord. This is of course reminiscent of the almost formulaic ἀποκριθεὶς εἶπεν in the Synoptic gospels. (The exception is in 14:2; but there the Ethiopic lacks the word. In addition, at 21:7 the Ethiopic has "We answered" where the Coptic is fragmentary.) In this case, the same compositional principle also applies to the earlier chapters; see 4:4, 6, 8, 15.

(3) *Again:* ⲡⲁⲗⲓⲛ is found in introductions to speeches six times in the extant Coptic (19:17; 23:1; 25:1; 29:5, 7; 40:3), always before speeches of the disciples.

resurrection / rest: Two somewhat later writings show the same versional variation as in the *Ep. apost.*: Melito *Pass. Hom.* Syriac frg. 15 line 58 "He is the *repose* of the dead," where the Greek has "resurrection"; AcThom 10 "the *rest* (ἀνάπαυσις) / *resurrection* (ἀνάστασις) of the oppressed."

13:3 *commander-in-chief:* Jesus himself is "commander-in-chief of the luminaries" and "commander-in-chief of the All" in *Melch.* (NHC IX,*1*) 6.3; 18.5–6.

Uriel and Raphael: Further references to lists of archangels in OTP 1. 350 n. p2. The *Liturgy of the Abyssinian* (i.e., Ethiopian) *Jacobites* lists "the four great luminaries" as "Michael and Gabriel, Raphael and Suriel" (Brightman, 1896: 230).

13:5 *the Father's merciful will: LPGL, s.v.* οἰκονομία C.3 (p. 941b) notes the noun's use "of God's special dispensations or interpositions, esp. of grace and mercy." Cf. AcAndMatt 17:3, where for τὴν μεγάλην οἰκονομίαν ("the great plan") the Latin recension has *misericordiam dei* ("the mercy of God") (Lipsius-Bonnet, 1891–1903: 2. 185; MacDonald, 1990: 105–7).

14:5 *laughed:* The fam. 1 and fam. 2 Ethiopic witnesses are unanimous in reading *saḥaqat*. This is the verb that translates ἐγέλασεν ("Sarah *laughed*") in the Ge'ez of Gen 18:12 (*DLLA*, *s.v. šaḥaqa* [col. 234b]; cf. Hebrew *ṣāḥaq*). The sense, then, would appear to be a laughter of *amusement* or even *scorn* (see LSJ, *s.v.* γελάω [p. 341b]). But Haile, a native Ethiopian, translates the phrase in *Ep. apost.* 14:5 "Her heart accepted (what I told her) and [she] believed and *smiled*" (1982: 216). The nuance here may therefore shade towards μειδιᾶν ("to smile"; LSJ, *s.v.* [p. 1092b], "opp. γελᾶν, *laugh aloud*), which from Homer on is used of one smiling because of special knowledge or insight, e.g., of secret or divine purposes. This latter sense is frequent in the Christian apocryphal acts; see, e.g., AcAndrGE 16:3; AcAndrPas 3:4; 55(5):2; AcPaulThec 4:1. Cf. also Herm. *Vis.* 1.1.8 "[Rhoda] laughed (γελάσασα) and said to me . . . "; *Ap. John* (NHC II,*1*) 22.12 "The savior smiled and said"; 26.25–26 "And he smiled and said to me"; *Soph. Jes. Chr.* (NHC III,*4*) 91.22–92.1 "The Savior laughed."

15:9 *until I come . . . :* The Coptic reading, "until *the day,*" may reflect the influence of the gospel tradition: Matt 26:29 = Mark 14:25 ἕως τῆς ἡμέρας ἐκείνης (but Luke 22:16 ἕως ὅτου; 26:18 ἕως οὗ). In the extant Coptic, the noun ϩοογε ("day") is found eleven times, including a reconstruction in 26:1 and fragment a2 (Schmidt, 1919: 25*), which parallels 37:2 in the Ethiopic. Only in fixed expressions, and where the sense is specifically "day" and not "time" or "era," does the parallel Ethiopic read *'elat* ("day"): see 13:4; 15:9; 22:3; 24:4; 26:1; 29:7; 37:2; 39:3; 43:13; 47:8.

with my wounds: The noun suggested by the Coptic reading is τραυματίας, "wounded, *slain*"; e.g., in Aristotle *Poet.* 14.13 "wounded Odysseus"; Lucian *V.H.* 2.38; in the LXX at Num 19:16, 18; Deut 21:1; Judg 16:24; 1 Kgdms 17:52; cf. also Isa 30:26; Zech 14:5; Hippolytus *C. Gaium* frg. 5 "when the King comes in glory with his slain" (Gwynn, 1888: 416). Precisely this proposed confusion between τραυμάτων and τραυματιῶν is found in the manuscript tradition of the fourth-century B.C.E. military writer Aeneas Tacticus *Poliorcetica* 26.7 (Loeb ed.: 134–35); in the singular, τραύματος is found in Num 19:18 (Alexandrinus) for τραυματίου (Vaticanus, Sinaiticus).

16:3 *shining seven times brighter . . .:* Further instances in *T. Abr.* A 7.3 "a luminous man descending from heaven, shining more than seven suns"; *Hist. Rech.* 23; *Apoc. Zeph.* A (*apud* Clement of Alexandria *Strom.* 5.11.77); *Apoc. Paul* (NHC V,*2*) 22.23–30; *Acts Phil.* 2.15: Jesus descends, "his face seven times brighter than the sun (ἑπταπλάσιον λάμπον ὑπὲρ τὸν ἥλιον)" (Bovon, et al., 1999: 1. 60–61; ANF 8. 505b); *T. Gal.* 7; Montanist saying 5 (*apud* Epiphanius *Adv. haer.* 48.10.3); *Gos. Bart.* 4.57; *Narr. Jos.* 4.3 "we beheld the undefiled cross shining like lightning . . . , gleaming with sevenfold the light of the sun" (Tischendorf, 1876: 468; ANF 8. 470b); *Apoc. Paul* (Arm. I) 14 "The light of the city was more brilliant than any light of this world—seven times brighter than the sun's rays" (Leloir, 1986–92: 1. 117); (Lat.) 21; (Syr.) 24.

17:2 *hundredth part and twentieth part:* On the "hundredth part and twentieth part" as the fraction 1/120, see Till, 1928: 104 and n. 6 (§233d). The difference between the versions ("years"; "part") may indicate that in the original Greek the noun was understood; for absent "part" (μέρις), see Smyth, 1956: §1027b (p. 273), coincidentally quoting εἰκοστή in Thucydides *Hist.* 4.96 "twentieth (part)."

The contention of Delazer (1929: 260–61, 272, 291–92), that "120" in the Coptic derives from Gen 6:3 ("My spirit shall not abide in man for ever, for he is flesh, but his days shall be a hundred and twenty years"), perhaps receives fresh support from the Gnostic writing *Concept of our Great Power.* In *Great Pow.* (NHC VI,*4*) 36.8–14, the revealer states that "every one in whom my form will appear will be saved, from <the age of> seven days up to one hundred and twenty years." Later, in *Great Pow.* 38.9–39.15 and 43.4–22, the period of Noah's preaching and salvation marks the first era of history. The second period, the era of the redeemer (the one who will "speak in parables" [40.30–31]), is of equal length: "He made the first aeon, going about it until it perished while preaching one hundred and twenty years in number. This is the perfect number [cf. *Ep. apost.* 18:2] that is highly exalted."

the feast of Unleavened Bread: Ge'ez *pāsikā* (*fāsikā*), like *fešḥ*, regularly translates πάσχα (*DLLA*, *s.v. fāsikā* [col. 1357]; *fešḥ* [col. 1351]); the rarer *p̣āsā*, "Passover" (*s.v.* [col. 1392]) is not relevant here. The more common terms for τὰ ἄζυμα (unleavened bread) are *maṣalat* (*s.v. ṣalala* III [col. 1257]); e.g., in Luke 22:7 ἡ ἡμέρα τῶν ἀζύμων = *'elata maṣalat*) and *nā't* (*s.v. nē'a* [col.

679]; in the NT only at 1 Cor 5:7). (As it happens, *maṣalat*—from root *ṣalala* I—also translates σκηνοπηγία, "Tabernacles," e.g., in John 7:21 (*LCDG, s.v.* [p. 223a]). Therefore the Ge'ez vocabulary associated with paschal chronology initially appears to be straightforward: (a) Passover (*fāsikā, pāsikā, fešḥ*), celebrated Nisan 14–15, followed immediately by (b) the feast of Unleavened Bread (*maṣalat, nā't*) on Nisan 15–21, and at length by (c) Pentecost (*panṭaqʷastē*), also called "the Feast of Weeks" (Exod 34:22; Deut 16:10).

However, "popular usage merged the two festivals [of Passover and Unleavened Bread], and treated them as a unity, as they were for practical purposes" (BAGD, *s.v.* πάσχα [p. 633b]; likewise *LPGL, s.v.* ἄζυμος 3 [p. 40b]: "feast of unleavened bread, Passover"). So, for example, Mark 14:1 has "it was now two days before the Passover and the feast of Unleavened Bread" (ἦν δὲ τὸ πάσχα καὶ τὰ ἄζυμα μετὰ δύο ἡμέρας: *wa-'eska sanuy mawā'ela fāsikā ba'āla maṣalat*—note the absence of the conjunction *wa-* ["and"], suggesting that Unleavened Bread is appositional). Luke 22:1 reports that "the feast of Unleavened Bread drew near, *which is called the Passover*" (ἤγγικεν ἡ ἑορτὴ τῶν ἀζύμων ἡ λεγομένη πάσχα: *wa-qarba ba'āla maṣalat za-semu fāsikā*—literally, "the name of which is Passover").

The result of this convergence of terms is that the Ethiopic NT can actually be found translating the festival named τὰ ἄζυμα ("Unleavened Bread") with *fešḥ* and *fāsikā* ("Passover"). Matt 26:17 has "on the first day of *Unleavened Bread* (τῶν ἀζύμων: *fešḥ*); Acts 12:3 "during the days of *Unleavened Bread*" (ἡμέραι τῶν ἀζύμων: *ba'āla fāsikā*); 20:6 "after the days of *Unleavened Bread*" (μετὰ τῶν ἡμερῶν τῶν ἀζύμων: *'em-dexra fāsikā*). In a most remarkable instance, the Ethiopic NT manuscript tradition even glosses "Unleavened Bread" with "the *fāsikā* at Mark 14:12 "And on the first day of Unleavened Bread, when they sacrificed the passover lamb" (καὶ τῇ πρώτῃ ἡμέρᾳ τῶν ἀζύμων, ὅτε τὸ πάσχα ἔθυον: *wa-'ama qadāmit 'elat ba-ba'āla maṣalat fāsikā 'ama yeṭabbeḥu fešḥa*—"And on the first day of the feast of Unleavened Bread, *the Passover* [?], when they sacrifice the passover lamb") (Zuurmond, 1989: 2. 260, 388).

The result of this brief survey is that the apparently incongruous Ethiopic reading in *Ep. apost.* 17:2 is compatible with the Coptic and Latin texts, and need not be suspected of deliberate or accidental scribal corruption.

18:2 *the ogdoad:* For this word's quite explicit identification here as "the Lord's Day," see also the several references in *LPGL, s.v.* ὀγδοάς 3 (p. 934b); also *Orig. World* (II,5) 117.32–118.2 "The third Adam . . . appeared on the eighth day [. . .] tranquility (ⲁⲛⲁⲡⲁⲩⲥⲓⲥ = ἀνάπαυσις) of poverty, which is called Sunday (ⲏⲙⲉⲣⲁ ⲏⲗⲓⲟⲩ = ἡμέρα ἡλίου)"; Justin *1 Apol.* 67.3.

19:11 *right hand of the Father:* See also *Teach. Silv.* (NHC VII,4) 115.3–10 "Only the hand of the Lord has created all things. For this hand of the Father is Christ, and it forms all. Through it, all has come into being since it became the Mother of all. For he is always (ⲛ̄ⲟⲩⲟⲉⲓϣ ⲛⲓⲙ) Son of the Father" (Janssens, 1983: 88–89). Paired with "fully" (see also 17:4, 8) the term "right hand" is reminiscent of Ps 73:11 LXX ἵνα τί ἀποστρέφεις . . . τὴν δεξιάν σου ἐκ μέσου τοῦ κόλπου σου εἰς τέλος; where κόλπος ("bosom, chest, breast") will find a NT echo in John 1:18, and whose final phrase is capable of the sense "altogether, completely" (LSJ, *s.v.* τέλος II.2.b [p. 1773b]).

19:12 *we said to him:* Fam. 1 and ms M also have "twelve," but lack the explicit pronominal phrase "and we"; they also have the conjunction "and" *after* "twelve" and *before* "we said"—so that in fam. 1 the verse can be read as beginning, "We said to him." As for the end of the previous verse, which in fam. 1 includes "twelve" immediately after *yefēṣṣem* ("[who] brings perfection") with no end-of-verse sign, no completely satisfactory explanation can be offered. But it is just possible that the Ethiopic translator or copyist recalled the consonantally very similar Herm. *Man.* 12.3.2 *wa-faṣṣim 'ašarta wa-kel'ēta te'zāza wa-yebēlani* "So he finished the twelve commandments, and he said to me . . ." (Abbadie, 1860: 74; for συνετέλεσεν οὖν τὰς ἐντολὰς τὰς δώδεκα καὶ λέγει μοι [Lake, 1912–13: 2. 128–29]). On this hypothesis, in fam. 2 mss this intrusive "twelve" was subsequently supplied with the pronoun "we" for context's sake. Cf. also *Ap. Jas.* (NHC I,2) 1.24–25 "all of us, his twelve disciples"; AcAndMatt 12.1 "we twelve disciples" (MacDonald, 2005: 25; ANF 8. 519b).

19:15 *you who will not perish:* The same misreading of forms is found elsewhere, e.g., in Matt 15:11 (twice), where, for "not what goes into the mouth *defiles* (κοινοῖ)," D (i.e., Codex Bezae) has "*participates in* (κοινωνεῖ)" (also in Matt 11:18, 20); and 4 Macc 7:6 ("you neither defiled your sacred teeth nor profaned your stomach, . . . by *eating defiling foods*"), where for ἐκοίνωσας the Alexandrian text has ἐκοινώσησας.

19:18 *O Lord . . . :* The following Greek words in the Coptic text are also in the LXX of Psalm: 3:2 "to my *soul*"—τῇ ψυχῇ μου; 3:4 "*but* you, O Lord"—σὺ δὲ κύριε; 3:6 "of ten thousand *people*"—ἀπὸ μυριάδων λαοῦ; 3:8 "for his *people*" ἐπὶ τὸν λαόν σου.

21:6 *Do you believe . . . ?* In the Ethiopic version of Herm. *Sim.* 6.44, βλέπεις ("you see") is likewise rendered with what is formally the imperative, *'a'mer* (Abbadie, 1860: 58); again, cf. 1 John 2:29, where γινώσκετε = *'a'meru*.

21:8 *all authority* (*kʷello šelṭāna*): At Matt 28:18, Zuurmond's five Geʻez texts show some variation: A-text *selṭān* (without "all"); B-text *kʷellu kʷennanē*; D- and E-texts *kʷellu šelṭāna* [E *šelṭān*]; C-text *kʷellu seltān kʷennanē* (Zuurmond, 2001: 298; 299; 406–7; 421). Zuurmond's B-text shows probable influence from John 5:22, where "all judgment" (only here in the NT) = *kʷello kʷennanēhu*.

24:4 *without grudging:* The phrase is a Hellenistic commonplace to describe the dispensing of divine knowledge and attributes. See further *Teach. Silv.* (NHC VII,*4*) 101.17–18 "Christ without being jealous (ⲛ̄ⲟⲩⲱϣ ⲛ̄ⲣ̄ⲫⲑⲟⲛⲓ) receives and gives"; *Corp. herm.* 5.2 "For the Lord manifests himself ungrudgingly through all the universe" (ἄφθονος [Scott: ἀφθόνως] γὰρ ὁ κύριος φαίνεται διὰ πάντος τοῦ κόσμου (Nock-Festugière, 1945–54: 1. 61; cf. 1. 58 n. 8); similarly already, Wis 7:13 "I learned without guile (ἀδόλως) and I impart without grudging (ἀφθόνως); I do not hide [wisdom's] wealth"; Plato *Phaedr.* 247a "for jealousy is excluded from the celestial band" (φθόνος γὰρ ἔξω θείου χοροῦ ἵσταται); *Tim.* 29e "For (the Creator) was good, and therefore not jealous, and being free from jealousy he desired that all things should be like himself" (ἀγαθὸς ἦν, ἀγαθῷ δὲ οὐδεὶς περὶ οὐδενὸς οὐδέποτε ἐγγίγνεται φθόνος); Ps.-Aristotle *De mund.* 391a τοῦτο δὲ ἔπαθε, καθ' ὅσον οἷόν τε ἦν, πᾶσιν ἀφθόνως μεταδοῦναι βουληθεῖσα τῶν παρ' αὐτῇ τιμίων. The idea of the Lord's imparting his revelation "ungrudgingly" is also close to the Matthean saying with adverbial δωρεάν: "*Freely* you have received, *freely* give" (Matt 10:8).

25:4 *we were joyful:* The Greek text of *Asc. Isa.* 7.6, recovered from the *Greek Legend* published by R. H. Charles, reads καὶ εὐφράνθησαν πάνυ ὅτι πραέως ἐλάλησέν μοι (*Gr. Leg.* 2.8; Charles, 1900: 143); the Latin witnesses have *simpliciter* (L1: "simply, gently"), *mansuete* (L2: "openly"). Alternatively, in *Ep. apost.* 25:4 fam. 1 mss lack the phrase by homoioteleuton: it ends with the syllable *-na*, as does the word immediately preceding it. The Coptic reading ⲁⲛⲣ̄[ⲉⲩⲫⲣⲁⲛⲉ ϫⲉ, filling out a gap at the end of the line, might with the same meaning be completed thus: ⲁⲛⲣ[ⲉϣⲉ ϫⲉ (Schmidt, 1919: 81 n. 10).

25:8 *what has fallen will arise:* In the later church order literature, Jer 8:4 is applied to the reconciliation of a penitent; so Latin *Didasc.* 2.14.2 (= *Const. apost.* 2.14.2; Funk, 1905: 1. 50—51); Syriac *Didasc.* 6 (Connolly, 1929: 43); Ethiopic *Didasc.* 3 (Platt, 1834: 28; Harden, 1920: 22).

27:1 *Abraham, Isaac, and Jacob:* See further the Syriac *Didasc.* 26 "who was crucified in the days of Pontius Pilate and slept, that he might announce to Abraham and to Isaac and to Jacob . . ." (Connolly, 1929: 258–59; p. 258 n. 17: "a remarkable creed-doxology"). In AcAndrMatt 15, Jesus sends a sphinx to secure the testimony of Abraham, Isaac, and Jacob; after which "the three patriarchs went with the sphinx, came to Jesus, and refuted the high priests" (15:13). *Const. apost.* 8.41.2 preserves a prayer for the deceased who have entered "the land of Abraham, Isaac, and Jacob" (Funk, 1905: 550; ANF 7. 497b); similarly the *Liturgy of St. James* (Brightman, 1896: 57); and the liturgies of various Jacobite rites: *Syrian* (Brightman, 1896: 95; 108); *Coptic* (Brightman, 1896: 170); *Abyssinian* (Brightman, 1896: 236). In later Christian art, the abode of the just is frequently depicted as the "bosom of Abraham" (Nunn, 1920: 23).

28:1 *children of life:* See *LPGL*, *s.v.* ζωή (p. 594a) for further references to "God as life and giver of life." For "children of light," see 39:11; 1QS i 9; ii 16; iii 13, 24, 25; 1QM i 9; et al.; Luke 16:8;

John 12:36; Eph 5:8; 1 Thess 5:5; Ignatius *Philad.* 2.1; *Soph. Jes. Chr.* (NHC III,*4*) 119.6; *1 Apoc. Jas.* (NHC V,*3*) 25.17–18; *Trim. Prot.* (NHC XIII,*1*) 37.19–20; 41.1; 42.16; Syriac *Didasc.* 1; 9; 11 "If one of them be found to be of the sons of God . . ., he is a son of light" (Connolly, 1929: 6–7, 93, 110). With regard to the reading of Ethiopic fam. 2 mss CN ("children of light and children of God"), it is presumably a coincidence that in the Ethiopic *Didasc.* 1, where on the authority of the best manuscripts Harden (1920: 4) has "O ye sons [= children] of God," there is a variant in Platt's text (1834: 5): "O ye *sons* [= children] *of light* and sons of God" (the probable antecedent is in *Const. apost.* 1.3.1: δοῦλοι καὶ υἱοὶ θεοῦ).

28:5 *choice kingdom: LPGL, s.v.* ἐκλεκτός (p. 434a) offers no precedent for the combination "kingdom" and "elect," though the latter is common with saints, the church, Christ, etc.

29:2 *another teaching:* In the NT the word *temhert* is used to translate a wide range of nouns, including εὐαγγέλιον (e.g., in Rom 1:1; 15:16; 1 Cor 15:14; Phil 1:27; 4:15; 1 Thess 1:5) and διδασκαλία (1 Tim 4:6); these references in *DLLA, s.v.* (col. 144). With *Ep. apost.* 29:2 and 50:8 cf. especially 2 Cor 11:4 and Gal 1:6 ἕτερον εὐαγγέλιον ("a different gospel") = *kale' temhert* ("another teaching"); also Gal 1:7 "the gospel of Christ" = *temherto la-Kerestos.*

31:3 *Do everything . . . :* In the phrase that begins 31:3, the scribe or corrector who produced ms B** appears to have transliterated Greek ἐγώ where we would expect the Ethiopic pronoun, *'ana*. This led Guerrier (1913: [32–33] 172–73) to suspect that the corrector actually read a Greek text of the *Epistula*. This possibility is rejected by Wajnberg (in Schmidt, 1919: 18–19), however, since in Ethiopic script the pronoun *'ana* and this tentative reading *'ego* are very similar in appearance.

31:8 *wall . . . fall:* The prayer before the Epistle reading in the *Liturgy of the Syrian Jacobites* asks God for strength to keep the commands of "thy divine apostles and of Paul the architect and builder of thine holy church" (Brightman, 1896: 78). Apparently, later veneration for Paul also favored architectural metaphor, e.g., in the conclusion of the Coptic *Apocalypse of Paul*: "Greetings, Paul, roof and foundation of the Church!" (*NTApoc*[2] 2. 742).

33:6 *and my bride:* Cf. Ps.-Hippolytus *De consumm.* 3 (on Isa 1:7) "It is not of the Jews that he [Isaiah] spake this word of old, nor of the city of Zion, but of the Church. For all the prophets have declared Sion to be the bride brought from the nations."

39:3 *will they not . . . ?* Cf. 1QH iv 35 "I said in my sinfulness, 'I am forsaken by Thy covenant'"; *Apoc. Mos.* 27.4 "The Lord said to his angels, 'Why have you stopped driving Adam out of Paradise? Is the guilt mine, or did I judge badly?' "

presided over: The text has *'amrāxka*, a lexically possible CG form of *marḥa* ("to lead, guide, show"), hence Duensing-Mueller "You caused to lead. . . ." But under that heading, itself acknowledged to be doubtful ("ut videtur"), Dillmann quotes only this passage ("Kid. f. [= *Maṣḥafa Kidān*, folio] 40"), with an annotation suggesting its dubiousness ("si quidem lectio sana est") (*DLLA, s.v.* [col. 164]; *GSLLA, s.v.* [p. 82] supplies a definition but no reference). The Coptic "you did not pursue" probably belongs with the next Ethiopic verb, "you separated"; hence Schmidt's suggestion (1919: 125 n. 6; 179) of a primitive confusion: διώκειν ("to pursue") for διακρίνειν ("to distinguish, separate"). Also possible, in light of the probable allusion to Gen 1:4 ("God *separated* the light from the darkness"), is corruption to διώκειν (a) from διαχωρίζειν (as in Genesis); (b) from διαχωρεῖν (also "to separate"); or (c) in the Coptic manuscript tradition, from πωϣ ("to divide"), πωϩ ("to reach, attain"), or πωρϫ̅ ("to divide, separate").

39:4–5 *Adam . . . :* In addition to the verses in Sirach (15:14–17) referred to in the principal note, another verse in Sirach, outside the mainstream LXX tradition, is of special interest here: 16:16 "His mercy is manifest to the whole creation, *and he divided his light and darkness with a plumb line* (καὶ ἐμέρισεν τὸ φῶς αὐτοῦ καὶ τὸ σκότος τῷ ἀδαμάντι)" (see, e.g., Rahlfs, 1935: 2. 403, apparatus). For τῷ ἀδαμάντι ("with a plumb line"), Rahlfs asks if τῷ Ἀδάμ (or even more promising, perhaps, the declinable form as in Josephus: τῷ Ἀδάμι) is to be read, in light of Sir 40:1 "Much labor was created for every man, and a heavy yoke is upon the sons of Adam."

39:11 *so then:* Alternatively, ⲁⲣⲁ (whether inferential or anticipating a question, as, e.g., in Luke 18:8; Acts 18:30; Gal 2:17) may be followed by the Coptic existential particle ⲟⲩⲛ ("there is / are"; Crum, s.v. [p. 481a]); hence Till's decision (1928: §169a and n. 7) to supply a ligature between this and the following "everyone": ⲟⲩⲛ̄–ⲡⲟⲩⲉ ⲡⲟⲩⲉ.

40:3 *does no one then entreat you?* Concerning the difference between the Coptic and Ethiopic readings, it is also possible that a mistake occurred at the level of the earlier Greek text, e.g., (1) αἰτεῖσθαι ("to ask," as in the Ethiopic) misread as αἰσχύνεσθαι ("to be ashamed"; see Crum, *s.v.* ϣⲓⲛⲉ [p. 576b], and Schmidt, 1919: 128 n. 14); (2) δεῖσθαι ("to beg, ask," again as in the Ethiopic) misread as δείδειν / δείδεσθαι ("to fear"); or, even more likely, (3) αἰτεῖσθαι ("to ask") for αἰδεῖσθαι ("to be ashamed, fearful"; see Crum, ibid. [p. 577a]).

41:1 *laborers:* It is striking that the the ordination prayers in the *Testamentum Domini*, while describing the presbyter (or priest) as one who is to "govern [God's] people in *labour*" (*T. Dom.* 1.30), reserves the noun uniquely for the ordination of a deacon: "Grant him, O Lord, to be *a lawful labourer* without shame" (1.38) (Sperry-White, 1991: 43; Cooper and MacLean render the phrase "a *worker in the law* without shame" [1902: 104]).

42:3 *by my hand:* Cf. the *T. Dom.* 2.10 : "Let the deacon, when the presbyter is not present, of necessity baptize" (2.10). Cooper and MacLean (1902: 225) point out that "in Spain, at the beginning of the fourth century, the Council of Elvira (can. [canon] 77) allows deacons to baptize if there is no priest in the place; and (can. 38) permits laymen to baptize in case of necessity."

42:8 *ten thousand tongues:* For an inventory and discussion of instances of this figure in literature down to the twelfth century, see Courcelle, 1955; Pascucci, 1959.

43:5 *the five:* See also *1 Clem.* 62.2; *Barn.* 2.2–3; Herm. *Vis.* 3.8.7; *Sim.* 9.15.2; *Ap. Jas.* (NHC I,*2*) 1.2–7 "Peace [be with you from] Peace, [love from] Love, [grace from] Grace, [faith] from Faith, life from Holy Life" (*NHLE* 30); *Untit. Text* 2; 15; and especially 10: "In the midst of the immeasurable deep there are five powers which are called by these unutterable names: <1.> The first is called *love*, . . . ; 2. The second <is called> *hope*, . . . ; 3. The third is called *faith*, . . . ; 4. The fourth is called *gnosis*, . . . ; 5. The fifth is called *peace*" (Schmidt-MacDermot, 1978: 256–57).

43:6 *joy / peace:* See further the variant readings in 2 Cor 1:15; Phlm 7; 3 John 4; Ignatius *Eph.* (long recension) *proem.*; 12.1; Melito *Pass. Hom.* 661.

43:16 *Knowledge . . . :* Similar lists are found, e.g., in Hegemonius *Acta disp. Arch.* 9 "Now these are the designations of the soul,—namely, intelligence, reflection, prudence, consideration, reasoning" (ANF 6. 184b); AcThom 27 "Come, elder messenger of the five members, understanding, thought, prudence, consideration, reasoning"; Lactantius *Div. inst.* 7.27 "[At death], that man will appear before God with abundant resources . . . to whom there shall belong self-restraint, mercy, patience, love, and faith" (ANF 7. 222b).

44:2 *for they will remain:* There are several NT examples of the misreading of the liquid future of μένειν; see the Greek (and some versional variants) in John 14:17; 15:10 (see the Coptic in Horner, 1926: 3. 249); 1 Cor 3:14; 1 John 3:17; also *T. Abr.* (recension B) 7 μένει for μενεῖ (Stone, 1972: 73). The Ethiopic cannot be decisive here, because its imperfect form *yekawwenu* ("they will be") might equally be rendered as a present.

46:3 *benefactor:* Guerrier's suggestion is strengthened by the fact that the allegedly omitted word, *šānnayt*, is similar in appearance and sound to the verb, which follows immediately: *yessamay* ("he will be called"). The single NT occurrence of εὐεργέτης, in Luke 22:25, is rendered *radā'eyān* ("helpers") rather than *gabārē [šānnayt]*. It is possible that the verb in the Greek of *Ep. apost.* 46:3 was not active (as in the Coptic) or passive (as in the Ethiopic) but a reflexive middle: "he will call himself"; cf. καλοῦνται in the same Lukan verse, an ambiguous form (middle and passive) for which "the middle voice suits the context better" (Fitzmyer, 1985: 1416). If so, it has now been given an explicit (if generic) agent (ⲛ̄ⲣⲱⲙⲉ, *sab'*), and any middle sense has been lost.

47:6 *'whose god is their belly':* Whatever the derivation of the phrase, it seems to have achieved the status of an independent rhetorical flourish; see, e.g., *Apoc. Elij.* 1.13; Ignatius *Magn.* (long recension) 9; Cyril of Jerusalem *Catech.* 19.6; similarly, Clement of Alexandria *Paed.* 2.1.4 οἷς οὐδὲν ἀλλ' ἢ γαστήρ ἐστιν ὁ βίος ("whose life is their belly, and nothing else").

51:1 *after three days and three hours:* In 17:2, it is easier to imagine "part" (Coptic) becoming "year" (Ethiopic) than vice versa. The latter ("one hundred and fifty years") looks like an attempt to derive an absolute chronology from an obscure phrase. Late medieval Ethiopian tradition, in particular 15th-century millennial expectation, would take it thus (Haile, 1981: 314 and n. 8). But if the Coptic "100" and "20" as "parts" are *portions of years* rather than whole years, then it is possible that what is being specified is a much briefer period: 120th of a year is a little more than three days; the "three hours" can perhaps then mean "early" or "in the first period."

While "three days" clearly echoes the time of the resurrection "on the third day" (Matt 16:21; 17:22; 20:19; Mark 8:31; 9:31; 10:34; Luke 9:22; 18:33; 1 Cor 15:4; et al.), "three hours" has no obvious biblical antecedent. But two occurrences of the phrase may be relevant, especially the second: (a) the uniquely Markan statement about the moment of crucifixion: "it was the third hour" (Mark 15:25 ἦν δὲ ὥρα τρίτη), and (b) the note in Acts 2:15, during the events of Pentecost, that those speaking in diverse languages are not drunk "since it is only the third hour of the day (ἔστιν γὰρ ὥρα τρίτη τῆς ἡμέρας)." The whole phrase in *Ep. apost.* 51:1 may therefore reflect the combination of "three days" (from death to resurrection) and "third hour" as "three hours" (from dawn to the coming of the Holy Spirit).

One further textual witness is worth mentioning here: Mark 16:3 in the 4th- or 5th-century Old Latin Codex Bobbiensis (*k*), where the account of the resurrection is embellished, the result apparently being a combination resurrection-ascension event (note that "third hour of the day" and "he rose" are not grammatical, and are rendered according to probable sense):

> Suddenly at the third hour of the day there was darkness throughout the whole circuit of the land, and angels descended from heaven, and he rose in the brightness of the living God, [and] at once they ascended with him, and immediately there was light. Then they [the women] drew near to the tomb. (Metzger-Ehrman, 2005: 269)

It is of course a nice coincidence that the fragmentary Latin witness to the *Epistula* once resided in the same monastic library at Bobbio (in northern Italy); see Bick, 1908: 3–10.

51:4 *in the name . . . :* Mss PV have a major punctuation mark (usually reserved for the separation of sentences, rather than words) after the preceding "in peace." But this is somewhat deceptive, because, while ms V lacks "in the name. . . ," after the major punctuation ms V has "Believe in the name of our Lord Jesus Christ." It is striking that the text ends with the name and title, "Jesus Christ," only. That this is not extended into a concluding *trinitarian* flourish in any of the manuscripts marks a commendable reserve on the part of the scribes.

THE COLOPHONS

The colophons deserve a special kind of respect, since they are often our best link to the actual scribes who copied the manuscripts. The oldest and best Ge'ez manuscript, ms O, has no colophon. Its final page has only two and one-half words on it. There follows a line of dots across the full width of the page (not merely across one of two or three possible columns), the rest being completely blank. This does not mean that the colophons quoted below—their formulaic phrases in particular—are necessarily of later invention; indeed, that is most improbable. A variety of factors might account for the presence or absence of colophons. It is interesting but not surprising to observe that the pairings of manuscripts already noticed within "family 1" and "family 2" (mss AT, BK, CN, QR) can be discerned in the colophons as well; mss CN are only an apparent exception to this since, though they differ from one another, they both include extensive personal matter.

According to the punctuation of ms O and most other fam. 1 and fam. 2 witnesses, the actual text of the *Epistula* ends with the words "in the name our Lord Jesus Christ" (though, as already noted, punctuation is not a certain guide). Mss MQRS are noteworthy exceptions: they include these words (ms M lacks "Christ"), but, in the absence of end-of-sentence punctuation, in effect they continue Jesus' parting speech with phraseology generally found later, in the colophons (see below). One late witness, ms V, lacks "in the name . . . Christ," but has an exhortation with very similar wording in its colophon (see below).

For clarity and economy of space, the phrases that make up the colophons (including the personal materials in mss CN) are set out here as an inventory of numbered elements. In the collation of colophons that follows the list, periods (full-stops) after the numbers reflect sentence separators (typically 4 dots, forming a square : :), commas reflect word separators (two dots, like a colon :).

INVENTORY OF FEATURES

1 And believe in the name of our Lord Jesus Christ

2a The Testament is completed
2b The Book of the Testament is completed
2c The Testament of our Lord Jesus Christ is completed

3a in peace
3b in his peace
3c in the peace of God
3d in the peace of God the Father

4a Love is the bond of perfection [cf. Col. 3;14]
4b For love is the bond of perfection

5a And righteousness [*or* truth: *ṣedq*] is the name of the holy Church
5b And <likewise?> righteousness [*or* truth: *ṣedq*]. The name of the holy Church is
5c And righteousness is also the name of the holy Church.

6 To him who wrote it and to him who caused it to be written
and to him who reads and to him who hears its words:
May God have mercy on us together
and may he cause us to inherit the kingdom of heaven
with all the saints for ever and ever.

7 And he said to them, "Peace be with you, children of peace."

8 And may the peace of God be with us

9a May he protect his servant Absalom
9b May mercy and pity be with his beloved (*masc.*)
9c and with his mother

10 For ever and ever.

11a Amen.
11b Amen. And amen.
11c Amen. Amen. And amen.
11d Amen. And amen. And amen.

12 So may it be

13 This Book was bought <by> Abba Yostos Romawi
from his disciples
for 1 silver piece (*berur*)
in the Canopy of Mary,
on the 20th of Maskaram
the year of the birth of Christ 1849 (?) [YEAR OBSCURED BY LIBRARY STAMP]
in the time of Mark.

Note: (1) "the Canopy [*or* Umbrella: *tadbāb*] of Mary," is here taken to be a church, or shrine, or town. In addition to being a "canopy" or "balcony," in Ethiopian Christianity the *tadbāb* is a "large umbrella held over the king or the ark" and "the umbrella that priests carry in a procession" (*LCDG*, *s.v.* [p. 195a]).
(2) "the 20th of Maskaram," i.e., Sept. 30, Maskaram being the first Ethiopian month, Sept. 11–Oct. 10.

14 The book of Arkanyos, and which he caused to be written
by his hand, without any help, either in writing
or by the gift of a <writing> implement,
but <it was> with his own <resources>
that he began it and inscribed it.
Whoever, then, takes it by force,
or whoever steals it away,
whether it be voluntarily
or involuntarily : :
Like Simon <the> Magician
and like Arius the Foolish
by the power of the Father
and the Son and the Holy Spirit,
may this one, too, be excommunicated. : : : :

Note: (1) "Simon <the> Magician": Simon is not called "the Magician" (*masrey* = *mašarey*) in the *Epistula* itself, nor in Acts 8. An equivalent term (*za-šerāy*) is used of a certain μάγος in Acts 13:6, 8. "Simon the Magician" (*mašarey*) does appear in the Ethiopic *Didasc.* 4; 21 (Harden, 1920: 23, 103; Platt, 1834: 29).
(2) It is of course fitting that Simon, in the *Epistula* paired with the relatively obscure "Cerinthus," is here named with Arius. In the scribe's circle, the two were likely held to be respectively the first and the last of the great heretics. The Ethiopian national religious epic, the *Kebra Nagast* ("Glory of the Kings"), identifies "those who <after the time of Constantine and Helena> corrupted the faith of Christ and introduced heresy into the Church of God" as "Nestorius, Arius, and Yabâsô (?)" (Budge, 1932: 164).

15 O, my Lord Jesus Christ,
By the Testament of your word
keep my soul and my body from all evil.
And do not let me be ashamed of my hope
in your handmaid, the maidservant of Jesus,
in this world and in that which is to come. Amen.

16 In the name of the Father, and of the Son,
and of the Holy Spirit, Amen.

These various features appear in the colophons of the manuscripts as follows (see the Inventory of Features, above):

A (and see T) "…Jesus Christ." : : 2c 3d 10 11a 6 11b
THERE IS A FULL LINE OF ORNAMENTATION
THEN THREE ICONIC IMAGES (FACES WITH HALOS)
THE REST OF THE COLUMN IS BLANK

B (and see K) "…Jesus Christ." : : 4a 5a 7
A LINE OF DOTS FILLS ONE MORE LINE;
THE REST OF THE PAGE HAS ONLY A FEW POORLY-WRITTEN WORDS

C (and see N) "…Jesus Christ," 11b ONE LINE OF MAJOR PUNCTUATION : : : : : : : :
THEN ONE LINE OBSCURED; THEN, IN A DIFFERENT HAND: 13
NO FURTHER WORDS OR ORNAMENTATION IN THE COLUMN

K (and see B) "…Jesus Christ." : : 4a 5c 7
THE REST OF COLUMN AND PAGE ARE BLANK

L "…Jesus Christ." : : ONE LINE OF LARGE DOTS, THEN: 2b 3c 9 10 11a
NEXT LINE: ORNAMENTATION ACROSS ALL THREE COLUMNS OF THE PAGE.
THE BOTTOM HALF OF THE PAGE IS BLANK.

M "…Jesus" 2a 3d 11b 12 12 : : : :
A FINAL LINE HAS 9 END-OF-SENTENCE PUNCTUATION MARKS

N (and see C) IN THE SAME HAND THROUGHOUT; CONTRAST ms C
"…Jesus Christ NO END-OF-SENTENCE PUNCTUATION
for ever and ever, Amen and Amen.
ONE LINE OF HEAVY ORNAMENTATION, THEN 14
THE REST OF THE COLUMN IS BLANK

O "…Jesus Christ." : :
THERE ARE NO FURTHER WORDS ON THE PAGE

P "…Jesus" NO END-OF-SENTENCE PUNCTUATION 2a 3d 11d
ONE LINE OF MAJOR PUNCTUATION : : : : : : THEN 15 : :
NO FURTHER WORDS OR ORNAMENTATION IN THE COLUMN

Q (and see R) "…Jesus Christ" NO END-OF-SENTENCE PUNCTUATION 4a 2a 5a 7 8 10 11a
NEXT LINE: 4 FULL PUNCTUATION MARKS: : : : : : : : :
NEXT LINE: THE NEW TEXT BEGINS

R (and see Q) "…Jesus Christ" NO END-OF-SENTENCE PUNCTUATION 4a 2a 5a 7 8 10 11a
NEXT LINE: 4 FULL PUNCTUATION MARKS: : : : : : : : :
NEXT LINE: NEW TEXT BEGINS

S "…Jesus Christ" NO END-OF-SENTENCE PUNCTUATION 4a : :
2b 5b 7, 8 9b [THREE-WORD GAP, FOR NAME]
9c [A SIMILAR GAP] 10 11b 12 12
ORNAMENTATION COMPLETES THE LINE, THEN APPEARS ACROSS ALL THREE COLUMNS;
THE LOWER 2/3 OF THE PAGE IS BLANK

T (and see A) "…Jesus Christ." : : 2c 3d 10, 11a 6 11b
THERE IS FULL LINE OF ORNAMENTATION
THE REST OF THE COLUMN IS BLANK

V LACKS "in the name … Christ." (BUT SEE 1*) 4b 1* 2b 3d 11c
THEN, IN RED, 16

BIBLIOGRAPHY

TEXTS AND TRANSLATIONS

Abbadie, Antoine d', ed., *Hermae Pastor: Aethiopice primum edidit et aethiopica latine vertit* (Abhandlungen für die Kunde des Morgenlandes 2/1; Leipzig: Brockhaus, 1860).

Abraha, Tedros, *The Ethiopic Version of the Letter to the Hebrews* (Studi i Testi 419; Città del Vaticano: Biblioteca Apostolica Vaticana, 2004).

Beylot, Robert, ed. and trans., *Testamentum Domini éthiopien: Édition et traduction* (Louvain: Peeters, 1984).

Bick, Josef, "Wiener Palimpseste, I. Teil: Cod. Palat. Vindobonensis 16, olim Bobbiensis," Sitzungsberichte der Wiener Akademie der Wissenschaften, philosophisch-historische Klasse 159/7 (1908) 90–99 with Plate 4. See also the response by Pius Bihlmeyer, in *Revue bénédictine* 28 (1911) 271. Bick (p. 90) credits Josef von Eichenfeld with the earliest modern reference (in the Vienna *Jahrbuch* for 1824) to this apocryphal letter. This is presumably the work catalogued separately in WorldCat as Eichenfeld, *Ein Bobbeser Codex rescriptus der Wiener Hof-Bibliothek*, 1824 (OCLC number: 2492-04931; the only library holding listed: Staatsbibliothek zu Berlin).

Bonwetsch, G. N., and H. Achelis, eds., *Hippolyt Werke*, vol. 2 (Die griechischen christlichen Schriftsteller der ersten drei Jahrhunderte 1/2; Leipzig: Hinrichs, 1897; reprinted Berlin: Akademie Verlag, 2000).

Bovon, François, Bertrand Bouvier, and Frédéric Amsler, eds., *Acts Philippi*, vol. 1: *Textus;* Frédéric Amsler, *Acta Phillipi*, vol. 2: *Commentarius* (Corpus Christianorum Series apocryphorum 11–12; Turnhout: Brepols, 1999).

Brightman, F. E., *Liturgies Eastern and Western: Being the Texts, Original or Translated, of the Principal Liturgies of the Church*; vol. 1 *Eastern Liturgies* (Oxford: Clarendon, 1896; reprinted 1965; also Piscataway, N.J.: Gorgias, 2002).

Buchholz, Dennis D., *Your Eyes Will Be Opened: A Study of the Greek (Ethiopic) Apocalypse of Peter* (Society of Biblical Literature Dissertation Series 97; Atlanta, Ga.: Scholars Press, 1988).

Budge, Ernest A. Wallis, trans., *The Contendings of the Apostles* (2d ed.; 2 vols.; 1935; reprinted Amsterdam: Philo, 1976).

———, trans., *The Queen of Sheba and Her Only Son Menyelek (1), or, The Kebra Nagast* (London: Martin Hopkinson and Medici Society, 1922; 2d ed.; London: Oxford University Press, 1932; reprinted London: Research Associates School / Times Publications, 2000; and often).

Butterworth, Robert, ed. and trans., *Hippolytus of Rome: Contra Noetum* (Heythrop Monographs 2; London: Heythrop College, University of London, 1977).

Charles, R. H., ed. and trans. *The Ascension of Isaiah: Translated from the Ethiopic Version Which, Together with the New Greek Fragment, the Latin Versions and the Latin Translation of the Old Slavonic, is Here Published in Full* (London: A. & C. Black, 1900).

———, *The Assumption of Moses: Translated from the Latin sixth century ms., the unemended text of which is published herewith, together with the text in its restored and critically emended form, edited with introduction, notes, and indices* (London: A. & C. Black, 1897).

———, *The Ethiopic Version of the Book of Enoch: Edited from Twenty-Three Mss. Together with the Fragmentary Greek and Latin Versions* (Anecdota Oxoniensia 11, Semitic series; Oxford: Clarendon, 1906).

Charlesworth, James H., ed., *The Old Testament Pseudepigrapha* (2 vols.; Garden City, N.Y.: Doubleday, 1983–85).

Connolly, R. Hugh, *Didascalia Apostolorum: The Syriac Version Translated and Accompanied by the Verona Latin Fragments* (Oxford: Clarendon, 1929; reprinted 1969).

Cooper, James, and Arthur John MacLean, *The Testament of Our Lord: Translated into English from the Syriac with Introduction and Notes* (Edinburgh: T&T Clark, 1902).

Cureton, William, *Corpus Ignatianum: A Complete Collection of the Ignatian Epistles, Genuine, Interpolated, and Spurious* (London: Rivington, 1849).

Dix, Gregory, ed. and trans., Henry Chadwick, rev., *ΑΠΟΣΤΟΛΙΚΗ ΠΑΡΑΔΟΣΙΣ: The Treatise on the Apostolic Tradition of St Hippolytus of Rome, Bishop and Martyr* (London: S.P.C.K., 1968; "Reprinted with additional corrections," London: Alban; Ridgefield, Conn.: Morehouse, 1992).

Duensing, Hugo, ed. and trans., *Epistula Apostolorum: nach dem äthiopischen und koptischen Texte* (Kleine Texte 152; Bonn: Marcus & Weber, 1925).

See also Hennecke, below.

Reviews: Rudolf Bultmann, in *Christliche Welt* 39 (1925) 1064–65; Carl Schmidt, in *Orientalistische Literaturzeitung* 28 (1925) 855–59; Ernest B. Allo, in *Revue biblique* 36 (1927) 305–6; Bernhard Vandenhoff, in *Theologische Revue* 26 (1927) 345–46.

Erbetta, Mario, "L'epistola degli Apostoli," in idem, ed., *Gli Apocrifi del Nuovo Testamento*, vol. 3: *Lettere e Apocalissi* (Turin: Marietti, 1969; reprinted 1998) 37–62.

Field, Frederick, *Origenis Hexaplorum quae supersunt: sive Veterum interpretum graecorum in totum Vetus Testamentum fragmenta* (2 vols.; Oxford: Clarendon, 1875; reprinted Hildesheim: Olms, 1964).

Funk, Franz Xaver, ed., *Didascalia et constitutiones apostolorum* (2 vols.; Paderborn: Schoeningh, 1905; reprinted Turin: Bottega d'Erasmo, 1970).

Funk, Franz Xaver, and Karl Bihlmeyer, *Die apostolischen Väter* (Sammlung ausgewählte Kirchen- und dogmengeschichtlicher Quellenschriften 2/1/1; 3d ed.; rev. Wilhelm Schneemelcher; Tübingen: Mohr-Siebeck, 1970).

Garcia-Martinez, Florentino, *The Dead Sea Scrolls Translated: The Qumran Texts in English* (trans. Wilfred G. E. Watson; Leiden / New York: Brill, 1994.

Geffcken, Johannes, ed., *Die Oracula Sibyllina* (Die griechischen christlichen Schriftsteller der ersten drei Jahrhunderte 8; Leipzig: Hinrichs, 1902; reprinted 1967).

Goodspeed, Edgar J., ed., *Die ältesten Apologeten: Texte mit kurzen Einleitungen* (Göttingen: Vandenhoeck & Ruprecht, 1914; reprinted 1984).

Guerrier, Louis, and Sylvain Grébaut, "Le testament en Galilée de notre-Seigneur Jésus-Christ," Patrologia Orientalis 9/3 (1913) 1–96 (= vol. pp. 141–236).

Reviews: Anton Baumstark, in *Theologische Revue* 13 (1914) 165–69; Montague Rhodes James, in *Journal of Theological Studies* 14 (1913) 601–6; 21 (1920) 334–38.

Gwynn, John, "Hippolytus and His 'Heads against Gaius,' " *Hermathena* 6 (1888) 403–4, 415–16.

Haile, Getatchew, "The Homily of Zar'a Ya'qob of Ethiopia in Honor of Saturday," *Orientalia lovaniensia periodica* 13 (1982) 185–231. Cited as Haile, 1982a.

———, "The Homily of Zar'a Ya'qob in Honor of St. John the Evangelist (EMML 1480, ff. 48r–52v)," *Oriens christianus* 67 (1983) 144–66.

Hall, Stuart George, ed. and trans., *Melito of Sardis: On Pascha and Fragments* (Oxford Early Christian Texts; Oxford: Clarendon, 1979).

Hannah, Darrell D., *Epistula Apostolorum* (Oxford Early Christian Gospel Texts; Oxford: Oxford University Press, forthcoming). This edition is announced in Hannah, "Four-Fold Canon" (see Studies, below).

Harden, J. M. *The Ethiopic Didascalia* (Translations of Christian Literature; Series IV Oriental Texts; London: S.P.C.K.; New York: Macmillan, 1920).

Hauler, Edmund, "Zu den neuen lateinischen Bruchstücken der Thomas-apokalypse und eines apostolischen Sendschreibens im Codex Vind. Nr. 16," *Wiener Studien* 30 (1908) 308–40.

Hennecke, Edgar, ed., *Neutestamentliche Apokryphen: in Verbindung mit Fachgelehrten in deutscher Uebersetzung und mit Einleitungen* (2d ed.; Tübingen: Mohr-Siebeck, 1924). The *Epistula Apostolorum* (a brief report, with summary, by Hennecke): 146–49.
In subsequent editions:
3d German ed., 1959–64 (2 vols.; ed. with Wilhelm Schneemelcher; *Epistula Apostolorum* trans. by Hugo Duensing): 2. 126–55;
English translation of the 3d ed.: Edgar Hennecke and Wilhelm Schneemelcher, eds., R. McL. Wilson, trans. ed., *New Testament Apocrypha* (2 vols.; London: Lutterworth; Philadelphia: Westminster, 1963–65); ET of Duensing, *Epistula Apostolorum*, by Richard Taylor: 1. 191–227;
4th German ed., 1971 = a corrected reprint of the 3d ed. (no English translation published);
5th German ed., 1987–89 (2 vols.; ed. by Schneemelcher; *Epistula Apostolorum* translated by C. Detlef G. Müller): 1. 205–33;
6th German ed., 1990–97 = a corrected reprint of the 5th ed.;
English translation of the 5th/6th eds.: Wilhelm Schneemelcher, ed., R. McL. Wilson, trans. ed., *New Testament Apocrypha* (2 vols.; rev. ed.; Cambridge: Clark; Philadelphia: Westminster, 1991); ET of Müller, *Epistula Apostolorum*: 2. 249–84.

Horner, G., ed. and trans., *The Statutes of the Apostles or Canones ecclesiastici: Edited with Translation and Collation from Ethiopic and Arabic mss., also a Translation of the Saidic and Collation of the Bohairic Versions, and Saidic Fragments* (London: Williams & Norgate, 1904).

———, *The Coptic Version of the New Testament in the Northern Dialect: Otherwise Called Memphitic and Bohairic: With Introduction, Critical Apparatus, and Literal English Translation* (4 vols.; Oxford: Clarendon, 1898–1905; reprinted Osnabrück: Zeller, 1969; Springfield, Ill.: Scholarly Reprints, 2002).

———, *The Coptic Version of the New Testament in the Southern Dialect, Otherwise Called Sahidic and Thebaic: With Critical Apparatus, Literal English Translation, Register of Fragments and Estimate of the Version* (7 vols.; Oxford: Clarendon, 1911–24; reprinted Osnabrück: Zeller, 1969).

Hotchkiss, Robert V., ed. and trans., *A Pseudo-Epiphanius Testimony Book* (Society of Biblical Literature Texts and Translations 4; Early Christian Literature 1; Missoula, Mont.: Scholars Press, 1974).

James, Montague Rhodes, "The Epistula Apostolorum," in idem, *The Apocryphal New Testament* (Oxford: Clarendon, 1924; with additions, 1953; reprinted 1959 and often) 485–503.

Janssens, Yvonne, *Les Leçons de Silvanos (NH VII, 4): Texte établi et présenté* (Bibliothêque copte de Nag Hammadi, Section "Textes" 13; Québec: Les Presses de l'Université Laval, 1983).

Kleist, James A., trans., *The Didache, The Epistle of Barnabas, The Epistles and the Martyrdom of Polycarp, The Fragments of Papias, The Epistle to Diognetus* (Ancient Christian Writers 6; Westminster, Md.: Newman; London: Longmans, Green; Cork: Mercier, 1948; reprinted New York, N.Y. / Mahwah, N.J., Paulist, [1948]).

Klostermann, Erich, *[Eusebius:] Das Onomastikon der biblischen Ortsnamen = Eusibius Werke*, vol. 3 part 1 (Die griechischen christlichen Schriftsteller der ersten drie Jahrhunderte 11/1; Leipzig: Hinrichs, 1904; reprinted Hildesheim: Olms, 1966).

Lagarde, Paul A. de, *Constitutiones apostolicae graece ad fidem versionis syriacae recensuit Paulus Boetticher* (Leipzig: Teubner; London: Williams & Norgate, 1862).

Lake, Kirsopp, trans., *The Apostolic Fathers* (2 vols.; Loeb Classical Library; London: Heinemann; Cambridge, Mass.: Harvard University Press, 1912–13; reprinted often).

Leloir, Louis, ed. and trans., *Écrits apocryphes sur les Apôtres: Traduction de l'édition arménienne de Venise* (2 vols.; Corpus Christianorum: Series apocryphorum 3–4; Turnhout: Brepols, 1986–92).

Lightfoot, J. B., *The Apostolic Fathers: Revised Texts with Introduction, Notes, Dissertations and Translations* (2 parts in 5 vols.; 1889–90; reprinted Grand Rapids: Baker, 1981).

Lipsius, Richard Adelbert, ed., and Maximilian Bonnet, *Acta apostolorum apocrypha* (2 vols. in 3 parts; 1891–1903; reprinted Hildesheim: Olms, 1959, 1990).

MacDonald, Dennis Ronald, *The Acts of Andrew and the Acts of Andrew and Matthias in the City of the Cannibals* (Society of Biblical Literature Texts and Translations 33; Christian Apocrypha Series 1; Atlanta, Ga.: Scholars Press, 1990).

———, *The Acts of Andrew* (Early Christian Apocrypha 1; Santa Rosa, Ca: Polebridge, 2005).

Moraldi, Luigi, ed., "Lettera degli apostoli," in idem, ed., *Apocrifi del Nuovo Testamento* (2 vols.; Classici delle religioni 5: Le altre confessioni cristiane; Turin: Unione Tipografico-Editrice Torinese, 1971; reprinted 1975) 2. 1669–1702.

Müller, C. Detlef G. See Hennecke-Schneemelcher, above.

Musurillo, Herbert, ed. and trans., *The Acts of the Christian Martyrs: Introduction, Texts and Translations* (Oxford Early Christian Texts; Oxford: Clarendon, 1972; reprinted as "Special edition," London: Sandpiper, 2000).

The New Testament in Ge'ez (London: British and Foreign Bible Society, 1979). See also Abraha, *Hebrews*; Wechsler, *Evangelium Iohannis*; Zuurmond, *Synoptic Gospels*.

Nock, A. D., ed., and A.-J. Festugière, trans., *Corpus Hermeticum* (4 vols.; Collection des universités de France; Paris: Les Belles Lettres, 1945–54).

Pérès, Jacques-Noël, trans., *L'Épître des Apôtres et le Testament de notre Seigneur et notre Sauveur Jésus-Christ: Présentation et traduction de l'éthiopien* (Apocryphes: Collection de poche de l'Association pour L'Étude de la Littérature Apocryphe Chrétienne [LAELAC] 5; Turnhout: Brepols, 1994).

———, trans., "Épître des apôtres," in François Bovon and Pierre Geoltrain, eds., *Écrits apocryphes chrétiens,* vol. 1 (Bibliothèque de la Pléiade; Paris: Gallimard, 1997) 357–92.

Platt, Thomas Pell, *The Ethiopic Didascalia: Or, The Ethiopic Version of the Apostolical Constitutions as Received in the Church of Abyssinia, with an English Translation* (Oriental Translation Fund [Series] 37; London: Oriental Translation Fund / Richard Bentley, 1834).

Rahmani, Ignatius Ephaem II, ed. and (Latin) trans., *Testamentum Domini nostri Jesu Christi: Nunc primum edidit, Latine reddidit et illustravit* (Mainz: Kirchheim, 1899; reprinted Hildesheim: Olms, 1968).

Roberts, Alexander, and James Donaldson, eds., A. Cleveland Coxe, rev., *The Ante-Nicene Fathers: Translations of the Writings of the Fathers Down to A.D. 325* (10 vols.; 1886; New York: Scribner, 1925).

Robinson, James M., ed., *The Nag Hammadi Library in English* (3d rev. ed.; San Francisco: Harper & Row, 1988).

Schmidt, Carl, and Isaak Wajnberg, *Gespräche Jesu mit seinen Jüngern nach der Auferstehung: Ein katholisch-apostolisches Sendschreiben des 2. Jahrhunderts* (Texte und Untersuchungen 43; Leipzig: Hinrichs, 1919; reprinted Hildesheim: Olms, 1967).

Reviews: Hermann J. Cladder, in *Theologische Revue* 18 (1919) 452–53; J. De Zwaan, in *Nieuw theologische studien* 2 (1919) 281–86; Arnold Ehrhardt, in *Historisch-politische Blätter für das katholische Deutschland* 165 (1920) 645–55, 717–29; Gustav Krüger, in *Literarisches Zentralblatt für Deutschland* 71 (1920) 817–20; Montague Rhodes James, in *Journal of Theological Studies* 21 (1920–21) 334–38; Gustave Bardy, in *Revue biblique* 30 (1921) 110–34; Anton Baumstark, in *Theologische Revue* 20 (1921) 260–65; Leopold Fonck, in *Biblica* 2 (1921) 244–45; Hans Lietzmann, in *Zeitschrift für die neutestamentiche Wissenschaft* 20 (1921) 173–76; Hans von Soden, in *Zeitschrift für Kirchengeschichte* 39 (1921) 140–47; Hugo Duensing, in *Göttingische gelehrte Anzeigen* 184 (1922) 241–52; Felix Haase, in *Oriens christianus* n.S. 10/11 (1923) 170–73; Walter Till, in *Zeitschrift für ägyptische Sprache und Altertumskunde* 63 (1928) 92.

Schmidt, Carl, ed., Violet MacDermot, trans., *The Books of Jeu and the Untitled Text in the Bruce Codex* (Nag Hammadi and Manichaean Studies 13; Leiden: Brill, 1978).

Schoedel, William R., *Ignatius of Antioch: A Commentary on the Letters of Ignatius of Antioch* (Hermeneia; Philadelphia: Fortress, 1985).

Scott, Walter. ed. and trans., *Hermetica: The Ancient Greek and Latin Writings which Contain Religious or Philosophic Teachings Ascribed to Hermes Trismegistus* (4 vols.; Oxford: Clarendon, 1924–36; reprinted Boston, Mass.: Shambhala, 1985–93).

Smith, Joseph P., ed. and trans., *St. Irenaues: Proof of the Apostolic Preaching, Translated and Annotated* (Ancient Christian Writings 16; London: Longmans, Green; Westminster, Md.: Newman, 1952).

Sperry-White, Grant, trans., *The Testamentum Domini: A Text for Students, with Introduction, Translation, and Notes* (Alcuin/GROW Liturgical Study 19; Grove Liturgical Study 66; Bramcote, Notts., England: Grove, 1991).

Stone, Michael E., ed. and trans., *The Testament of Abraham: The Greek Recensions* (Society of Biblical Literature Texts and Translations 2; Pseudepigrapha Series 2; New York: Society of Biblical Literature, 1972).

Tischendorf, Constantin, *Evangelia apocrypha: adhibitis plurimis codicibus graecis . . . collegit atque recensuit* (1853; 2d ed.; Leipzig: Mendelssohn, 1876; reprinted Hildesheim: Olms, 1987).

Wechsler, Michael G., ed., *Evangelium Iohannis aethiopicum* (2 vols.; Corpus scriptorum Christianorum orientalium 617: series aethiopicum 109; Louvain: Peeters, 2005).

Zuurmond, Rochus, *Novum Testamentum aethiopice: The Synoptic Gospels*, Part 1: *General Introduction*; Part 2: *Edition of the Gospel of Mark* (2 parts in one vol.; Äthiopische Forschung 27; Stuttgart: Steiner, 1989). Originally published as *Research into the Text of the Synoptic Gospels in Ge'ez* (see below).

———, *Novum Testamentum aethiopice: The Synoptic Gospels*, Part 3: *The Gospel of Matthew* (Wiesbaden: Harrassowitz, 2001).

———, *Research into the Text of the Synoptic Gospels in Ge'ez* (2 vols.; privately published, Oxford: Delft and Faringdon, 1987).

STUDIES AND OTHER WORKS CITED

Abbadie, Antoine d', *Catalogue raisonné de manuscrits éthiopiens* (Paris: L'Imprimerie impériale, 1859).

Amann, Émile, "La lettre des apôtres," in Louis Pirot and André Robert, eds., *Dictionnaire de la Bible: Supplément* (10 vols.; Paris: Letouzey et Ané, 1928–) 1. 523–25.

Amiot, F., ed., "La Lettre des Apôtres," in idem, *La Bible Apocryphe: Evangiles Apocryphes* (Textes pour l'histoire sacrée 5/2; Paris: Librairie Arthème Fayard, 1952) 275–85. Summary of contents (including paragraphs from Guerrier's translation), with brief bibliography.

Attridge, Harold W., "Liberating Death's Captives: Reconsideration of an Early Christian Myth," in James E. Goehring et al., eds., *Gnosticism and the Early Christian World in Honor of James M. Robinson* (Forum Fascicles 2; Sonoma, Calif.: Polebridge, 1990) 103–15.

Bardenhewer, Otto, "Eine 'Epistola apostolorum,' " *Geschichte der alterkirchlichen Literatur* (5 vols.; 1913–32; reprinted Darmstadt: Wissenschaftliche Buchgesellschaft, 1962) 1. 589–98.

Bauckham, Richard, "Synoptic Parousia Parables Again," *New Testament Studies* 29 (1983) 129–34.

Bauer, Johannes Baptist, "Ein Rundschreiben der Elf Apostel," *Die neutestamentlichen Apokryphen* (Die Welt der Bibel 21; Düsseldorf: Patmos, 1968) 87.

Bauer, Walter, *A Greek-English Lexicon of the New Testament and Other Early Christian Literature* (2d ed.; rev. Frederick W. Danker; trans. William F. Arndt and F. Wilbur Gingrich; Chicago / London: University of Chicago Press, 1979).

Baumstark, Anton, "Alte und neue Spuren eines außerkanonischen Evangeliums (vielleicht des Ägypterevangeliums)," *Zeitschrift für die neutestamentliche Wissenschaft* 14 (1913) 232–47.

———, "Hippolytos und die außerkanonische Evangelienquelle des äthiopischen Galiläa-Testaments," *Zeitschrift für die neutestamentliche Wissenschaft* 15 (1914) 332–35.

Blass, F., A. Debrunner, and R. W. Funk, *A Greek Grammar of the New Testament and Other Early Christian Literature* (Chicago: University of Chicago Press, 1961).

Brockington, L. H., "The Septuagintal Background to the New Testament Use of ΔΟΞΑ," in D. E. Nineham, ed., *Studies in the Gospels: Essays in Memory of R. H. Lightfoot* (Oxford: Blackwell, 1967) 1–8.

Brown, Francis, S. R. Driver, and Charles A. Briggs, *A Hebrew and English Lexicon of the Old Testament* (Oxford: Clarendon, 1907).

Bultmann, Rudolf, *The Gospel of John: A Commentary* (trans. G. R. Beasley-Murray; Philadelphia: Westminster, 1971).

———, *History of the Synoptic Tradition* (rev. ed.; trans. John Marsh; Oxford: Blackwell, 1963).

———, *Theology of the New Testament* (2 vols.; trans. Kendrick Grobel; London: S.C.M.; New York: Scribner, 1951–55).

Cameron, Ron, *Sayings Traditions in the Apocryphon of James* (Harvard Theological Studies 34; Philadelphia: Fortress, 1984; rev. ed., Cambridge, Mass.: Harvard University Press, 2005).

Cerulli, Enrico, *Inventario dei manoscritti Cerulli etiopici: Introduzione, integrazioni e indici a cura di Osvaldo Raineri* (Studi e testi 420; Città del Vaticano: Biblioteca Apostolica Vaticana, 2004).

Chaîne, Marius, *Éléments de grammaire dialectale copte: bohairique, sahidique, achmimique, fayoumique* (2 vols.; Paris: Librairie Orientaliste Paul Guethner, 1933). Includes numerous references to the Coptic text, referred to by Chaîne according to page numbers in Schmidt's edition, identified as "TU43."

Charlesworth, James H., with James R. Mueller, *The New Testament Apocrypha and Pseudepigrapha: A Guide to Publications, with Excursuses on Apocalypses* (American Theological Library Association Bibliograpjhy Series 17; Metuchen, N.J. / London: Scarecrow, 1987). Pp. 168–71 on the *Epistula apostolorum*.

Courcelle, Pierre, "Histoire du cliché virgilien des cent bouches (*Georg.* II, 42–44 = *Aen.* VI, 625–627)," *Revue des études latines* 33 (1955) 231–40.

Cowley, R. W., "The Biblical Canon of the Ethiopian Orthodox Church Today," *Ostkirchliche Studien* 23 (1974) 318–23.

Crum, W. E., *A Coptic Dictionary: Compiled with the Help of Many Scholars* (originally issued in fascicles, 1929–39; Oxford: Clarendon, 1939; reprinted 2000).

Daniélou, Jean, "Les traditions secrètes des apôtres," *Eranos-Jahrbuch* 31 (1962) 199–215.

Deissmann, (Gustav) Adolf, *Light from the Ancient East: The New Testament Illustrated by Recently Discovered Texts of the Graeco-Roman World* (German original, 1908; new ed.; trans. Lionel R. M. Strachan; London: Hodder & Stoughton, 1927; reprinted Grand Rapids: Baker, 1980).

Delazer, Jakob, "Disquisitio in argumentum Epistolae apostolorum," *Antonianum* 3 (1928) 369–406.

———, "De tempore compositionis Epistolae Apostolorum," *Antonianum* 4 (1929) 257–92, 387 –430.

Denniston, J. D., *The Greek Particles* (2d ed.; Oxford: Clarendon, 1954).

Dillmann, August, *Ethiopic Grammar* (2d ed.; rev. Carl Bezold; trans. James A. Crichton; London: Williams & Norgate, 1907; reprinted Amsterdam: Philo, 1974; Eugene, Or.: Wipf & Stock, 2005).

———, *Lexicon linguae aethiopicae cum indice Latino* (Leipzig: Weigel, 1865; reprinted New York: Ungar, 1955; Osnabrück: Biblio, 1970).

Duensing, Hugo, Review of Schmidt, *Gespräche Jesu*, in *Göttingische gelehrte Anzeigen* 184 (1922) 241–52.

Ehrhardt, Arnold, "Eine neue apokryphe Schrift aus dem 2. Jahrhundert," *Historisch-politische Blätter für das katholische Deutschland* 165 (1920) 645–55, 717–29.

———, "Judaeo-Christians in Egypt, the Epistula Apostolorum, and the Gospel to the Hebrews," in F. L. Cross, ed., *Studia Evangelica III: Papers Presented to the Second International Congress on New Testament Studies Held at Christ Church, Oxford, 1961*, part 2: *The New Testament Message* (Texte und Untersuchungen 88; Berlin: Akademie Verlag, 1964) 360–82.

Ehrman, Bart D., "Cephas and Peter," *Journal of Biblical Literature* 109 (1990) 463–74.

Ehrman, Bart D. and Michael W. Holmes, eds., *The Text of the New Testament in Contemporary Research: Essays on the Status Quaestionis* (Grand Rapids: Eerdmans, 1995).

Eijk, A. H. C. van, " 'Only that can rise which has previously fallen': The History of a Formula," *Journal of Theological Studies* NS 22 (1971) 517–29.

Ferreiro, Alberto, *Simon Magus in Patristic, Medieval, and Early Modern Traditions* (Studies in the History of Christian Traditions 125; Leiden / Boston: Brill, 2005).

Fitzmyer, Joseph A., *The Gospel According to Luke: Introduction, Translation, and Notes* (2 vols.; Anchor Bible 28/28A; Garden City, N.Y.: Doubleday, 1981–85).

Funk, Franz Xaver, *Das Testament unseres Herrn und die verwandten Schriften* (Forschungen zur christlichen Litteratur- und Dogmensgeschichte 2/1–2; Mainz: Kirchheim, 1901).

Geerard, Maurice, *Clavis apocryphorum Novi Testamenti* (Corpus Christianorum; Turnhout: Brepols, 1992).

Pp. 11–12 on the *Epistula apostolorum*.

Gerlach, Karl. *The Antenicene Pascha: A Rhetorical History* (Liturgia condenda 7; Louvaine: Peeters, 1998).

Pp. 95–103 on the *Epistula apostolorum*.

Gry, Léon, "La date de la parousie d'après l'Epistula Apostolorum," *Revue biblique* 49 (1940) 86–97.

Grébaut, Sylvain, *Supplément au Lexicon linguae aethiopicae de August Dillmann (1865) et Édition de Lexique de Juste d'Urbin (1850–1855)* (Paris: L'Imprimerie nationale, 1952).

Guerrier, Louis, "Un 'Testament de Notre-Seigneur et Sauveur Jésus-Christ' en Galilée," *Revue de l'Orient chrétien* 12 (1907) 1–8.

Haile, Getatchew, "A New Look at Some Dates of Early Ethiopian History," *Le Muséon* 95 (1982) 311–22. Cited as Haile, 1982b.

Hammerschmidt, Ernst, *Äthiopische Handschriften vom Tanasee* I (Verzeichnis der orientalischen Handschriften in Deutschland 20/1; Wiesbaden: Steiner, 1973).

Hannah, Darrell D., "The Four-Fold 'Canon' in the *Epistula Apostolorum*," *Journal of Theological Studies* NS 59 (2008) 598–633.

Hill, Charles E., "The *Epistula Apostolorum*: An Asian Tract from the Time of Polycarp," *Journal of Early Christian Studies* 7 (1999) 1–53.

Hillmer, Melvyn Raymond, "The Gospel of John in the Second Century" (Th.D. dissertation, Harvard University, 1966). Pp. 28–50 on the *Epistula apostolorum.*

Hills, Julian V., "Apostles, Epistle of," in David Noel Friedman, ed., *Anchor Bible Dictionary* (6 vols.; New York: Doubleday, 1992) 1. 311–12.

———, "The *Epistula Apostolorum* and the Genre 'Apocalypse,'" Society of Biblical Literature Seminar Papers 25 (1986) 581–95.

———, "Proverbs as Sayings of Jesus in the *Epistula Apostolorum*," *Semeia* 49 (1990) 7–34.

———, *Tradition and Composition in the Epistula Apostolorum* (Harvard Dissertations in Religion 24; Minneapolis: Fortress, 1990; rev. ed., Harvard Theological Studies 57; Cambridge: Harvard University Press, 2008).

———, "Tradition, redaction, and Intertextuality: Miracle Lists in Apocryphal Acts as a Test Case," *Society of Biblical Literature Seminar Papers* 29 (1990) 375–90.

Hofmann, Josef, "Limitations of Ethiopic in Representing Greek," in Metzger, *Early Versions*, 240–56.

Holland, David Larrimore, "The Third Article of the Creed: A Study in Second- and Third-Century Theology," in Elizabeth A. Livingstone, ed., *Papers Presented to the Sixth International Conference on Patristic Studies, Held in Oxford, 1971* (3 vols.; Studia Patristica 12–14 = Texte und Untersuchungen 115–117; Berlin: Akademie Verlag, 1975–1976) 2. 145–54.

Hornschuh, Manfred, "Das Gleichnis von den zehn Jungfrauen in der Epistula Apostolorum," *Zeitschrift für Kirchengeschichte* 73 (1962) 1–8.

———, *Studien zur Epistula Apostolorum* (Patristische Texte und Studien 5; Berlin: De Gruyter, 1965).

Reviews: Walter J. Burghardt, in *Theologische Studiën* 26 (1965) 443–44; M. van Esbroeck, in Analecta Bollandiana 83 (1965) 417–18; Otto Betz, in *Theologische Literaturzeitung* 91 (1966) 516–18; Antonio Orbe, in *Gregorianum* 47 (1966) 125–26; Christopher G. Stead, in *Journal of Theological* Studies NS 17 (1966) 171–73; Pedro Vanovermeire, in *Revue d'histoire ecclésiastique* 61 (1966) 539–41;Robert McL. Wilson, in *Journal of Ecclesiastical History* 17 (1966) 105; Anon, in *Irenikon* 40 (1967) 443; Gilles Quispel, in *Vigiliae christianae* 22 (1968) 61–63.

James, Montague Rhodes, "Epistola Apostolorum: A Possible Quotation?" *Journal of Theological Studies* 23 (1922) 56.

———, "The 'Epistola Apostolorum' in a New Text," *Journal of Theological Studies* 12 (1910–11) 55–56.

Jastrow, Marcus, *A Dictionary of the Targumim, the Talmud Babli and Yerushalmi, and the Midrashic Literature* (2 vols.; London: Luzac; New York: Putnam, 1903; reprinted 2 vols. in 1, Brooklyn, N.Y.: Traditional Press, n.d.).

Kelly, J. N. D., *Early Christian Creeds* (3d ed.; New York: McKay; London: Longmans, 1972; reprinted London: Continuum, 2006).

Knibb, Michael A., *Translating the Bible: The Ethiopic Version of the Old Testament* (Oxford / New York: The British Academy / Oxford University Press, 1999).

Koester, Helmut, "One Jesus and Four Primitive Gospels," *Harvard Theological Review* 61 (1968) 203–47; reprinted in idem and James M. Robinson, *Trajectories Through Early Christianity* (Philadelphia: Fortress, 1971), 158–204.

Lake, Kirsopp, "The Epistola Apostolorum," *Harvard Theological Review* 14 (1920) 15–29.

Lambdin, Thomas O., *Introduction to Classical Ethiopic (Ge'ez)* (Harvard Semitic Studies 24; Missoula, Mont.: Scholars Press, 1978).

———, *Introduction to Sahidic Coptic* (Macon, Ga.: Mercer University Press, 1983).

Lampe, G. W. H., *A Patristic Greek Lexicon* (Oxford: Clarendon, 1961).

Layton, Bentley, *A Coptic Grammar, with Chrestomathy and Glossary: Sahidic Dialect* (Porta linguarum orientalium, n.S. 20; Wiesbaden: Harrassowitz, 2000).

Leslau, Wolf, *Comparative Dictionary of Ge'ez: Ge'ez-English, English-Ge'ez, With an Index of Semitic Roots* (Wiesbaden: Harrassowitz, 1987).

———, *Concise Dictionary of Ge'ez (Classical Ethiopic)* (Wiesbaden: Harrassowitz, 1989).

Liddell, Henry George, and Robert Scott, *A Greek-English Lexicon* (rev. Henry Stuart Jones; Oxford: Clarendon, 1940).

Louw, Johannes P., and Eugene A. Nida, eds., *Greek-English Lexicon of the New Testament Based on Semantic Domains* (2d ed.; 2 vols.; New York: United Bible Societies, 1989).

Macomber, William F., and Getatchew Haile, *A Catalogue of Ethiopian Manuscripts Microfilmed for the Ethiopian Manuscript Microfilm Library, Addis Ababa, and for the Hill Monastic Manuscript Library, Collegeville, Minnesota* (Collegeville, Minn.: St. John's University, 1976–).

McNeil, Brian, "Jesus and the Alphabet," *Journal of Theological Studies* NS 27 (1976) 126–28.

Metzger, Bruce M., *The Early Versions of the New Testament: Their Origin, Transmission, and Limitations* (Oxford: Clarendon, 1977).

———, and Bart D. Ehrman, *The Text of the New Testament: Its Transmission, Corruption, and Restoration* (1964; 4th ed.; New York/Oxford: Oxford University Press, 2005).

———, *A Textual Commentary on the Greek New Testament* (2d ed.; Stuttgart: Deutsche Bibelgesellschaft; London / New York: United Bible Societies, 1994).

Miles, John Russiano, *Retroversion and Text Criticism: The Predictability of Syntax in an Ancient Translation from Greek to Ethiopic* (Society of Biblical Literature Septuagint and Modern Studies 17; Chico, Calif.: Scholars Press, 1985).

Moule, C. F. D., *The Origin of Christology* (Cambridge / New York: Cambridge University Press, 1977).

Moulton, James Hope, and George Millligan, *The Vocabulary of the Greek Testament* (London: Hodder & Stoughton, 1929; reprinted Peabody, Mass.: Hendrickson, 1997).

Nock, Arthur Darby, "The Apocryphal Gospels," *Journal of Theological Studies* NS 11 (1960) 63–70.

Nunn, H. P. V., *Christian Inscriptions* (Texts for Students 11; London: S. P. C. K., 1920; reprinted Eton: Saville, 1951; New York: Philosophical Library, 1952).

O'Leary, De Lacy, *The Apostolical Constitutions and Cognate Documents: With Special Reference to Their Liturgical Elements* (Early Church Classics; London: S.P.C.K.; New York: Gorham, 1906).

Pascucci, "Ennio, *Ann.*, 561–62 V[2] e un tipico procedimento di ΑΥΞΗΣΙΣ nella poesia latina," *Studi italiani di filologia classica* NS 31 (1959) 79–99.

Payne Smith, J., *A Compendious Syriac Dictionary Founded Upon the Thesaurus Syriacus of R. Payne Smith, D.D.* (Oxford: Clarendon, 1903).

Pérès, Jacques-Noël, "Le baptême des patriarchs dans les Enfers," *Études théologiques et religieuses* 68 (1993) 341–46.

———, "Gabriel, qui se tient devant Dieu," *Positions luthériennes* 39/3 (1991) 247–56.

Piovanelli, P., "Les aventures des apocryphes en Éthiopie," *Apocrypha* 4 (1994) 197–224.

Plumley, J. Martin, "Limitations of Coptic (Sahidic) in Representing Greek," in Metzger, *Early Versions*, 141–52.

Richardson, C. C., "A New Solution to the Quartodeciman Riddle," *Journal of Theological Studies* NS 24 (1973) 74–84.

Schmidt, Carl, "Eine bisher unbekannte altchristliche Schrift in koptischer Sprache," Sitzungsberichte der preußischen Akademie der Wissenschaften (1895) 705–11.

———, "Eine Epistola apostolorum in koptischer und lateinischer Überlieferung," Sitzungsberichte der preusßischen Akademie der Wissenschaften (1908) 1047–56.

Schnackenburg, Rudolf, *The Gospel according to St John*, vol. 1 (London: Burns and Oates; New York: Herder and Herder, 1968).

Schneider, T., "Das prophetische 'Agraphon' der Epistola apostolorum," *Zeitschrift für die neutestamentliche Wissenschaft* 24 (1925) 151–54.

Schodde, George H., *Hêrmâ Nabî: The Ethiopic Version of Pastor Hermae Examined* (Leipzig: Brockhaus, 1876).

Schumacher, H., "The Discovery of the 'Epistola Apostolorum,'" *Homiletical and Pastoral Review* 22 (1921–22) 856–65.

———, "The 'Epistola Apostolorum' and the New Testament," *Homiletical and Pastoral Review* 22 (1921–22) 967–75.

———, "The Christology of the 'Epistola Apostolorum,'" *Homiletical and Pastoral Review* 22 (1921–22) 1080–87, 1303–12.

———, "The 'Epistola Apostolorum' and the 'Descensus ad Inferos,'" *Homiletical and Pastoral Review* 23 (1922–23) 13–21, 121–28.

Smyth, Herbert Weir, *Greek Grammar* (rev. Gordon M. Messing; Cambridge: Harvard University Press, 1956; reprinted often).

Staats, Reinhart, "Die törichten Jungfrauen von Mt 25 in gnostischer und antignostischer Literatur," in Walther Eltester, ed., *Christentum und Gnosis* (Beihefte zur Zeitschrift für die neutestamentliche Wissenschaft 37; Berlin: Töpelmann, 1969), 98–115.

Stewart-Sykes, Alistair, "The Asian Context of the New Prophecy and of *Epistula Apostolorum*," *Vigiliae christianae* 51 (1997) 416–38.

Streeter, Burnett Hillmann, *The Four Gospels: A Study of Origins* (London: Macmillan, 1924; reprinted often).

Till, Walter C., *Achmîmisch-koptische Grammatik: mit Chrestomathie und Wörterbuch* (Leipzig: Hinrichs, 1928). Includes numerous references to the Coptic text, cited as "TU43."

———, *Koptische Grammatik (saïdischer Dialekt): mit Bibliographie, Lesestücken, und Wörterverzeichnissen* (1955; Lehrbücher für das Studium der orientalischen Sprachen 1; 6th ed.; Leipzig: Enzyklopädie, 1986).

———, *Koptische Dialektgrammatik: mit Lesestücken und Wörterbuch* (1931; 2d ed.; Munich: Beck, 1961).

Ullendorff, Edward, *Ethiopia and the Bible* (Schweich Lectures of the British Academy1967; Oxford: Oxford University Press, 1968; reprinted 1988).

Van Groningen, B. A., *Short Manual of Greek Paleography* (Leiden: A. W. Sijthoff's Uitgeversmaatschappij N.V., 1940).

Vanovermeire, Pedro, "Livre que Jésus-Christ a révélé à ses disciples: étude sur l'apocryphe, connu sous le nom d'Epistula Apostolorum : premier témoin de l'influence littéraire du quatrième Evangile sur la littérature chrétienne de la première moitié du second siècle" (Dr. Théol. dissertation, Institut catholique de Paris, 1962).

Vitti, Alfredo M., "De 'Epistula Apostolorum' apocrypha," *Verbum domini* 3 (1923) 367–73.

Wisse, Frederick, "The Coptic Versions of the New Testament," in Ehrman and Holmes, *The Text of the New Testament*, 131–41.

Wright, William, *Catalogue of the Ethiopic Manuscripts in the British Museum Acquired Since the Year 1847* (London: British Museum / Longmans, 1877).

Zuurmond, Rochus, "The Ethiopic Version of the New Testament," in Ehrman and Holmes, *The Text of the New Testament*, 142–56.

Zwaan, J. de, "Date and Origin of the Epistle of the Eleven Apostles," in H. G. Wood, ed., *Amicitiae Corolla: A Volume of Essays Presented to James Rendel Harris, D. Litt., on the Occasion of His Eightieth Birthday* (London: University of London Press, 1933) 344–55.

INDEX OF TEXTS

OLD TESTAMENT

References are to the notes, indicated by the chapter and verse numbers in the translation. References marked with a dagger (†) are in the Additional Notes found after the translation. Entries lacking chapter and verse reference but marked "Coloph." will be found among the Colophons, following the Additional Notes.

DEAD SEA SCROLLS

OTHER JEWISH WRITINGS

NEW TESTAMENT

APOSTOLIC FATHERS

NEW TESTAMENT APOCRYPHA

NAG HAMMADI AND RELATED WRITINGS

OTHER EARLY CHRISTIAN WRITINGS

CLASSICAL AUTHORS

INDEX OF NAMES

INDEX OF GREEK WORDS

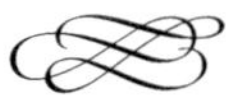

Lightning Source UK Ltd.
Milton Keynes UK
01 December 2009

146950UK00002B/19/P